JAMES JOYCE

and

HERALDRY

JAMES JOYCE and HERALDRY

Michael J. O'Shea

State University

of

New York Press

Grateful acknowledgment is given for permission to use the following:

Excerpts from *Finnegans Wake* by James Joyce. Copyright 1939, renewed © 1967 by George and Lucia Joyce. Reprinted by permission of Viking Penguin and The Society of Authors as the literary representative of the Estate of James Joyce.

Excerpts from *Ulysses* by James Joyce. Copyright, 1914, 1918, by Caroline Anderson. Copyright renewed, 1942, 1946 by Nora Joseph Joyce. Copyright, 1934, by Modern Library, Inc. Copyright renewed, 1961, by Lucia and George Joyce. Reprinted by permission of Random House, Inc., The Bodley Head, Garland Publishing, Inc., and The Society of Authors as the literary representatives of the Estate of James Joyce.

Arms of Joyce (Illustration 3-D). Reprinted with the permission of The Poetry/Rare Books Collection of the University Libraries, State University of New York at Buffalo.

Arms of Dublin (Illustration 5-I), from *Intelligible Heraldry* by Christopher and Adrian Lynch-Robinson. Reprinted by permission of Genealogical Publishing Co.

Published by
State University of New York Press, Albany

Printed in the United States of America

For information, address State University of New York
Press, State University Plaza, Albany, N.Y., 12246

Library of Congress Cataloging in Publication Data

O'Shea, Michael J., 1955–
James Joyce and heraldry.

Bibliography: p. 135.
Includes index.
1. Joyce, James, 1882–1941—Knowledge—Manners
and customs. 2. Heraldry in literature. I. Title.
PR6019.09Z774 1986 823'.912 85-26260
ISBN 0-88706-269-5
ISBN 0-88706-270-9 (pbk.)

10 9 8 7 6 5 4 3 2 1

For Robert Boyle

TABLE OF CONTENTS

A NOTE ON THE TEXT

Following are the abbreviations used to refer to works by James Joyce throughout this study, and the editions to which they refer:

CP	Joyce, James. *Collected Poems.* New York: Viking, 1957.
CW	———. *Critical Writings.* Ed. Ellsworth Mason and Richard Ellmann. London: Faber and Faber, 1959.
D	———. **Dubliners:** *Text, Criticism, and Notes.* Viking Critical Library. Ed. Robert Scholes and A. Walton Litz. New York: Viking, 1969.
FW	———. *Finnegans Wake.* 1939, 1945 with corrections; rpt. New York: Viking, 1982.
GJ	———. *Giacomo Joyce.* Ed. Richard Ellmann. New York: Viking, 1968.
Letters	———. *Letters of James Joyce.* Vol. 1, ed. Stuart Gilbert. New York: Viking, 1966. Vol. 2 and 3, ed. Richard Ellmann. New York: Viking, 1966.
P	———. **A Portrait of the Artist as a Young Man:** *Text, Criticism, and Notes.* Viking Critical Library. Ed. Chester G. Anderson. New York: Viking, 1968.
SH	———. *Stephen Hero.* Ed. Theodore Spencer. New York: New Directions, 1963.
SL	———. *Selected Letters of James Joyce.* Ed. Richard Ellmann. New York: Viking, 1975.
U	———. *Ulysses.* Critical and Synoptic Edition. Ed. Hans Walter Gabler, Wolfhard Steppe, and Claus Melchior. 3 vols. New York: Garland Publishing, 1984.

All references are by abbreviation and page number only, with the following exceptions:

Letters references are by volume and page number.

Finnegans Wake references are by page and line number (e.g. *FW* 546.5–11 = page 546, lines 5 through 11). In addition, references to Chapter 10 of *FW* (260–308) use the page/line arrangement described above for the text at the center of the page, and for the notes on the left, right, and foot of the page, the page number is followed by the initials "R," "L," or "F," followed by the number of the note (e.g. 277.F7 refers to the seventh note at the foot of page

277). Finally, as far as possible, use of roman numerals is reserved for the four books of *FW:* "I.7" refers to chapter 7 of Book I, etc.

Ulysses references use the reading text of the Critical and Synoptic Edition produced by Galber *et al.* The numbers refer to episode and line (e.g., 7.40 refers to the fortieth line of Chapter 7). For the reader's convenience, all *U* references are followed by the page and line numbers for the same passage in the 1961 Random House edition of *Ulysses,* in these brackets: { }. The reference {0} refers to a passage in the new edition that was omitted from the Random House edition.

In addition, the following references are used for secondary works:

AWN *A WakeNewslitter.*

Boutell *Boutell's Heraldry.* Rev. J. P. Brooke-Little. London: Frederick Warne, 1978.

Burke's Burke, Sir Bernard Burke. *The General Armory of England, Scotland, Ireland, and Wales.* 1884; rpt. London: Heraldry Today, 1984.

All references to "Burke's" are to the *General Armory,* unless another work is specified.

CG Fox-Davies, A. C. *A Complete Guide to Heraldry.* 1909; rpt. New York: Bonanza Books, 1978.

JJ Ellmann, Richard. *James Joyce.* New and rev. ed. New York: Oxford Univ. Press, 1982.

JJQ *James Joyce Quarterly.*

MBK Joyce, Stanislaus. *My Brother's Keeper: James Joyce's Early Years.* New York: Viking, 1958.

McHugh McHugh, Roland. *Annotations to* **Finnegans Wake.** Baltimore: Johns Hopkins, 1980.

All references to glosses from McHugh's annotations will simply be identified as such without giving a page number, since McHugh's pagination precisely matches that of *FW.* Thus a gloss by McHugh used in reference to *FW* 546.5 will be found on page 546 of McHugh's text. All references to McHugh are from the *Annotations,* except where another work is specified.

Full bibliographic references for these and all other sources used in this study are found in the "Bibliography and Works Cited" at the end of the text.

LIST OF ILLUSTRATIONS

ACKNOWLEDGEMENTS

This book would have been impossible without the generous assistance of many individuals, only a few of whom can be acknowledged here. The Reverend Robert Boyle, S.J., Professor of English at Marquette University, taught me how to stop worrying and love *Finnegans Wake.* More than any other individual, Father Boyle made this book possible. His contagious enthusiasm made me realize that scholarship can be—and should be—a labor of love. Since I studied *Finnegans Wake* in his seminar at the University of Delaware in 1981, I have filled his mailbox with notes and queries, and, despite ill health, he has generously and copiously responded, sharing his expert and sensitive appreciation of Joyce. I presume to dedicate this effort to him; I mean it as a compliment.

I am grateful to many individuals at the University of Delaware, where this study began as a doctoral dissertation. Professor Zack Bowen encouraged my interest in my subject at an early stage, directed my research, and provided extensive assistance with my manuscript. Other individuals who read my manuscript and provided advice and corrections were Professor Bonnie K. Scott and Professor Jay L. Halio in the English Department at the University of Delaware; Professor John S. Crawford of the Department of Art History at Delaware; Professor Patrick McCarthy of the University of Miami; and Professor A. Nicholas Fargnoli of Molloy College.

Mr. Daniel Brooks produced original artwork which appears herein; his talent greatly relieves the tedium of these pages. For assistance with the photographic reproductions used herein, I am grateful to the Library of the State University of New York, Buffalo, and the Library of Congress. Also, I am grateful to the Instructional Systems Department at Drexel University for their assistance with many of the illustrations.

I am indebted to many people in the United States and abroad who answered queries by mail. I am particularly grateful to Mr. Stephen Joyce, who very kindly replied to my queries concerning the coat of arms used by his grandfather. At Emory University, Professor Richard Ellmann, Woodruff Professor of English, provided biographical information on Joyce, and some very sound advice on my research at an early stage. In Dublin, I thank Mr. Patrick J. Smyth, and Mr. Eilís Ní Dhuibhne, Assistant Keeper, Dublin Castle. At the College of Arms in London, I am indebted to Sir

Colin Cole, K.C.V.O, T.D., F.S.A., Garter Principal King of Arms; and Mr. Thomas Woodcock, Somerset Herald. I am grateful to Mrs. Rosemary Pinches of Heraldry Today in London for her bibliographic assistance.

The contribution of my wife, Catherine L. O'Shea, to this project has been inestimable; in addition to patiently suffering my heraldic hobbyhorse, she also provided Italian translations and taught me everything I know about medieval English history. Her parents, Mr. and Mrs. E. K. Large, took a very active interest in this project and assisted me in many ways; I am particularly indebted to Mrs. Large, who glossed many classical allusions, read the manuscript, and prevented my making many blunders. The interest, encouragement and example of my parents, Mr. and Mrs. Arthur K. O'Shea, have been invaluable at all times.

The University of Delaware generously facilitated this project by granting me University Fellowships from Fall 1982 through Spring 1984. Parts of Chapter Two appeared in *Enquiry* (Vol. 4, No. 3, Spring 1984), copyright University of Delaware, and are used here by permission. Parts of Chapter Three appeared in *Collections* (Vol. 1, 1984), copyright, Library Associates of the University of Delaware, and are used here by permission.

CHAPTER ONE

"His crest of huroldry"

—*Finnegan's Wake* 5.6

I

In *A Portrait of the Artist as a Young Man,* Stephen Dedalus laments that the language with which he described art and beauty "was held no higher by the age he lived in than the subtle and curious jargons of heraldry and falconry" (180). When he mentions the jargon of heraldry, Stephen refers to the specialized language used to describe coats of arms, and such related displays as badges, pennons, banners, and flags. Ruth von Phul pointed out in a 1971 essay that Joyce had sufficient interest in the arcane language of heraldry to pass some on to Stephen Dedalus in the "Proteus" chapter of *Ulysses,* where Stephen's thoughts take the form of blazon, or the formulaic language used to describe coats of arms and the devices that they display (von Phul 399–405). When Stephen contemplates the activities of a dog on Sandymount Strand, he thinks, "[The dog] turned, bounded back, came nearer, trotted on twinkling shanks. On a field tenney a buck, trippant, proper, unattired" (*U* 3.336–37 {46.11–13}). In his mind, Stephen transforms the dog into a hornless ("unattired") buck on a brown ("tenney") heraldic field. Later, as Stephen leaves the beach, his attitude is described in terms appropriate to an heraldic lion: "He turned his face over a shoulder, rere regardant" (3.503 {51.4}).

Nor is Stephen's heraldic interest limited to the "subtle and curious jargons" associated with blazon. In *A Portrait,* he implies that he is entitled by his distinguished lineage to a coat of arms. When Davin impugns the Dedalus Irish heritage, the affronted Stephen replies, "Come with me now to the office of arms and I will show you the tree of my family" (*P* 202).

The "office of arms" was the Dublin Castle office of the Ulster King of Arms, who was the principal heraldic officer in Ireland until this British office was replaced by that of the Chief Herald in 1943.[1]

It is a little-noted fact that this office is a constant in *A Portrait*, *Ulysses*, and *Finnegans Wake*.[2] In addition to this mention of the office by the defensive Stephen of *A Portrait*, there is the procession honoring Bloom in "Circe," which includes "the Athlone poursuivant and Ulster King of Arms" (*U* 15.1413 {480.10–11}). The Ulster King of Arms we have met; the Athlone Pursuivant was the sub-officer of the Dublin Office of Arms, who also appears with his boss at HCE's wake in the "Yawn" chapter of *Finnegans Wake:* "Ulster Kong and Munster's Herald with Athclee Ensigning and Athlone Poursuivant" (498.11–12).

In Dublin, the function of these officers was to record and authenticate grants of heraldic bearings. It is appropriate that the Irish king of arms and his officers are so well represented in Joyce's three major works, because they are needed there: each book contains characters who claim the right to arms. Stephen's reference to the office in *Portrait* is an implicit claim to be an "armiger" (a gentleman of coat-armor); in *Ulysses*, there are two prominent would-be armigers. First, Leopold Bloom, who in the "Oxen of the Sun" chapter is granted heraldic bearings when he appears as "good sir Leopold that had for his cognisance the flower of quiet, margerain gentle" (*U* 14.330–31 {392.23–24}), later imagines himself with "a family crest and coat of arms" (*U* 17.1610 {715.31}). The second armiger of *Ulysses* is Stephen, who sees his father in the form of a bird of prey, swooping overhead and crying out, "Keep our flag flying! An eagle gules volant in a field argent displayed. Ulster king at arms!" (*U* 15.3948–49 {572.16–17}). Joyce's gesture of legitimizing his characters' lineage through armorial bearings is repeated in *Finnegans Wake.* To name two instances: first, under examination in the "Yawn" chapter, Yawn modestly admits to his armorial bearings, laying a claim "to Lowman Catlick's patrician morning coat of arms with my High tripenniferry cresta and caudal mottams: Itch dean. . . ." (*FW* 485.1–3). Yawn has appropriated a device belonging to the Prince of Wales: the "tripenniferry cresta" with motto "Itch dean" is, in distorted form, the badge of the heir apparent to the British throne—three ostrich plumes over the motto "Ich dien" (I serve). Not to be outdone, HCE proclaims at the end of the same chapter:

> These be my genteelican arms. At the crest, two young frish, etoiled, flappant, devoiled of their habiliments, vested sable, withdrewers argent. For the boss a coleopter, pondant, partifesswise, blazoned sinister, at the slough, proper. In the lower field a terce of lanciers, shaking unsheathed shafts, their arms crossed in

saltire, embusked, sinople. Motto, in letters portent: *Hery Crass Evohodie.* (*FW* 546.5–11)

Understanding what all of this gibberish might mean involves more than defining the individual heraldic terms: heraldry itself must be defined, and the traditions associated with it identified. To begin my study of such wondrous examples of Joycean blazon as the above passage, then, I consider heraldry in the context of history, and some aspects of the language and graphic conventions of heraldry.

II

Possible sources for Joyce's heraldic allusions seem to precede the history of heraldry itself. For Giambattista Vico, whose cyclic view of history was an acknowledged template for that of *Finnegans Wake* (Beckett 3–22; N. Brown 102), heraldic blazon is the "official" language in the heroic age. Vico's *New Science* describes the age in which expression was "symbolic, [expressed] by signs or by heroic devices" (*New Science* 140); in other words, in Vico's scheme of history, heraldry precedes the genesis of articulate speech. In his *Autobiography*, Vico recounts his discovery of: "new origins of heroic insignia, which were the dumb language of all the first nations at a time when they were incapable of articulate speech. Thence he [the author] discovers new principles of the science of heraldry. . . ." (168)

"Heraldry" in this sense is not strictly limited to the armorial cognizances of medieval Europe; Vico's heraldry consists of several ancient emblematic codes which may or may not pertain to heraldry in the strictest sense. Northrop Frye invokes this broad, Viconian view of heraldry in his *Anatomy of Criticism* when, in his discussion of the theory of symbols, he describes "the heraldic symbol, the central emblematic image which comes most readily to mind when we think of the word 'symbol' in literature" (92). In this category, Frye includes "Hawthorne's scarlet letter,[3] Melville's white whale, James's golden bowl, and Virginia Woolf's lighthouse": in other words, symbols not likely to be found on an heraldic shield.

Although these emblematic codes are relevant to this study, I am primarily interested in a more precise definition of heraldry. In his *Complete Guide to Heraldry*, A. C. Fox-Davies addresses the problem of defining heraldry by first considering the puzzling but apparent fact that heraldic allusions in literature predate heraldry as we know it (*CG* 6–9). Classical writings contain some of literature's most famous emblazoned shields, including the five-fold shield of Achilles, which is an epic in itself: in the *Iliad* of Homer, the description of the elaborate (in fact, physically impossible) ornamentation on Achilles' shield occupies nearly 150 lines of Book 18. The "Aegis," the shield of Athena, emblazoned with the head of a Gorgon, figures prominently in the *Odyssey* and other Greek legends. For another striking example of pre-heraldic heraldry, Fox-Davies refers to Aeschylus's *Seven Against Thebes,* in which a scout (a "herald" in the translation Fox-Davies uses) describes the seven captains to Eteokles, King of Thebes, in terms of the devices on their shields. The first, Tydeus, bears:

> . . . this top-lofty blazon:
> heaven forged with flaming stars, and at the
> center
> the triple goddess of the three ways,
> a brilliant full moon. . . . (471–74)

This emblazoned shield carries what C. S. Pierce would call a "symbolic" sign; the other champions bear "iconic" charges, that literally depict and underscore the dramatic action. The arms of Kapaneus are blazoned:

> . . . a naked man
> armed with a flaming torch
> who is crying out in golden letters
> "I shall burn the city." (534–37)

The shield of Eteoklos is blazoned with "A man, fully armed, [who] mounts a ladder against the walls. . ." (574). Each shield functions in the fashion of the names in Bunyan's *Pilgrim's Progress* (Christian, Atheist, By-Ends, Obstinate, and so forth), providing an immediate, telegraphic summary of the character and the external forces guiding him. The descriptions of the shields of the seven culminate in the revelation of the shield of Eteokles himself, who bears a shield blazoned with the representation of the forces underlying his character and actions, the Fury.

In similar fashion, Virgil's tale of "arms and a man," the *Aeneid,* makes use of "arms" to characterize Aventinus, who is seen, "Bearing his father's blazon on the shield— / The Hydra wreathed in snakes, a hundred snakes" (vii, 656–57). This particular literary use of heraldry seems to anticipate European heraldry, by assigning Aventinus arms that are not only emblematic, but also patrilineally transmitted: Aventinus' shield bears the emblem of his father, Hercules. But, as Fox-Davies points out, it is misleading to equate the ancient blazoned shields with their counterparts in medieval Europe: the ancient devices were not assumed and used according to the highly sophisticated, hereditary system that governed medieval arms. This code emerged about the time of the Crusades, and was somewhat regularized in the modern sense of heraldry by 1300. *Boutell's Heraldry* states that "these insignia of antiquity are to be regarded as the predecessors and not as the ancestors of modern heraldry" (3). If one defines heraldry—once known as "armory"—as the art and science associated with "coats of arms," then many problems of definition are solved, since the term "coat of arms" does not accurately describe armorial devices predating the Crusades: the armorial "surcoat," which emerged during the Crusades, is the origin of the "coat" associated with modern heraldic display. All authorities agree that the "1066" of studies of European heraldry seems to be the year 1127, when Henry I granted a shield of gold lions (*"clipeus leunculos aureos ymaginarios habens"* [*Boutell* 4]) to his son-in-law, Geoffrey of Anjou, whose tomb features the first known funerary monument (an enamel) featuring heraldic bearings in the modern sense. When one hears boasts of an hereditary coat of arms dating back to William the Conqueror, it is pleasant to remember (but rude to say aloud) that no such arms existed.

Although the emblazoned shields of medieval Europe are distinguished from most of those in ancient history by the development of hereditary transmission, there are broad similarities between the ancient and medieval devices. Both are military in origin: the armorial shield bears an ensign that proclaims the identity, and perhaps the virtues, of the great warrior bearing it. The shield serves the function implied in Vico's "mute speech." Historically, arms have seldom been as loquacious as those Aeschylus grants to Kapaneus (Admiral Nelson's arms, which struggle to depict his victories, being a hideous exception), which seem not only to announce his character and destiny, but also his military strategy; but arms have always served as a form of expression, in some sense proclaiming the identity of the bearer. The primitive hero fighting under the ensign of a lion, or an eagle, might be thought to possess the ideal characteristics of these beasts; this idea has survived in the pervasiveness of these beasts as symbols of power, from the eagles of the Caesars, the Holy Roman Empire, the Russian Czars, and Napoleon, to the royal lions of England and Scotland.

In practical terms, the heraldic ensign was a recognizable emblem under which adherents of a warrior might rally. While symbolic cognizances predate armor with visored helmets, it is generally agreed that the rise of heraldic insignia stems in part from the anonymity of the steel mask in battle; heraldist Julian Franklyn, noting the difficulty of distinguishing friend from foe in battle, describes the rise of the painted shield, with a design that would also likely be displayed on the heraldic standard, or banner; the ensign: "was usually simple in [its] conception and forceful in its execution so that it could be recognized at a distance. [The leader] had but to hold his painted shield aloft for his men to rally around him. . . ." (4).

If this simple explanation of the origins and use of heraldry threatens to strain one's credulity, one need only reflect on the fate of the Lancastrian leader De Vere, Earl of Oxford, whose heraldic badge of a silver star so closely resembled the Yorkist white rose that confusion between the two caused him to lose the Battle of Barnet in 1471 (*Boutell* 165). For all of its romantic and fantastic connotations, heraldry was, at its inception, a very practical art.

Another term that fixes the historical origin of heraldry as we know it is the word "heraldry" itself—meaning the offices of a herald. Sir Anthony Wagner traces early references to heralds in twelfth-century France, and finds heralds active as retainers in noble and royal households in England from the reign of Edward I (Wagner 1–4). These officers issued proclamations and officiated at tournaments; over time, their duties came to include examining and recording the armorial bearings of those participating in tournaments. In England, the Sovereign began to assume authority over the right to "bear arms" in the heraldic sense; by 1338, records indicate that the "Norroy King of Arms" was exercising control over the granting and recording of arms under Royal authority (Wagner 20–21), and in 1484, the Herald's College (now the College of Arms) was incorporated. The College continues to operate in England as the sole arbiter of legitimate armorial bearings, as do the Lyon King of Arms in Scotland, and the Chief Herald in the Republic of Ireland. Consequently, "heraldry," once connoting the various offices of a herald, which in the early days might even have included minstrelsy, has come to mean the old science of "armory." *Boutell* quotes Sir Anthony Wagner's definition of heraldry: "The systematic use of hereditary devices centred on a shield" (4). Geoffrey of Anjou's arms meet this definition because his insignia were transmitted to his heirs.

The emergence of the heralds as a corporate institution supported by royal authority influenced the development of heraldry as more than the haphazard repetition of certain graphic emblems; heraldry is a highly refined code of signs. Of this system, the medieval historian V. H. Galbraith is able to make this succinct statement:

> Heraldry as a science was already complete by 1300 and has remained unchanged ever since. It preserves a complicated technical language which must be learnt by any student [of history] who wants to use heraldic evidence in order to identify, not only families, but individual members of families; there is, for example, a range of "cadency" marks, which were added to a coat of arms, and often to

crests as well, to indicate a son's place in his family—and whether—if he were the eldest son—his father was alive at the time. (16)

To give an example of what Professor Galbraith means, to the trained observer, the paternal arms of the novelist Henry Fielding (Illus. 1-A) indicate that Fielding was the eldest son of the third son of a fifth son (of George Fielding, Earl of Desmond). The evidence is the mark of "cadency" at the top of the shield: a mullet (five-point star), the mark of a third son, within an annulet (a ring), the mark of a fifth son (von Volborth 100).

This level of precision leads writers such as Galbraith (and, in a passage cited earlier, Giambattista Vico) to describe heraldry as a "science." This is justified in a sense: heraldry as a semiotic code has graphic intricacy (and an elaborate jargon to match) sufficient to make a semiotician dizzy. But many writers describe heraldry not as a science, but as an art. Perhaps this distinction stems from the true nature of heraldry, which may not be quite as immutable and fixed as Professor Galbraith implies. A case in point: the marks of cadency, so brilliantly employed above, are not used consistently in British heraldry, and the specific marks of cadency above are not used at all in Scottish heraldry; moreover, cadency is virtually unknown in continental heraldry. In other words, heraldry has the institutional integrity of British common law, or the unwritten constitution: it exists as a systematic code, but its existence is predicated more on precedent and usage than on prescriptive standards. Consequently, for every heraldic "rule," there is at least one duly matriculated coat of arms that violates it.

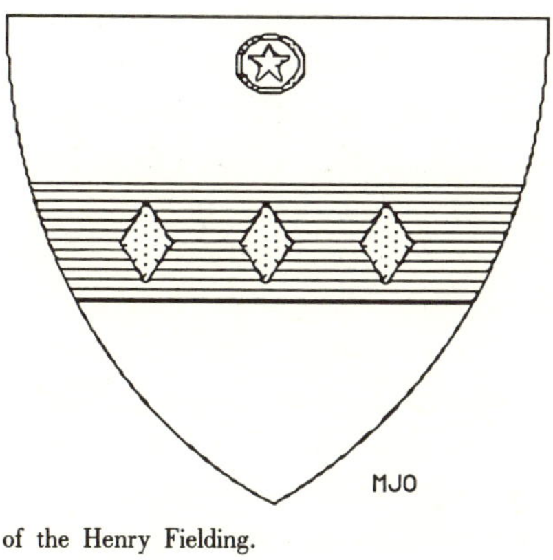

Illustration 1-A Arms of the Henry Fielding.

But heraldry has a great deal of graphic and symbolic integrity, and its significance is organically linked with other legal, social, political, and historical codes of western culture. The military significance of heraldry has already been mentioned; interestingly, while the military use of armor became obsolete with the advent of gunpowder, the military significance of heraldry remains unabated. In the United States, a country popularly thought to have no "official" heraldry, there is in fact one heraldic authority: the Institute of Heraldry of the U. S. Army. The medieval tradition of the soldier fighting under the ensign of the liege-lord or sovereign is preserved in the heraldic badges and escutcheons adorning modern military uniforms, aircraft, and the like.

As a social code, heraldry proclaims the rank of the "armiger"—one entitled to bear arms. Fox-Davies expresses the fact succinctly: "Arms are the sign of the technical rank of gentility" (*CG* 23). Because the gentry as a discrete social class found its origins in men who, in feudal times, were obligated to raise armies for the liege lord, the ensign by which those armies were identified—the leader's coat of arms—became the symbol of gentility. Fox-Davies notes a further refinement of the relationship between a gentleman, his land, and his arms: the landowner would require a device with which to authenticate legal documents, and this would typically be heraldic: "Every landowner was at one time required to have his seal—presumably, of arms—and as a result arms were naturally then considered to possess something of a territorial character" (*CG* 478).

As an historical code, heraldry proclaims personal and national history—both, in the case of Royal Arms. The appearance of the paternal arms of Saxony in an inescutcheon on the arms of Albert Edward, Prince of Wales, in the nineteenth century, tells a story about the family history of the bearer, and also describes a chapter in European history. Perhaps an even more interesting family and national story is that told by the sudden disappearance of the arms of Saxony from the armorial achievement of the Prince of Wales in 1911, during a time of strained relations between England and Germany.[4] This heraldic change presaged a similarly-motivated change of name in 1917, when the Teutonic Royal family of England suddenly became the eponymous "Windsor" family (which prompted the King's first cousin, the Kaiser, to wonder when he might see a production of the *Merry Wives of Saxe-Cobourg-Gotha* [Lacey 96]). On the level of family history, we get a brief account of the relative sexual continence of Edward IV, Henry VIII, and William IV in the "differenced" (or modified, in these cases by batons and bendlets sinister) versions of the Royal Arms assigned to Arthur, Viscount Lisle; Henry, Duke of Richmond; and the

Earl of Munster; respectively. The observer trained in heraldry will recognize the distinctive bearings of royal bastards.

III

It is not my purpose here to provide a comprehensive guide to heraldry; even were I qualified to do so, it would be appropriately pointed out that the world needs another guide to heraldry even less than it needs another specialized volume of Joycean exegesis. But I would like to follow the lead of C. W. Scott-Giles, whose *Shakespeare's Heraldry* provides a Shakespearean introduction to heraldry; I hope not only to discuss heraldry in Joyce, but also, in so doing, to produce a "Joycean guide to heraldry": an exposition of heraldry in the light cast by Joyce's use, and ultimate transformation, of it. The logical starting place is to discuss the "subtle and curious jargon" that fascinated Stephen Dedalus.

One can always go a long way in heraldic discussion simply by considering "what everybody knows" about heraldry. To wit: "everybody knows" that heraldry has to do with heralds, who historically played trumpet fanfares for royal personages as they moved from room to room. Heraldry is also concerned with "crests," which are synonymous with coats of arms; everyone knows that "crests" are connected with surnames, so that any Smith can find the Smith crest in Burke's *General Armory*, and on that authority display it on his wall, stationery, or automobile, unless said Smith be a bastard (I mean a *real* bastard), in which case he need merely differentiate his Smith crest from the others by using a "bar sinister."

As the humorist Josh Billings said a century ago, "The trouble with people is not that they don't know but that they know so much that ain't so." To undo the damage of the paragraph above, let me first address this pernicious matter of trumpets. This is a favorite subject of writers on heraldry, but none have expressed it better than the co-authors of *Intelligible Heraldry:*

> But as regards that romantic figure, the *Herald of England*—who is always depicted in the cinema and in pictures advertising patent medicines and tinned foods, blowing spirited fanfares on the trumpet, it should be noted that proficiency on the trumpet or any wind instrument was not one of the accomplishments ever demanded of the herald. In fact we doubt very much whether there is a single herald to-day in any of the three Offices of Arms who could be relied upon for even a recognisable interpretation of "The Death of Nelson" on the euphonium. (Lynch-Robinson 113–14)

The matter of the "crest" is far more serious. In 1909, A. C. Fox-Davies wrote: ". . . a few years ago the habit of the uneducated in styling anything stamped upon a sheet of note-paper 'a crest,' was fast becoming stereotyped into current acceptance" (*CG* 59). Fox-Davies's statement needs the following qualifications: this trend was limited neither to a few years before 1909, nor to the "uneducated." In November of the same year, James Joyce made a manuscript of *Chamber Music* for Nora Barnacle, into which he bound an illustration of the coat of arms of Joyce of Galway. In writing to his brother, Stanislaus, to ask for the coat of arms, he asked him "to take my crest out of its frame . . ." (*Letters* 2: 262). Joyce makes a common error here that he would not have made several years later: there are many heraldic passages in Joyce's works which distinguish a crest from a coat of arms. The new critical edition of *Ulysses* restores two such references: in "Scylla and Charybdis," Stephen alludes to Shakespeare's "coat and crest" (9.925; cf. "coat of arms" {210.2–3}); also, the reference to the crest of Sir Frederick Falkiner ("the engraved initials, crest, coat of arms. . ." [12.1873]) had been omitted in the Random House editions {344.21–22}. Even Leopold Bloom seems to know the difference between shield and crest in "Ithaca," when he envisions achieving gentility, "with a family crest and coat of arms" (*U* 17.1610–11 {715.31}). In the passage from *Finnegans Wake* to which my chapter heading refers, a clear (at least by *Wake* standards of clarity) distinction is made between crest and shield: Wassaily Booslaeugh's armorial bearings are described first by referring to his crest: "His crest of huroldry, in vert with ancillars. . ."; and then to his shield (or escutcheon) "His scutschum fessed. . ." (*FW* 5.6–8).

A crest is a *part* of a coat of arms: not every coat of arms has a crest; but those that do, have it as an ornament on the helmet, usually on a wreath. In the arms of Joyce of Galway, for example, the crest is the wolf issuing forth from the helmet (or, in the case of the rendering that Joyce owned, from the wreath over the shield: the artist dispensed with the helmet). Thus it is misleading when the indefatigably meticulous Adaline Glasheen says "There is a phoenix on Joyce's family crest. . ." (233) not only because the eagle on the Joyce escutcheon is not, strictly speaking, a firebird (although the connection between the red eagle and the Phoenix is an inspired perception on Mrs. Glasheen's part), but because the Joyce crest is a "demi-wolf ducally gorged." Another scholar from whose meticulousness I have benefitted is Richard Ellmann, but even he follows Joyce's lead in misusing "crest" to refer to an entire coat of arms when he says ". . . in *A Portrait* . . . Stephen offers to show a doubting classmate the family crest at the Ulster king-at-arms' office in Dublin Castle" (*JJ* 11). Actually, in the passage referred to, Stephen offers to show Davin his family tree (*P* 202), but perhaps Ellmann has picked up Joyce's use of "crest" from the 1909 letter, which is in one of the volumes of the *Letters* that Ellmann edited. It is not my purpose here to berate my betters for a semantic *faux pas;* but I wish to illustrate that something that "everyone knows"—that "crest" is synonymous with coat of arms—is a solecism foisted upon us by purveyors of bogus heraldic stationery and school ties; it is a solecism that I oppose with the fervor appropriate to a holy crusade, first, because it is so pervasive, and second, because it interferes with a sensitive reading of heraldic allusions in Joyce's works. I will have done riding this hobby-horse for the moment, closing with a stirring passage from the *Oxford English Dictionary* on this vital subject: "It is a vulgar error to speak of the arms of such bodies [as colleges or cities] as *crests*" (*OED* 1: 602).

The very existence of the College of Arms and the Irish Genealogical Office (formerly the Office of Arms) belies another popular entry in the encyclopedia of heraldic misinformation, which has to do with the assumption of arms "by right of name" (a phrase coined by stationers for marketing reasons). Arms belong to specific people, not to names, and even though members of Scottish clans and Irish septs *display* the arms of chieftains in the fashion that a British subject might display the Royal Arms, the coat of arms actually belongs to the one person to whom it is granted, and to his direct descendants. One can understand how the assumption of arms by "right of name" emerged if one compares the cost of a grant of arms (typically over £800 in England [Olmert 90]), and the cost of printing stationery with someone else's arms, taken from a book. To illustrate this distinction between a legitimate grant of arms and "irregular assumption," suffice it to remark that neither the College of Arms in England, nor the Chief Herald of the Republic of Ireland, could attach any meaning to the phrase "the arms of James Joyce"; the arms of the Joyces of Galway, however, are another matter.

To move to another heraldic "ghost," in his chapter on marks of bastardy, Fox-Davies observes: "It has been remarked that the knowledge of 'the man in the street' is least incorrect when he knows nothing. Probably the only heraldic knowledge that a large number possess is summed up in the assertion that the heraldic sign of illegitimacy is the 'bar sinister' " (*CG* 508).

The heraldic bar, being horizontal, can tend neither dexter nor sinister; Fox-Davies explains that this solecism stems from the French expression "barre sinistre," which is translated "bend sinister" in English heraldry, the English bend being the equivalent of the French diagonal "barre." But even the "bend sinister" is not invariably a mark of illegitimacy, as Vladimir Nabokov points out in the 1963 preface to his 1947 novel, *Bend Sinister* (vi). Bends sinister have, on occasion, been used as a difference for bastardy, just as they occur in the arms of Shiffner and Burne-Jones with absolutely no connotation of bastardy (*CG* 512).

Finally, before leaving sinister subjects of discussion, let me point out that everybody knows that "dexter" refers to the right side of the heraldic field, and "sinister" to the left. And this is perfectly true; but what *not* everybody knows is that this holds true only *from the standpoint of a shield bearer:* the sinister side of a field is the right side *as viewed*, and vice versa.

The point of this pompous diatribe is to demonstrate that for reading an author like Joyce, who is both meticulous and subtle in his use of heraldic language, a little "common knowledge" about heraldry is worse than useless. On the other hand, because Joyce distinguishes between shield and crest, dexter and right, sinister and left in his works (if not in his letters), some understanding of the "subtle and curious jargon" of heraldry can significantly inform and expand a reading of Joyce's works.

IV

The focus of heraldry is the shield, or escutcheon. Shields of many shapes have been used in heraldic art over the centuries; the Norman shield was elongated, but later shields gradually tended toward the equilateral shape common in heraldic illustration today. In addition to the numerous roughly triangular heraldic shields, there is the "lozenge" (shaped like the diamond of a deck of cards), used to display the arms of unmarried heiresses, or of the widows of armigers; and the cartouche, an oblong shield often associated with ecclesiastical heraldry. Treating the "conventional" shield, Ottfried Neubecker catalogues some 200 discrete shield shapes, including elaborate fifteenth-century shields with lance-notches in the dexter, and the highly ornate shields of the period many writers consider heraldry's most "decadent," the eighteenth and nineteenth centuries (Neubecker 76–77). Most of the illustrations herein will use the equilateral, so-called "heater-shaped" shield (not a particularly technical term, but one used in many recent heraldry books, including *Boutell* and Fox-Davies).

The two main divisions of the shield are dexter and sinister (which, incongruously, appear to be left and right, respectively). A more detailed division of the shield recognizes nine "points," as seen in Illus. 1-B. The surface of the shield, or the "field," is distinguished by its tinctures, and its charges. The tinctures include two metals—or (gold) and argent (silver; generally also equivalent to white),[5] and a number of "colors." How many heraldic colors there are has been a matter of controversy in heraldic circles. Oswald Barron, whose *Encyclopaedia Brittanica* article on heraldry has been described by Ruth von Phul as one of the sources of Joyce's heraldic allusions, recognizes five colors, and contemptuously dismisses attempts to augment the heraldic spectrum (323a-24a). Most writers agree on the five: azure (blue), gules (red), vert (green), sable (black), and purpur (purple).

Von Phul argues that Joyce's use of heraldic language in "Proteus" reflects a satiric sympathy with the strongly-held classical views expressed in Barron's essay. Barron not only excludes such so-called "stains" as "tenné" (brown-orange; the "tenney" of *U* 3.336–37 {46.11–13}), or "murrey" and "sanguine" (shades of red introduced, according to Fox-Davies, to obviate encroachment on the Royal livery color), but also strongly advocates simplified heraldic language bordering on "plain language." For example, he favors the use of "gold" and "silver" instead of "or" and "argent." While, on the one hand, Barron's direct and concise approach to heraldic language seems sensible, it also tends to take some of the sport out of the language of blazon. Since such controversies as those that existed between Barron and Fox-Davies (indeed, between Barron and almost everybody else) are never resolved, this study employs only those heraldic conventions appropriate to explicating Joyce's allusions. In fact as von Phul points out, Joyce's references in "Proteus" are replete with many of the terms eschewed by Barron, and his references throughout the works tend toward more elaborate blazon than Barron favors. For instance, he favors

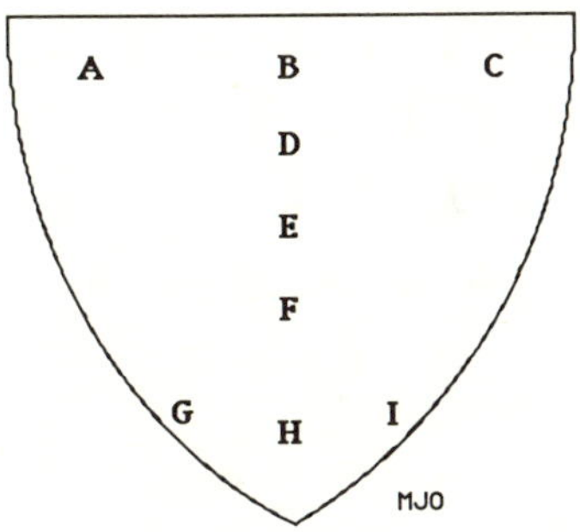

Illustration 1-B The Nine Points of an Heraldic Shield. A—Dexter Chief; B—Middle Chief; C—Middle Chief; D—Honour Point; E—Fess Point; F—Nombril Point; G—Dexter Base; H—Middle Base; I—Sinister Base.

the use of "or" and "argent" rather than "gold" or "silver." The strongly-held preferences of Barron and others notwithstanding, neither the "or/argent" school nor the "gold/silver" school is more or less correct than the other: while "gold/silver" seemed to be preferred by heralds in Shakespeare's day (and more recently, in the 1950s), current usage leans toward the more antique "or/argent." Gold/silver will undoubtedly have further comebacks, and so forth.

In addition to the two metals, five colors, and various "stains" (all of which comprise "tinctures"), one other term related to hue is "proper," meaning "in the color of nature." For example, a Cornish chough (a bird) described as "sable" would be depicted in black, while a Cornish chough "proper" would be portrayed with black feathers, and red feet and beak. A tree "vert" would be completely green, whereas a tree "proper" would have green foliage, and bark of natural color. The "dexter handcoup" (or dexter hand, couped [cut at the wrist]) of *Finnegans Wake* 99.30–31, is, as one might expect of a hand so treated, "bloody proper."

A final category of terms related to tinctures is that of "furs." This includes *ermine* (white, with stylized black marks representing ermine tails; Illus. 1-C), and several related furs: *ermines*, which is like a negative image of ermine: black with white marks; and *erminites*, *erminetes*, and *erminois*, which are other variations on the ermine "theme" of different colors. Another fur is "vair," a parti-colored fur of argent and azure (Illus. 1-D). Although of unclear origin, vair was apparently a valuable fur, and it is a mistranslation of vair that is thought to be responsible for the improbable material of which Cinderella's slippers were made: of glass, or "verre."

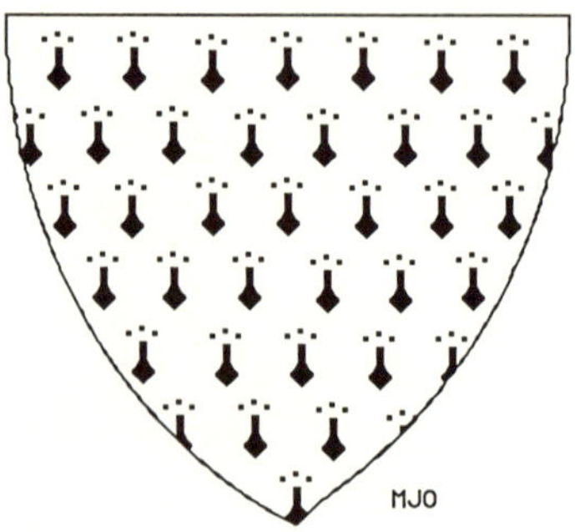

Illustration 1-C Ermine

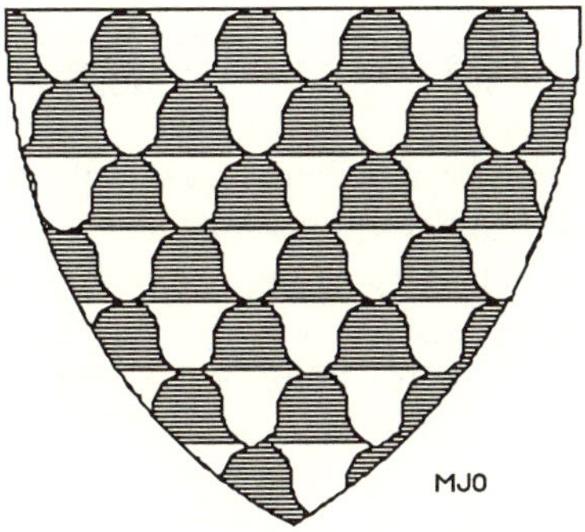

Illustration 1-D Vair

Another means of distinguishing fields is by partitions; I will discuss these in connection with the traditional geometric shapes of the heraldic field, since these so-called "ordinaries" and the partitions are inherently related. The "ordinaries" include an arbitrary group of seven to twelve shapes called by some writers the "honorable ordinaries" (a distinction which also elicits a sneer from Barron [317b]). There is no authoritative number of these, nor any authoritative explanation why they are "honorable"; *The Observer's Book of Heraldry* lists ten, as does *Boutell* (counting the bends dexter and sinister as one ordinary).

The one name among many distinguished writers on heraldry likely to be widely recognized is that of John Ruskin, who wrote extensively on heraldry, including an introduction to the subject in *The Eagle's Nest;* Ruskin gives a list of twelve ordinaries, along with some colorful derivations of them. I do not know for certain that Ruskin was one of Joyce's heraldic sources; it is demonstrable that Joyce read widely on heraldry, and it is known that he read much of Ruskin (see Feshbach 333–36). Whether or not Ruskin's heraldry was in Joyce's syllabus, however, Ruskin's advocacy of gothicism in general, and of heraldry in particular (he called heraldry "the most brilliant, and in its power on character, hitherto the most practically effective of the arts" [*Works* 22: 156]) was a major influence on Joyce's generation. For this reason, and also because of his far superior powers of exposition, I rely on Ruskin to introduce the heraldic ordinaries (Illus. 1-E):

> 1. The Chiefe; a bar of colour across the upper part of the shield, signifies authority or chief-dom, as the source of all order, power, and peace.

2. The cross, as an ordinary [a geometric shape], distinguished from the cross as a bearing [a physical object], consists simply of two bars dividing the shield into four quarters; and, I believe, that it does not in this form stand properly as a symbol of Christian faith, but only as one of Christian patience and fortitude. The cross as a symbol of faith is terminated within the field.

3. The Fesse, a horizontal bar across the middle of the shield, represents the knight's girdle, or anything that binds and secures, or continues. [. . .]

4. The Bend, an oblique bar descending from the right to left of the holder of the shield, represents the sword belt. [. . .]

5. The Pale, an upright bar dividing the shield in half, is simply an upright piece of timber in a palisade. It signifies either defence or enclosure.

6. The Pile, a wedge-shaped space of colour with the point downwards, represents what we still call a pile; a piece of timber driven into moist ground. . . .

7. The Canton, a square space of colour in either of the upper corners of the shield, signifies the cornerstone of a building. . . .

8. The Chevron, a band bent at an angle (properly a right angle), with its point upwards, represents the gable or roof of a house. [. . .]

9. The Orle, or a narrow band following the outline of the shield midway between its edge and centre, is a more definite expression of enclosure or fortification by moat or rampart. [. . .]

10. The Gyron, a triangular space of colour with its point in the centre of the shield, derives its name from the old Latin gyro [sic], a fold. . . .

11. The Flasque, a space of colour terminated by a curved line on each flank of the shield. . . .

12. The Saltire, from salir, represents the securest form of machine for mounting walls. . . . As a bearing, it is the St. Andrew's Cross. (*Works* 22: 280–83)

What validity some of Ruskin's interpretations may have is anybody's guess; he reveals his architectural orientation in many of his explanations, and his distinction between the cross of fortitude and the cross of faith is extremely suspect; on the one hand, heraldry as we know it does hail primarily from the Crusades, and consequently the cross has been of referential significance from heraldry's early days; on the other hand, crosses seem to appear on shields in the Bayeux tapestry, but, far from representing heraldic ordinaries *per se*, these may merely be structural supports. In fact, Ruskin recognizes this functional origin of the cross elsewhere (*The Laws of Fésole* [*Works* 15: 396]). Steering clear of either thematic or structural interpretations of heraldic ordinaries, Gerard Brault defends the abstractions of early blazon as abstractions: "Heraldic terminology is derived, for the most part from the specialized language of artists. Thus *besant* does not mean a Byzantine coin, *chevron* a rafter, *cotice* a leather thong,

Illustration 1-E The Heraldic Ordinaries

and *manche* a sleeve, but the stylized bezant, chevron, cotice, and maunch of artistic tradition" (5).

The principal partitions of the heraldic field derive from the ordinaries. A shield divided vertically down its center is divided "per pale"; a horizontal halving of the field is "per fess"; a diagonal division is "per bend"; a division in the shape of a chevron is "per chevron"; and a division by two diagonal lines (as in an "X") is "per saltire." In addition, shields are partitioned "quarterly" (divided as by a cross), and "gyronny" (in eight triangular sections partitioned per pale, per bends sinister and dexter, and per fess). A circular field partitioned gyronny is a pizza.

Beyond the ordinaries, there are the subordinaries. Like the ordinaries, the subordinaries are arbitrarily defined; for example, the gyron, the flasque (or flanche), the canton, and the orle, considered ordinaries by Ruskin, are deemed subordinaries in *Boutell's Heraldry,* and in Gough and Parker's *Glossary of Terms Used in Heraldry.* Additional subordinaries described in these two sources include:

Lozenge—a diamond-shaped figure; some writers consider a narrowed lozenge a "fusil," but Barron considers this an affectation (322). A "voided" fusil (a "hollow" outline in the shape of a fusil) is called a "mascle." (Illus. 1-F)

Fret—a device described by *Boutell* as "one bendlet [a diminutive of bend] and one bendlet sinister interlaced with a mascle" (56). (Illus. 1-G)

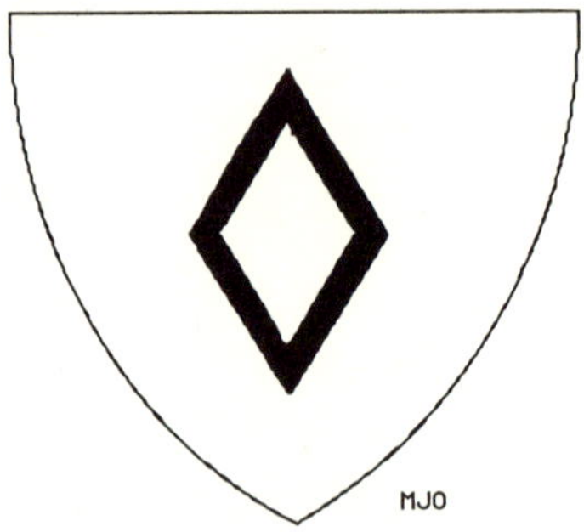

Illustration 1-F Mascle

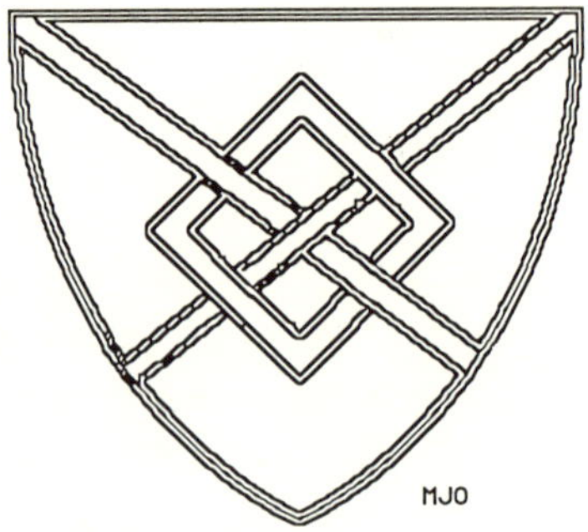

Illustration 1-G Fret

Roundel—circles on the heraldic field. These are classified by their tinctures; i.e., a silver roundel is a "plate," a gold one a "bezant," and so forth.

Billet—an upright rectangular shape.

Label—Commonly seen (with three "points") as the mark of "difference" (to distinguish the arms of members of the same family) for an eldest son (see Illustration of arms of Prince of Wales, Illus. 1-H). The label is described in *Boutell* as "a riband with several shorter ribands [the "points"] (usually three or five pendent from it)" (57).

Inescutcheon—A small shield within the shield. When the differenced Royal Arms of the Princes of Wales bore the arms of Saxony, it was on an inescutcheon (see Illus. 1-H); this has since been replaced by the arms of Wales. The husband of an heiress marshalls her arms on an inescutcheon at the center of his arms; this is called an "escutcheon of pretence."

In addition to these geometric shapes, numerous (innumerable, in fact) recognizable creatures and objects are "charges" on heraldic shields. These range from beasts, both real (as in the lion and eagle), and mythical (the unicorn, the griffin, the basilisk, and the heraldic tyger—not to be confused with the Bengal tiger); plants (including trees, flowers, and so forth), and inanimate objects (weapons, books, the sun, stars, and, in one case I once saw, a floppy diskette). The variety of charges found prohibits listing or discussing them here, since my purpose is not to provide a comprehensive guide to heraldry. Joyce's heraldic descriptions have variety enough, and the spears, women, fish, feathers, eagles, and insects that occur in his heraldic descriptions are discussed in their contexts in the following chapters.

The discussion thus far has been limited to the escutcheon. In addition to this, the one essential component of the heraldic display, the basic elements of a complete coat of arms, or "achievement," might include the following: (See Illus. 1-H)

Crest—Strictly speaking, it refers to the figure ornamenting the helmet of an heraldic achievement. It usually rests on the:

Torse—a stylized wreath atop the helmet, usually drawn to resemble twisted silk. The torse is of the principle metal and color (in that order) of the field, as is the:

Mantling, or *Lambrequin*—cascades of fabric surrounding the escutcheon. Many writers have suggested that the mantling is to represent the surcoat (a fabric coat worn over armor), tattered by swordplay and other misfortunes. Oswald Barron vigorously denies this "worthless tale" (317b); who knows whether he is right? Whether he is or not, however, a tale

Illustration 1-H Arms of Albert Edward, Prince of Wales. From Burke's *General Armory* (1884). A—Escutcheon, or Shield; B—Inescutcheon; C—Helm; D—Coronet; E—Crest; F—Badge; G—Dexter supporter; H—Sinister supporter; I—Compartment; J—Mantling.

so oft repeated over the centuries cannot be wholly "worthless" in heraldic exegesis. The mantling, by means of the torse, is connected to the:

Helm—or helmet.

Supporters—figures of men or beasts on either side of the shield, in the posture of supporting it. The presence of these is also indicative of rank: with the exception of some hereditary supporters granted (through an aberration) to baronets in Scotland (including Sir Walter Scott), the only persons granted hereditary supporters are of the rank (at least) of peers; cities and counties are also granted supporters in the United Kingdom.

Motto—not, strictly speaking, a part of the grant of arms in England, but often featured in a scroll over the crest or beneath the escutcheon of an armorial achievement.

Since there are no drawings of armorial bearings in the works of Joyce,[6] the most salient aspect of heraldry in this study is the language of heraldry: blazon. We have seen one example of blazon in *The Scarlet Letter:* "ON A FIELD, SABLE, THE LETTER A, GULES." This shares aspects of Joyce's use of blazon, of which I will recycle one example from "Proteus": "On a field tenney a buck trippant, proper, unattired" (*U* 3.336–37 {46.12–13}). I will defer precise discussion of this passage in its context to another chapter; for now, I use it to illustrate the syntax of blazon.

Blazon is formulaic: its obscurity derives not only from the ors, argents, bezants, propers, pales, piles, and chevrons of its recondite vocabulary, but also from its inverted structure. Brault suggests that the formulaic nature of blazon derives from an oral tradition, resulting from the need of early heralds to commit to memory many heraldic descriptions:

> For if classic blazon is typified by the sort of orderliness and telegraphic concision which would appeal to clerks, it is also a prime example of formulaic diction. The mnemonic requirements of effective oral delivery have always fostered stereotyped expressions and phrasing. The early French epics, which were designed for oral delivery, are replete with clichés which made the jongleurs' task easier. The same need for a system based upon readily assimilated patterns clearly played a key rôle in the development of blazon. (8)

The formulaic blazon of medieval France is the source of English blazon, just as the French vocabulary of heraldry is the basis of the English heraldic lexicon. Although the principles of blazon have been modified in practice, the following summary of basic principles holds as true for the blazon from Hawthorne and Joyce quoted above as it does for the "classic blazon" that emerged in the thirteenth century.

1. The Field. "*On a field tenney . . .*" In blazon, the first term defines the field itself. Stephen, like Hawthorne ("ON A FIELD, SABLE . . .") includes the phrase "on a field," which often is understood without being stated. In other words, to the heraldist, the blazon might simply begin "Tenney"; it would be understood that the first term refers to the tincture of the field.

2. The Ordinaries. If a coat of arms includes one of the ordinaries (i.e., a bend, a saltire, a fess, and so forth; the chief is an exception: see below), or is partitioned, this expression will follow the tincture. Stephen's blazoning of the buck/dog in "Proteus" includes no ordinary; in "Scylla and Charybdis," however, Stephen quotes the approximate blazon for Shakespeare's coat of arms, which features a gold field, and a spear on a black bend. Stephen omits to mention the gold field, but if this term is inserted, we get a blazoning illustrating the proper order: "[or] on a bend sable a spear or steeled argent. . ." (*U* 9.925 {210.3}). The blazon of the field, for which the single word "or" suffices, is followed by the blazon of the ordinary, the "bend sable."

3. The Charge. "*a buck trippant, proper, unattired. . . .*" The charge of Stephen's heraldic "field" is a buck (actually, a dog that Stephen has imaginatively transformed). The terms that follow the name of the charge elaborate on the charge's appearance. "Trippant" is the word used to describe a walking ("passant") deer; probably not coincidentally, the term is also applied to dogs when they occur in heraldry (*CG* 204, 208). In the blazon of Shakespeare's coat of arms, the charge is the spear; it is the same color as the field ("or"), and its tip is silver ("steeled argent").

In a more complicated blazon, the charge or charges would be followed with a description of the "bordure," if any. This would be followed by the blazon for the chief (partitioned upper third of the field), if any, and any charges found in the chief. If there are any marks of cadency (such as a label, to mark the arms of an eldest son, or the marks of cadency in Henry Fielding's arms, Illus. 1-A), or marks of augmentation, or badges, such as the Red Hand borne on an inescutcheon or canton by the Baronets of Great Britain, these would conclude the blazoning.

This brutally brief and general summary should aid understanding of the heraldic terminology in the following chapters; a glossary is also provided, keyed to relevant references in Joyce's works, as well as to technical terms introduced herein. Clearly, I have not covered all possible aspects of blazon that might be relevant to a reading of Joyce's heraldic allusions. The reader wishing a more detailed treatment of heraldry, its sources, and conventions, might consider Oswald Barron's article in the eleventh *Encyclopaedia Brittanica*, or A. C. Fox-Davies's *A Complete Guide to Heraldry* (either in the 1909 version that Joyce might have known, or in any of its several subsequent revisions); the hobby-horses of each respective writer notwithstanding, their writings have stood the test of time. *Boutell's Heraldry* is a nineteenth century work that has been frequently revised; the 1978 revision by J. P. Brooke-Little is lucid and thorough, and was my introduction to this subject. A surprising little book is Charles MacKinnon's *The Observer's Book of Heraldry*, which contains a wealth of precise and informative intelligence within its diminutive duodecimo format.

CHAPTER TWO

Heraldry in Literature

As a symbol of social station, of the legendary exploits of knights errant, of a nation's history, of life (in the hereditary legacy), and of death (in the heraldic funeral hatchment), heraldry is an evocative graphic code that has occupied a preëminent position in the Western imagination. It is not surprising, then, that many major figures in English and continental literature have been interested in (or, as in the case of Ben Jonson, obsessed with) heraldry. The playwright Sir John Vanbrugh not only held the office of herald, but ("due," says Sir Anthony Wagner with palpable contempt, "to an accident of patronage" [125]), actually held the post of Clarenceux King of Arms for a number of years. But Vanbrugh's acquaintance with heraldry was slight (perhaps almost nonexistent), and his tenure was without distinction.

The suggestion that there is a distinct heraldic "tradition" in European literature might arouse the reader's skepticism. Even those of us who have noticed heraldic language in the works of major poets are tempted to skip over the troublesome jargon, in the hope that the poet will soon move on to something more comprehensible. In this chapter, I hope to demonstrate that not only are there distinctive literary traditions involved in heraldic allusion, but also that these traditions emerge in the works of some of the most prominent English and continental writers. Northrop Frye mentions one instance of how this tradition functions: "When a critic meets St. George the Redcross Knight in Spenser, bearing a red cross on a white ground, he has some idea what to do with this figure. When he meets a female in Henry James's *The Other House* called Rose Armiger with a white dress and a red parasol, he is, in the current slang, clueless" (101).

As Frye implies, both references rely on a common heraldic allusion. He goes on to mention the problem of the lack of "a common cultural ground" between modern readers and poets: although the larger part of this common ground involves sources on the scale of the Bible and classical literature, one might also extrapolate from Frye's example that one element of this missing background includes allusions to heraldry. Such allusions have been used by Dante, Chaucer, Jonson, and Shakespeare, among others, as if the reader is expected to understand them; whether Henry James has similar hopes for his Rose Armiger allusion is open to question. Joyce's heraldic allusions, to go to another extreme, are important components of the "many puzzles and enigmas" which Joyce boasted of having put into *Ulysses* (*JJ* 521), and of the deeper and more various enigmas of *Finnegans Wake*.

I do not propose a comprehensive litany of allusions to heraldry in literature; this would require lengthy discussions of allusions in Dante, Chaucer, Malory, Spenser, Cervantes, Shakespeare, Jonson, Defoe, Sterne, Thackeray, Keats, Coleridge, Disraeli, Scott, Dickens, Ruskin, Tennyson—and this is only the "first string." My focus is on the most prominent writers using this tradition. Although this discussion is not intended to document specific instances of "influence" on Joyce, I will emphasize writers in whom Joyce was clearly interested. Short of determining influence, I seek to document the tradition that has surrounded heraldic allusions in European literature, and in which Joyce's allusions fall. Of greatest importance will be the emergence in literature of heraldry as the emblematic code of the knight errant on the one hand, and of the English gentleman on the other.

Elaborate literary use of heraldry occurs at the dawn of vernacular poetry, and not long after the dawn of European heraldry: several characters in the *Divine Comedy* of Joyce's favorite poet, Dante (*JJ* 4–5), are not identified by name, but would have been clearly recognizable to Florentine readers because of Dante's specific description of their heraldic bearings. In Canto 17 of the "Inferno," Virgil and Dante encounter a group of damned usurers. The poet looks them over carefully:

> Poi che nel viso a certi li occhi porsi,
>
> . . . .
>
> Non ne conobbi alcun, ma io m'accorsi
> che dal collo a ciascun pendea una tasca
> ch'avea certo colore e certo segno,
>
> . . . .
>
> in una borsa gialla vidi azzurro,
> che d'un leone avea faccia e contegno.
> Poi, procedendo di mio squardo il curro,
> vidine un'altra come sangue rossa,
> mostrando un'oca bianca più che burro.

E un, che d'una scrofa azzurra e grossa
segnato avea lo suo sacchetto bianco,
Mi disse: ««Che fai tu in questa
fossa?»» (17: 52–56)[1]

Heraldic arms identify their bearer in hell as well as on the battlefield. These arms identify three prominent Florentine families: the Gianfigliazzi ("Il leone azzuro in campo giallo" [Panaitescu 274]), the Ubriachi ("L'oca bianca in campo rosse"), and the Scrovegni ("d'una scrofa azzura" [Grandgent 71]). Illus. 2-A shows these arms, which appear in equally recognizable form in contemporary and later illustrations (one of which is attributed to Giotto) of this scene from the "Inferno" (Panaitescu 267, 271, 274, 280).

Dante's use of heraldry immediately and firmly connects arms with social privilege; that the emblem of social distinction should be borne on purses hanging around the necks of usurers in hell makes a moral point that is difficult to miss. In the "Paradiso," Dante meets his ancestor, Cacciaguida, a Crusader and knight; the poet's pride gives way to a meditation on the ephemeral nature of nobility: ("O poca nostra nobilità di sangue!" ["O, our petty blood nobility!"] 16: 1). In the course of the meditation, he refers to more noble families, again using arms rather than names to identify them: "la colonna del vaio" (the Column of Vair [16: 103]) refers to the arms of Pilli, which featured a pale of vair (one of the heraldic furs); "e la palle dell'oro / Fiorian Fiorenza in tutti suoi gran fatti" ("and the golden spheres / embellished Florence [lit. "flowered Florence"] in all of her great feats"; 16: 111) alludes to the bezants on the escutcheon of the Lamberti (Grandgent 257). As in the "Inferno," the heraldic allusions occur in the ironic context of the mighty who have fallen.

After Dante's death, heraldry received equally prominent attention in the works of Geoffrey Chaucer. Among the few facts that we know about Chaucer is that he was well-versed in heraldry (See Illus. 2-B). Sometime servant to John of Gaunt, controller under Richard II, and ambassador, Chaucer moved in noble and courtly circles, and would have had ample

Illustration 2-A Arms of the Gianfigliazzi, the Ubriachi, and the Scrovegni, as described in Dante, *Inferno* 17.

exposure to "practical heraldry"; moreover, he is thought to have been the son-in-law of a herald (Sir Payn Roet, Guienne King of Arms [Wagner 18]). Finally, we know that he testified at the 1386 Scrope-Grosvenor trial, a civil proceeding in the Court of Chivalry between two men claiming the same coat of arms.[2] Even without these facts, however, we could infer Chaucer's heraldic knowledge from references in his works. In "The House of Fame," for example, the narrator describes the arrival of a distinguished assemblage of heralds; in typical Chaucerian fashion, the speaker protests his inadequate grasp of heraldic matters, and in so doing reveals the impressive extent of his knowledge of how heralds functioned:

And somme corouned were as kynges,
With corounes wroght ful of losenges;
And many ryban and many frenges
Were on her clothes trewely.
   Thoo atte last aspyed y
That pursevantes and heraudes,
That crien ryche folkes laudes,
Hyt weren alle; and every man
Of hem, as y yow tellen can,
Had on him throwen a vesture
Which that men clepe cote-armure,
Embrowded wonderliche ryche,
Although they nere nought ylyche.
But noghte nyl I, so mote y thryve,
Ben aboute to dyscryve
Alle these armes that ther weren,
That they thus on her cotes beren. . . .
(*Works* 294–95; 11. 1316–32)

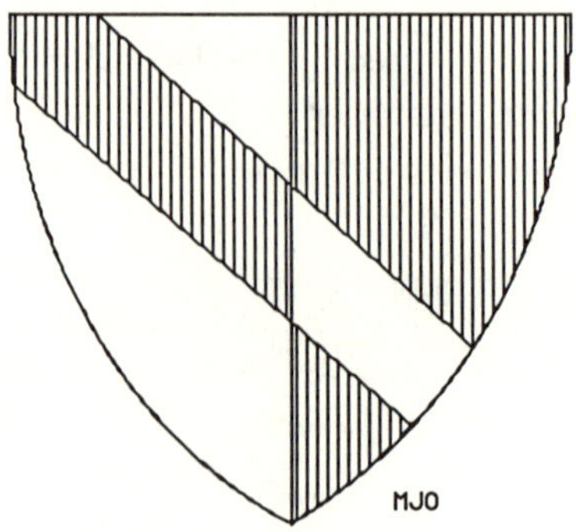

Illustration 2-B Arms of Chaucer: Per pale argent and gules a bend counterchanged.

Sir Anthony Wagner treats this passage as documentary evidence of the social status and functions of fourteenth-century heralds (Wagner 19). The kings crowned with lozenges and ribbons are "kings of arms"; a "pursevante" (pursuivant: literally, "follower") is a junior heraldic officer, and Chaucer's reference to pursuivants is the first recorded reference to the word in the *OED* (2: 2368). In *The House of Fame*, Chaucer's heralds are serving the social equivalent of their traditional function at the tournament: identifying the distinguished personages by their heraldic bearings. Arms are similarly used to identify, in their conventional chivalric context, in the "Knight's Tale" of the *Canterbury Tales:* among the dead and wounded after the battle at Thebes, the heralds identify Palamon and Arcite by their armorial bearings. They find the two:

> Both in oon armes, wroght ful richely,
> Of whiche two Arcita highte that oon,
> And that oother knyght highte Palamon.
> Nat fully quyke, ne fully dede they were,
> But by hir cote-armures and by hir gere
> The heraudes knewe hem best in special
> As they that weren of the blood roial
> Of Thebes, and of sustren two yborn
> (*Works* 27; 11. 1012–19)

That the two bear identical arms enables the heralds to determine the cousins' relation to one another, and to the Theban royal family. In the same Tale, heralds serve in their historical capacity as officials at Theseus' tournament: at lines 2533–34 "The heraud on a scaffold makes an 'Oo!'/ Til al the noyse of peple was ydo," and announces the rules of the tournament; finally, at line 2598 the heralds begin the tournament (*Works* 41–42).

For the most part, heraldry in Chaucer is the emblematic code of the "parfit gentil knyght." Although during Chaucer's lifetime the advent of firearms was rendering armor obsolete, and thereby diminishing the military significance of armorial bearings, their social significance was increasing. Nevertheless, the literary significance of heraldry in the two centuries following the death of Chaucer continued to pertain to knights, and especially to the knight-errant of Arthurian tradition. Thus while the proliferation of heraldic bearings as emblems of social rank and ancestry necessitated the incorporation of the College of Arms in 1484, the heraldic shield as the hallmark of the knight errant was a major symbol in a work published the following year: Malory's *Morte d'Arthur.*

Malory's heraldic allusions are not generally as learned as those of Chaucer, but there are a number of references that merit attention. Among these are references to heralds themselves, and to pursuivants, serving in their traditional tournament role. In Book 7, Ch. 30 (*MD* 1: 290), Gareth fights incognito in arms that (through the action of an enchanted ring) constantly change hue; despite his lack of recognizable arms, he is ultimately identified by the observant heralds, who notice that his helm is emblazoned in gold letters, "THIS HELM IS SIR GARETH OF ORKNEY." In a later episode (*MD* 1: 427; Bk. 9, Ch. 24), Sir Tristram learns of a tournament between the Kings of Scotland and Wales by consulting pursuivants.

References to armorial bearings themselves—to shields, crests, banners, and the like—are vague in the first eight books of the *Morte d'Arthur;* arms in these books generally serve to obscure identities rather than to identify, and seldom are the cognizances on the shields explicitly described. In Book 6, Ch. 6 (*MD* 1: 203) for example, Lancelot proposes to fight for King Bagdemagus anonymously, bearing only a plain white shield.[3] In Book 7, arms are distinguished by color only, as Gareth fights a succession of knights identified by their shields as a Black, Green, Red, and Blue knight. In the tournament (Bk 7, Ch. 29–30), Gareth himself is recognizable only as the knight of many colors until the heralds are able to identify him.[4] Similarly, Tristram fights as a white knight in tournament (*MD* 1 320; Bk. 8, Ch. 10) against Palomides, who is a black knight; in Book 9, Ch. 29 (*MD* 1: 436) Tristram is a black knight (like Leopold Bloom in "Cyclops").[5]

After Book 9, knights are more frequently identified by allusions to the bearings on their shields. We learn in Book 10, Ch. 12 (*MD* 2: 24) that Mordred bears "a shield of silver and black bends," when as a prank Dinadan persuades King Mark that these are the arms of Lancelot. Later in the same book, Dinadan, searching for Sir Palomides, describes his arms as: "a shield of silver and lions' heads." In Book 10, ch. 65, Epinogrus, son of the King of Northumberland, bears "a bended shield of azure" (*MD* 2: 135) and in chapter 83 of Book 10, Sir Safer bears "a green shield and therein a white lion . . ." (*MD* 2: 174).

The most famous arms in the *Morte d'Arthur* are those of Sir Galahad; but it is not necessarily as the arms of Galahad that they are famous. In Book 13 (ch. 9), Galahad obtains his shield, described as "white as any snow, but in the midst was a red cross" (*MD* 2: 252). Shortly thereafter, a white knight explains the origin of the arms to Galahad: the arms had been made thirty-two years after the death of Christ by "Joseph of Arimathea, the gentle knight" (*MD* 2: 254), who had painted the cross on the shield with his own blood. Brault notes that this same origin is accorded to the identical arms borne by "Perlesvaus" in the twelfth-century romance of that name (50); he also observes that this is the coat of arms often attributed to Christ in medieval and Renaissance sources (110). Fox-Davies discusses this medieval and Renaissance conceit, referring to "the statement in the 'Boke of St. Albans' that Christ was a gentleman of coat armour" (*CG* 2); similarly, Arthur Nason finds reference in Legh's 1562 *Accedens of Armory* to the genealogy of "Iesus Christ, a gentleman of great linnage . . ." (Nason 7).

The best known occurrence of these peculiarly Christian arms is in the traditional arms of St. George, prominently displayed in many flags of England (including the Union Jack), and which, in English literature, appears a century after *Morte d'Arthur* as the cognizance of Spenser's Redcrosse Knight in *The Faerie Queene:*

> A Gentle Knight was pricking on the plaine,
> Y cladd in mightie armes and siluer shielde, . . .
> . . . .
> But on his brest a bloudie Crosse he bore,
> The deare remembrance of his dying Lord. . . .
> (Bk 1, Canto 1: 1–2, 11. 1–2, 10)

A gentleman by birth, Spenser was employed in the households of the Earl of Leicester, and later, Lord Grey of Wilton, the Lord Deputy of Ireland. He consequently would have had the type of exposure to "practical heraldry" that Chaucer had. As one might expect, Spenser's heraldic references are specific, and his heraldic charges are integral to the symbolic texture of his works. His 70th Sonnet sustains the idea of spring as a herald:

> Fresh spring the herald of loves mighty king,
> In whose cote armour richly are displayed
> All sorts of flowers the which on earth do spring
> In goodly colours gloriously arrayed. (11. 1–4)

In *The Faerie Queene*, he attentively blazons the arms of the various knights-errant. In Book I, Prince Arthur bears a covered shield, which, when uncovered in Arthur's battle with the giant, proves not to bear a specific design, but rather:

> The light whereof, that heauens light did pas,
> That Such blazing brightnesse through the aier threw,
> That eye mote not the same endure to vew.
> (*FQ*, Bk 1, Canto 8: 19, 11. 3–5)

Arthur does wear a recognizable crest, however; Spenser describes:

> His haughtie helmet, horrid all with gold,
> [Which] Both glorious brightnesse, and great terrour bred;
> For all the crest a Dragon did enfold

> With greedie pawes, and ouer all did spred
> His golden wings. . . .
> (Bk 1, Canto 7: 31, 11. 266–70)[6]

Like Chaucer, Spenser takes occasion to protest his heraldic inadequacy when he avows that to describe the feast in Book 5, Canto 3 "Were worke fit for an Herauld, not for me . . ." (Stanza 3, 1. 6). Yet Spenser holds his own in blazoning the arms of his "Gentle Knights," and in recognizing the chivalric significance of these symbols. Redcrosse and Sir Guyon avoid a fatal conflict when they recognize one another's heraldic bearings in Book 2, Canto 1: Guyon recognizes Redcrosse's "sacred badge of my Redeemers death, / Which on your shield is set for ornament" (stanza 27), and Redcrosse identifies the "faire image of that heauenly Mayd" ([stanza 28] i.e., the Faerie Queene) that adorns Guyon's escutcheon. In Book 3, Arthegall appears in a vision to Britomart, bearing arms connecting him with Ajax and Achilles, with a "couchant Hound" for crest, and a shield bearing "crowned litle Ermilin, / That deckt the azure field with her faire pouldred skin" (Bk. 3, Canto 2: 25).

During the same year that Books 4–6 of *The Faerie Queene* were published, the Herald's College gave a grant of arms to John Shakespeare. Meanwhile, John Shakespeare's son, and another dramatist, Ben Jonson, were using heraldic allusions in a manner quite distinct from that of Spenser. For Spenser, the language of heraldic blazon was one of many devices that evoked the epic atmosphere appropriate to his epic of knight errantry; in this respect, Spenser's use of heraldic allusions is of a kind with that of his forebears, Chaucer and Malory, and of his literary descendants, Milton, Sir Walter Scott, and Alfred, Lord Tennyson.[7] The romantic strain of heraldic allusion, emphasizing the emblems of chivalry to evoke an heroic past, never quite disappears from English literature; indeed, heraldry's frequent occurrence in English novels might be attributed to its prominence in those two distinguished ancestors of the novel, *Morte d'Arthur*, and Cervantes' *Don Quixote.* The deluded knight of La Mancha begins his adventures with a blank shield—like the knights of Tennyson's *Idylls,* he bears a "shield of expectation" until he earns the right to a blazoned shield through his deeds—and ultimately he explains to Sancho his resolve to adopt a device that suitably proclaims his identity: "That is why I say that the sage I mentioned has put it into your thoughts and into your mouth to call me now *The Knight of the Sad Countenance,* a name which I intend to use from this day on; and to make it fit me better, I intend to have a very sad countenance painted on my shield when I have an opportunity" (147).

Without entirely giving way, the chivalric strain in literary allusion to heraldry began to coexist with a second idea that emerges in the English Renaissance: the heraldic emblem as the mark of a gentleman. In *Shakespeare's Heraldry,* C. W. Scott-Giles describes the emergence of the relationship between arms and gentility in Shakespeare's time:

> Shakespeare's outlook on heraldry was, naturally enough, Tudor rather than mediaeval, especially in his association of arms and gentility. In the age of chivalry, only persons holding land by military tenure, and leading their own unit in the feudal army, had occasion to use heraldic shields or banners.
>
> . . . .
>
> This association of heraldry with gentility was carried a stage further by the heralds of the Tudor period. Not content with holding that only a gentleman could possess arms, they asserted that only a person possessing arms could rank as a gentleman. (22)

As Scott-Giles documents, this understanding is amply demonstrated both in Shakespeare's work and his life—the critical dearth of intelligence on Shakespeare's biography notwithstanding. In the plays, references range from the gravedigger's assertion that Adam "was the first that ever bore arms" (*Hamlet* 5: 1, 1. 31), to the numerous references to the various royal arms in the histories. Scott-Giles observes that the sun/son imagery in *Richard III,* from the famous "Now is the winter of our discontent / Made glorious summer through this son of York" (1: 1, 11. 1–2) on, "is used with such method and consistency that Shakespeare must have been well aware that the sun was that King's particular badge" (19).

But as much as Shakespeare's heraldry is the emblematic code of history, it is also above all the badge of gentility: when Bolingbroke (who later becomes Henry IV) laments the effacement of his "household coat" in *Richard II,* it is because he is left with no cognizance "To show the world I am a gentleman" (3: 1, 1. 27).

Shakespeare, who was so manifestly conscious of the idea of gentility and its connection with heraldry, was probably also keenly aware of the disparity between gentility and his literary endeavor. Not only did Shakespeare bear the stigma of being a writer, but he was a writer for the *stage:* in short, a low life. In contrast to Lord Olivier, the entertainer of Shakespeare's day was unlikely to be recognized as a gentleman, let alone be raised to the peerage. Yet Shakespeare came to be recognized as a gentleman in 1596 when the College of Heralds in effect bestowed that hereditary dignity upon Shakespeare's father, John, through a grant of arms. Because of the prohibitive cost of such a grant, it is generally believed that the fees were paid for, not by the insolvent John Shakespeare, but by his successful son, William, whose affluence at that point in his career is indicated by his returning to Stratford in 1597 to buy the biggest house in town.

From the time of the grant of arms, Shakespeare was styled "William Shakespeare, Gentleman," and he established a tradition among English literary artists of dignifying their calling by claiming gentility—the evidence of which is a coat of arms. Thus, whatever Shakespeare's humble origins may have been, the 1596 grant of arms made both his father and him gentlemen, a point stressed by the defiant Shakespeare heraldic motto, "Non sans droit" ("Not without right"). Scott-Giles adds the observation:

> If [Shakespeare's motto, "Non sans droit"] was a challenge, it seems to have been taken up by Ben Jonson. In *Every man out of his humour* (1599) he introduced a wealthy rustic named Sogliardo who obtained a grant of arms which included a boar's head, whereupon Puntarvolo suggested the motto should be *Not without mustard.* (32)

Ben Jonson's use of heraldry, like that of Shakespeare, has been the subject of a book (Nason, 1907). Because Joyce was known to have had considerable interest in Jonson, and (according to Stanislaus Joyce [*MBK* 198]) read the entire Jonson canon in the winter of 1903, Jonson's elaborate attention to heraldry is of particular interest. Even if Joyce had not studied any books of heraldry, his reading of Jonson alone would have exposed him to an encyclopedic amount of heraldic language and detail. Jonson was a close friend of William Camden, Clarenceux King of Arms, to whom he dedicated *Every Man in His Humour.* Nason suggests that Jonson's heraldic erudition was such that, when in *The Staple of News* he commits "false heraldry" (depicting a color on a color, or a metal on a metal) by placing a silver (argent) tassel within a gold (or) canton, it is not an unwitting error, but rather is a deliberate elaboration of the satiric effect of the coat of arms (Nason 20).

Jonson adds two distinctive features to literary allusion to heraldry: first, a heightening of the type of satiric commentary on armorial pretensions introduced by Dante (for example, Jonson's jab at Shakespeare's motto); and, second, a great deal of technically learned mastery of blazon. Both of these features reflect the distinctive character of the heraldry of Jonson's day: complex blazon does not come into play in Dante or Chaucer, because they are describing the simple heraldry of medieval Europe, often characterized by a single, simple charge on a shield of one tincture. By Jonson's time, however, the proliferation of armorial bearings, and the need to differentiate arms, led to many elaborations in heraldic design. An additional factor reflected in Jonson's heraldic allusion is the matter of social rank we have been considering: persons desirous of proving distinguished pedigree did so not merely by bearing arms, but by using arms marshaling the bearings of several distinguished families. These are the "quartered" arms, which, contrary to what the term might lead one to expect, are not limited to four different sets of arms. Among Jonson's contemporaries, it had become a vogue to establish rights to arms of many quarterings;[8] in a 1929 essay on "The Abuse of Arms" (xxiv), Fox-Davies states that the record for the largest number of quarterings in the College of Arms was 323, for the family of Lloyd of Stockton. Scott Giles observes that: "In these complex [multiply-quartered] 'achievements of arms,' and not in the plain, practical shields of an earlier day, we find justification for Gray's words, 'the boast of heraldry' " (16).

In addition, Jonson's day was marked by corruption in the Herald's College, so that grants of arms were predicated upon nothing so much as money. This is what Jonson parodies in the passage from *Every Man Out of His Humour*, referred to above. Sogliardo is said to have "purchast armes, . . . and rare ones too: of as many colours, as e're you saw [on] any foole's coat in your life" (*EMOH* 3: 2, 11. 28–30). In his 1907 study of heraldry in Jonson, Arthur Nason demonstrates Jonson's extensive knowledge of heraldic blazon; Jonson brings much of this versatility to bear in blazoning the coat of arms that Sogliardo assumes. Appropriately, the result is the heraldic equivalent of a fool's motley (See Illus. 2-C). The blazon is (as read by Sogliardo):

GYRONY, of eight *peeces; AZVRE* and *GVLES,* betweene three *plates;* a *CHEV'RON, engrailed checkey, OR, VERT,* and *ERMINES;* on a *cheefe ARGENT* betweene two *ANN'LETS, sables;* a Bores head, *Proper.* (EMOH 3:4, 11. 75–79)

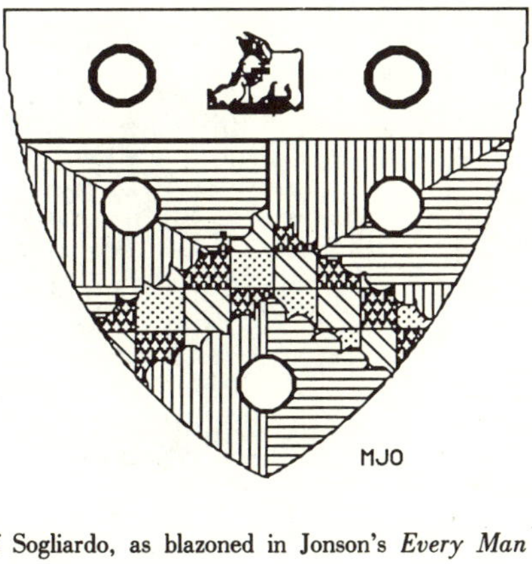

Illustration 2-C Arms of Sogliardo, as blazoned in Jonson's *Every Man Out of his Humour* (3: 4).

The issues that are raised in the heraldic allusions of Shakespeare and Jonson illustrate the basic ideas underlying heraldic interest in the following centuries. As Scott-Giles points out, the idea of armigerous gentility is manifest not only in Shakespeare's works, but in his life; that this did not escape Joyce's notice (or Stephen Dedalus's) will be the subject of Chapter Three. That this did not escape Jonson's notice has already been suggested by Jonson's allusion to Shakespeare's motto in *Every Man Out of His Humour*. But Shakespeare's gesture of affirming his gentility by obtaining a grant of arms is the first of many instances of English literary figures' gentling their social condition in this manner, with or without legitimate grants. Such diverse and unlikely figures as Daniel Defoe, Laurence Sterne, Robert Burns, and James Joyce made ostentatious (although perhaps tongue-in-cheek, in the cases of Burns and Joyce) use of coats of arms, apparently without grants to the same. Defoe used a coat of arms blazoned "Gules, a chevron or between three griffins rampant" as the frontispiece of his 1703 *A True Collection of the Writings of the Author of the True Born English-man* (Shinagel 73–74; See Illus. 2-D). Like Shakespeare, Defoe wished to ameliorate the low prestige of his calling (in Defoe's case, journalism) by establishing himself as a gentleman. The question of whether or not Defoe was entitled to the arms he displayed in 1703 is complicated by the appearance of a different achievement as frontispiece to Defoe's 1706 *Jure Divino:* the chevron disappears, and the griffins change from the rampant attitude to "passant" (walking on all fours).

Asked by a reader about his heraldic bearings, Charles Dickens once wrote that he made no use of a coat of arms. He wrote, "I have never

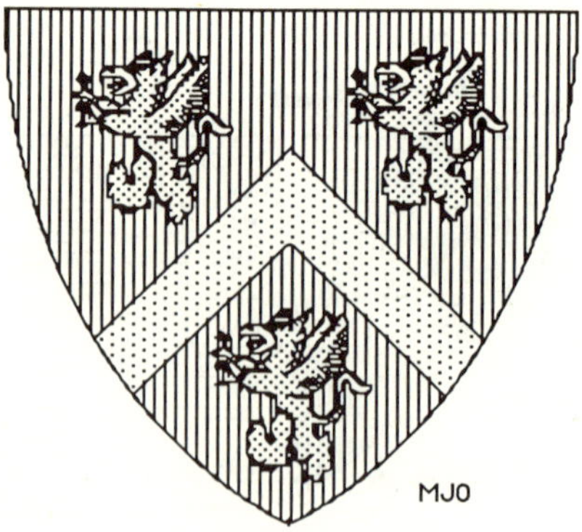

Illustration 2-D Arms used by Daniel DeFoe, circa 1703.

used any other armorial bearings than my father's crest; a lion couchant, bearing in his dexter paw a Maltese cross."[9]

Dickens is not making an error in terminology here: when he says crest, he means crest, as the bookplate he used bearing this insignia indicates. Dickens, whose sensitivity to social class compelled him to conceal scrupulously from his children his father's descent from servants, somehow came to believe that the crest granted to William Dickens in 1625, was his father's crest (Lee 102). That Dickens troubled to preserve this legacy on a bookplate (Illus. 2-E) is a fair measure of how indifferent he was to "such ceremonies," and the social status that they imply.

Some men of letters achieved the distinction of legitimate heraldic grants, like that of Shakespeare. In the nineteenth century, Sir Walter Scott achieved his "Sir" when he was the first man to be "created" a baronet by George IV. Despite being a distant relation to the ducal Buccleuch family, Scott was able to maintain enough proportion regarding his pedigree to admonish his son that the Scotts were but "cadets of cadets" (younger sons of younger sons), when the younger Walter had expressed an aversion to marry a woman connected with trade. But Scott was far from immune to social aspirations, and these ambitions were satisfied in the grant of arms that coincided with his creation as a baronet (1820). As Herbert Grierson notes in his biography of Scott: "Like Shakespeare a couple of centuries earlier, he would make for himself a place among those who, not by birth alone but by actual possession and status, were landed gentleman, *armigeri*" (3).

As the instances above would suggest, heraldry in the eighteenth and nineteenth centuries became the preoccupation of the socially ambitious, and uses of heraldry in the English novel reflected this. Laurence Sterne's

Illustration 2-E Crest used by Charles Dickens in a bookplate.

Tristram Shandy makes clear that the coat of arms on Walter Shandy's carriage features a bend sinister only because of the painter's ineptitude; Tristram's concern with his social rank is revealed in the title of the novel, *The Life and Opinions of Tristram Shandy, Gent.* Similarly, as I will discuss further in Chapter Three, Yorick in Sterne's *A Sentimental Journey* makes a point not only of blazoning his crest verbally, but also of providing the reader a drawing of his entire armorial achievement. The occurrence of heraldic emblems in Sterne's two novels suggests both connotations of the heraldic motif in English literature: Yorick and Tristram are not only self-proclaimed gentlemen, but they also have much in common with knights errant. Tristram's name links him with Sir Tristram de Lyonesse, and at the same time the lugubrious root of his name, and his comic adventures, link him with the famous Knight of the Woeful Countenance. Yorick, too, shares much with the knight errant, on an obscure mission to redress an insult based on his lack of travel experience.

The nineteenth-century novel usually makes note of heraldic bearings with a slight sneer. In an era marked by sloppy genealogical practices (such as those by which the fictional Simon Stoke becomes Simon Stoke-d'Urberville in Hardy's *Tess of the d'Urbervilles*), Thackeray satirized the great sport of lineage hunting. In his *Book of Snobs*, he traces the pedigree of Sir Alured de Mogyns, Bart. (who, before his grant, was a smuggler named Muggins), with the assistance of "Fluke's Peerage":

> This gentleman is a representative of one of the most ancient families in Wales, who trace their descent until it is lost in the mists of antiquity. A genealogical tree beginning with SHEM is in possession of the family, and is stated by a legend of many thousand years' date to have been drawn on papyrus by a grandson of the patriarch itself. Be this as it may, there can be no doubt of the immense antiquity of the race of MOGYNS. (31)

Thackeray's satires of social pretension make ample use of armorial bearings, as in his description of the arms on the Southdown carriage in *Vanity Fair:* "[on the carriage was] the Earl's coronet and the lozenge (upon which the three lambs trottant argent upon a field vert of the Southdowns, were quartered with sable on a bend or, three snuff-mulls gules, the cognizance of the house of Binkie). . . ." (324; Chapter 33) (see Illus. 2-F). Aside from the comic charges and the peculiar (even for heraldic blazon) term, "trottant," Thackeray's blazon demonstrates considerable familiarity with heraldry, down to the fact that the peer's widow would bear the arms on a lozenge, not on a conventional shield, and would bear the coronet of rank, but not the crest or supporters.

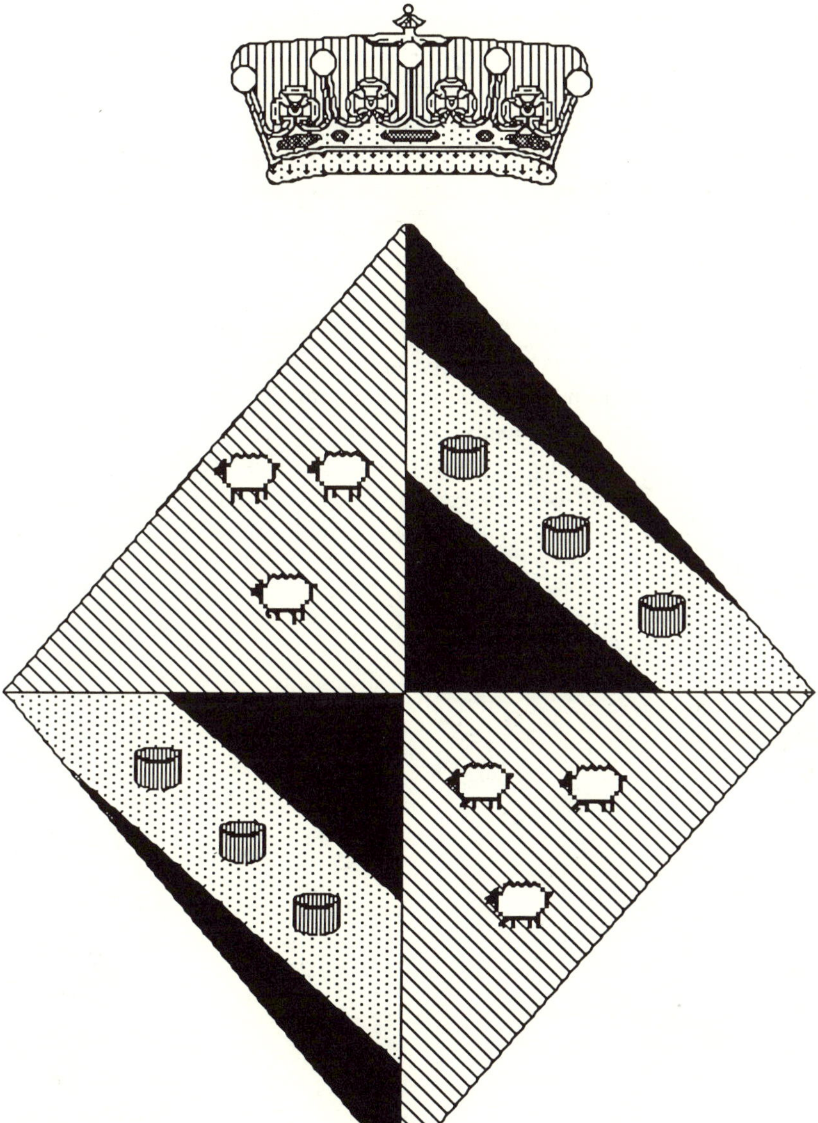

Illustration 2-F Arms borne by Lady Southdown in *Vanity Fair.*

In the nineteenth century, the coveted coat of arms becomes a target of ridicule in a fashion analogous to the emblazoned purses in Dante's "Inferno." A direct comparison can be made between these emblems of moral ruin and the prominent role played by the "ramping lion" of Hardy's d'Urbervilles: the appeal of the ancient escutcheon is part of the impetus behind John Durbeyfield's pursuit of gentility, and consequently of his daughter's doom. John Durbeyfield's ancestors are traced back to Norman knights; it is a peculiarity of pedigree hunting that pretenders to great arms and lineage have almost always tried to trace their armigerous status to the Norman conquest, even though hereditary heraldic bearings were unknown in 1066.

The similarity between the pretentious escutcheons lampooned by Thackeray, and those condemned to perdition by Dante, demonstrates one common thread running through heraldic allusions in literature: the symbols of genteel and aristocratic influence equally represent the moral decay behind the shield. This tradition, along with the chivalric codes evoked by heraldry, the ethic of the English country gentleman, and the power represented by the heraldry of sovereignty, will be significant in considering Joyce's use of heraldry.

CHAPTER THREE

"These be my genteelican arms . . ."

—*Finnegan's Wake 546.5*

In *Ulysses*, Stephen Dedalus's elaborations on his Shakespeare theories include some notice of the poet's interest in the hallmark of his gentility, his own coat of arms (Illus. 3-A):

> He has hidden his own name, a fair name, William, in the plays, a super here, a clown there, as a painter of old Italy set his face in the dark corner of his canvas. He has revealed it in the sonnets where there is Will in overplus. Like John o'Gaunt his name is dear to him, as dear as the coat and crest he toadied for, on a bend sable a spear or steeled argent, honorificabilitudinitatibus, dearer than his glory of greatest shakescene in the country. What's in a name? (*U* 9.921–27 {209.31–210.5})

The connection between Shakespeare's arms and his act of hiding his name in the sonnets is not casual. Just as several sonnets (including Sonnet 135, to which Stephen directly alludes),[1] contain references to Shakespeare's name, so does his coat of arms. The arms—blazoned in the extant drafts of the original grant (1596), "Gould on a Bend sables a Speare of the first steeled argent" (Scott-Giles 37)—illustrate the principle of "canting" arms; that is, they employ a visual pun (a "rebus") to allude to the bearer's name.[2] In the case of Shakespeare's arms, the canting effect is doubled: there is a hint of his name not only in the spear on the escutcheon (or heraldic shield), but also in the crest—"a falcon his wings displayed . . . supporting a speare gould." In other words, the falcon holds the spear, as if shaking it.[3] C. W. Scott-Giles suggests (with some reservations) an even more elaborate canting scheme in the crest:

I have toyed with the idea that the original thought was to make the bird a shag, so that the crest should be completely allusive to the name Shagspere (its form in William's marriage bond), but that the shag ('insatiate cormorant') had unpleasant associations and was replaced by the nobler falcon; but this is mere speculation. (31)

Just as Stephen's association of the sonnets with the arms is not casual, neither is that between the arms and John of Gaunt. In this respect, Shakespeare is indeed very much like Gaunt, the Duke of Lancaster, who (in *Richard II*) heralds his own demise in a speech punning on his name not once, but seven times.[4] Gaunt figures significantly in *Richard II*, a play written around the time of the Shakespeare grant of arms (1595). The play also features Gaunt's son, Bolingbroke (later Henry IV), a man much concerned with his father's good name, and his armorial legacy of a coat of arms. It is Bolingbroke who, his arms having been effaced from his windows, laments his lack of any sign "To show the world I am a gentleman." Scott-Giles also suggests that Bolingbroke's speech in the lists at Coventry contains reference to the author's sign that *he* was a gentleman. As Bolingbroke prepares to do battle with Mowbray, he invokes both of the charges in the Shakespeare armorial achievement: first, he refers to the falcon crest: "As confident as is the falcon's flight / Against a bird, do I with Mowbray fight" (1: 3, 11. 60–61). Later, he uses the image of steeled spear in an armorial shield, not in the symbolic sense of Shakespeare's escutcheon, but in the literal sense:

> Add proof unto mine armour with thy prayers,
> And with thy blessings steel my lance's point,
> That it may enter Mowbray's waxen coat
> And furbish new the name of John a Gaunt
> Even in the lusty haviour of his son.
> (1: 3, 11. 73–77)

That the composition of the play precedes the grant by a little under a year does not render this association anachronistic: Scott-Giles points out that the play was written about the time "when Shakespeare must have been dealing with the heralds about the arms" (35). Moreover, while the references to the falcon and the speared shield might seem tenuous allusions to the Shakespeare arms on first inspection, Scott-Giles concludes: ". . . at least it seems to be rather more than chance that, at a time when the grant of arms to his father was much in his mind, [Shakespeare] should allude to both the falcon and lance in a speech of filial sentiment" (35).

In the last chapter, I mentioned some men of letters, including Defoe, Burns, and Scott, who asserted their status as artists *and* gentlemen by

Illustration 3-A Arms of Shakespeare: Or, on a bend sable a spear of the first steeled argent. Crest: A falcon, its wings displayed, supporting a spear or. Illustration by Dan Brooks.

assuming armorial bearings. Below I will consider some literary figures who, like Shakespeare, have not stopped at merely assuming the arms, but have gone on to place them into their own works as symbols not only of the artist's gentility, but also of his identity, and of the genetic relationship between him and his works. This type of allusion is a distinctive feature of Shakespeare's works, and Stephen Dedalus notices it. Stephen connects

Shakespeare's nominal puns in the sonnets with the canting arms, and with the puns in *Richard II,* a play which brings the two types of allusion together, through Gaunt's nominal puns and Bolingbroke's allusions to his creator's arms. This device to which Stephen is so attentive is one which, not surprisingly, is given extended play by Joyce himself, as well as by the eighteenth-century novelist Laurence Sterne.

Like Shakespeare, both Joyce and Sterne were interested and somewhat learned in the symbols and language of heraldry, and, also like Shakespeare, the two writers shared their heraldic preoccupation with their characters. The Shakespearean clown from the fifth act of *Hamlet* lays claim to a coat of arms through his professional/genealogical link to Adam. Arguing for the gentility of his calling, the gravedigging clown claims that "There is no ancient gentleman but gard'ners, ditchers, and grave makers. They hold up Adam's profession." Asked if Adam was a gentleman—of the social class entitled to a coat of arms—the clown punningly replies, " 'A was the first that ever bore arms" (*Hamlet* 5: 1, 28–31). Expressing similar aspirations in the first chapter of Joyce's *A Portrait,* Stephen Dedalus answers the question "What is your father?" by saying, "A gentleman" (*P* 9); he later elaborates on this claim by offering to show Davin the family pedigree at Dublin Castle (*P* 202). Stephen's claim to gentility, like that of Shakespeare's clown, implicitly asserts the social rank that would entitle him to a coat of arms.

A more emphatic assertion of the Dedalus armorial legacy is found in the "Circe" chapter of Joyce's *Ulysses,* where an older Stephen Dedalus has a vision of his father, Simon Dedalus, in the form of a predatory bird who cries out: "Ho, boy! Are you going to win? . . . Head up! Keep our flag flying! An eagle gules volant in a field argent displayed. Ulster king at arms!" (*U* 15.3944–49 {572.14–17})

In a similar gesture in Sterne's *A Sentimental Journey,* the character Yorick (who was introduced in Sterne's earlier novel, *Tristram Shandy*) goes even further than Simon Dedalus: not content merely to render a verbal blazon of his family arms, he gives an extended history of the starling that he adopts as his heraldic crest, followed by inclusion of a highly ornate drawing of his arms (Illus. 3-B), with the verbal challenge, "—And let the herald's office twist [the starling's] neck about if they dare" (Sterne, *SJ* 100). Like Simon Dedalus and Tristram Shandy's father, Walter, Yorick displays his arms as a visual signature and as a token of his gentility.

According to Stephen Dedalus's theory, Shakespeare's hidden signature in the coat of arms and in the sonnets is an expression of his thwarted

Illustration 3-B Sterne arms, as displayed in *A Sentimental Journey.*

paternal impulse, frustrated in the death of his son, Hamnet. Whether or not this analysis is valid with regard to Shakespeare, it does work well in a consideration of Laurence Sterne's armorial signature in *A Sentimental Journey.* Sterne left no male heir, and Lodwick Hartley has demonstrated how this frustrated paternity becomes a dominant idea in *Tristram Shandy* (Hartley, " 'Tis a Picture . . ."). Elaborations of this theme include the protracted obstetrical focus of *Tristram Shandy* and Walter Shandy's various paternal frustrations: the death of his eldest son, the christening of his surviving son under the wrong name, the deficiencies of his bull, and the inadvertent "*bend sinister* [that] . . . had been drawn quite across the field of the *Shandy*-arms" (Sterne, *TS* 220).

Sterne's description of this latter misfortune reveals something of his technical understanding of heraldry.[5] Moreover, like Shakespeare and Joyce, Sterne exhibits an interest in blazon that extends to his family armorial bearings. In a note to his edition of *A Sentimental Journey*, Gardner Stout points out that Sterne used a personal seal incorporating the arms granted *circa* 1634 to Robert Sterne of Maldon, County Cambridge (Stout 206n). Laurence Sterne had no grant entitling him to these arms, but he used them, nevertheless, not only in the seal, but also early in Volume 2 of *A Sentimental Journey:* Yorick tells the story of the "imprisoned" starling that he subsequently adopts as his crest, and he presents to the reader a drawing of an armorial achievement that, for all its rococo embellishments, is unmistakably that of Robert Sterne (Illus. 3-B).

By introducing his presumed family arms into his novel, Sterne provides a hidden signature like that in Shakespeare's arms and sonnets. Furthermore,

Sterne's arms, like Shakespeare's, incorporate a canting reference to the author's name. The dialect form of starling is "starnel," or "starn." Thus Sterne identifies himself with Yorick, not only by using his putative family arms, but by using those arms in a form which signs his name in a rebus.[6]

But Yorick's connection to Shakespeare is not limited to his use of canting arms: Yorick is a self-proclaimed descendant of Shakespeare's Yorick from *Hamlet*. This link implies an analogy between Shakespeare and Sterne, the two creators of Yorick. For instance, Graham Petrie observes that the episode in which Sterne's Yorick obtains a passport with the aid of one Count de B*** parallels an event from Sterne's 1762 trip to Paris, when the author obtained a passport with the aid of the Comte de Bissy. Petrie points out that on this occasion, Sterne was pleased to find a copy of *Tristram Shandy* open on the Comte's table (in Sterne, *SJ* 152, n.51). In the parallel episode in *A Sentimental Journey*, the Count has the works of Shakespeare on his table. Yorick uses this expedient to identify himself: "Recollecting I was in [Shakespeare's] books, I took up *Hamlet*, and turning immediately to the grave-diggers scene in the fifth act, I laid my finger upon YORICK, and advancing the book to the Count, with my finger all the way over the name—Me, *Voici!* said I" (Sterne, *SJ* 109).

Sterne implies an equivalence between Shakespeare's creation of Yorick in *Hamlet* and Sterne-as-Yorick's creation of himself in *Tristram Shandy*. Sterne's use of his own (presumed) heraldic bearings signifies the fathering of fictive progeny, in the manner which Stephen Dedalus attributes to Shakespeare, and which Dedalus's creator, Joyce, adopts when he inserts his presumed heraldic bearings into *Ulysses*. Simon Dedalus's description of the Dedalus arms in "Circe"—an "eagle gules volant" appearing "in a field argent"—varies only slightly from the arms of the Joyces of Galway as blazoned in the 1884 Burke's *General Armory* (Illus. 3-C).

Joyce's possession of an armorial rendering was related to his deep personal interest in gentility. Joyce knew from his research on Shakespeare that, from Elizabethan times, the relation between gentility and heraldry has been one of definition: the right to bear a coat of arms is the mark that one is a gentleman. That Joyce had very specific acquaintance with this idea—and with its Elizabethan origins—is clear from the Cornell notes for his 1912 Hamlet lectures in Trieste, transcribed by William H. Quillian. On sheet "[I]" of the notes labelled "*Quaderno di Calligrafia di Shakespeare*," this note occurs: "n. John Shakespeare applies for a coat of arms / on Oct. 20 1596. Granted in 1599" (Quillian 17).[7] According to Quillian, a large red "J" next to the word "coat" connects this item with information

Illustration 3-C Arms used by James Joyce. Illustration by Dan Brooks.

on sheet "[11]" in the extensive background notes for the lecture, which includes the following, attributed to Sir Thomas Smith's *De Republica Anglorum*, 1583 (Quillian says the source is John Dover Wilson's *Life in Shakespeare's England*):

Ordinarily the king doth make only knights and create barons or higher degrees; for as for gentlemen they be made good cheap in England. For whosoever studieth the laws of the realm, who studieth in the universities, who professeth liberal sciences and, to be short, who can live idly and without manual labour and will bear the *port* charge and countenance of a gentleman he shall be called master (for that is the title which men give to esquires and other gentlemen). . . . And (if need be) a king of heralds shall also give him for money arms, newly made and invented, the title whereof shall pretend to have been found by the said herald in perusing and viewing of old registers where his ancestors in times past had been recorded to bear the same: or if he do it more truly and of better faith, he will write that for the merits of that man and certain qualities which he doth see in him and for sundry acts which he hath performed, he, by the authority which he hath as king of heralds and arms, giveth to him and his heirs these and these arms which being done I think he may be called a squire for he beareth ever after these arms. Such men are called sometimes in scorn gentlemen of the first head. (34–35)

We also know from several sources of Joyce's distinctive personal interest in gentility, which he inherited from the indefatigably genteel John Joyce. It is reflected in Stephen Dedalus's protestations of his gentle origins, discussed above. Ellmann quotes a letter from John Joyce to his son of 31 January 1903: "I have always looked up to your being a fitting representative of *our* family one that my father would be proud of. I now only hope that you may carry out *his* ideas and if you do, you may be sure you will not do anything unbecoming a gentleman" (*JJ* 122).

Ellmann notes that in the following year, Joyce avoided mentioning his elopement with Nora, "knowing that his father would consider a liaison with a Galway girl of no family foolhardy and, what was worse, ungentlemanly" (*JJ* 176). This was likely a prudent impulse on the part of one who had listened to a lifetime of his father's snobbish recriminations against the Murrays, the family of Joyce's mother (*JJ* 19–20). That Joyce inherited his father's interest in gentility is evident in facetious comments such as that in a letter from James Joyce to Frank Budgen of 3 January 1920, where Joyce laments his financial woes, including the loss of a patron, and remarks "It seems that gentility cannot be acquired in a single generation" (*SL* 245). A more serious reflection of Joyce's concern with the idea of gentility is recounted by Padraic Colum in *Our Friend James Joyce*. Asked by Joyce to bring back an account of John Joyce's final days in Dublin, Colum recalls that his report—to the effect that, to the family with whom John Joyce had lived at the end of his life, the novelist's father was "a battered, shabby old person"—was a source of distress to Joyce. Describing his own concern at being the bearer of such tidings, Colum comments: "Here was I in an apartment that had on the wall Tuohy's 'Portrait of a Dublin Gentleman' and other portraits of men and women in his family. And I was making my report to one for whom the tradition of gentlemanliness was important" (201).

As the heir to John Joyce's legacy of gentility, Joyce would, by post-Tudor definition, be a "gentleman of coat-armor." Ellmann notes that James Joyce's father "owned a framed engraving of the coat of arms of the Galway Joyces, and he used to carry it along, grandly and quixotically, on his frequent enforced *déménagements*" (*JJ* 11). Unlike Shakespeare, but like Sterne, the Joyces had no official grant of arms; moreover, no genealogical link has been demonstrated between the armigerous Galway Joyces and the author's Cork ancestors.[8] Nevertheless, John Joyce apparently treated his heraldic legacy with care, and both the legacy and the care were inherited by John Stanislaus's son and heir, James, who was known to have a version of the arms hanging on the wall of his various residences in Paris. That rendering (Illus. 3-D) is now at the State University of New York, Buffalo, and Illus. 3-C is based on that original.

To be precise, this coat of arms is not quite that of the Joyces of Galway. According to records in the Chief Herald's Office in Dublin Castle, the arms of the Galway Joyces feature a two-headed eagle, and the ermine device is a fess, or a horizontal band crossing the entire field—not merely two barlets (technically, a "bar gemel"—twin bars—on the Joyce rendering) crossing the eagle's breast (Illus. 3-E).[9] But this heraldic deviation gives us a clue to the origin of John Joyce's coat of arms: the 1884 edition of Burke's *General Armory* blazons the Joyce arms as follows: "Ar[gent] an eagle disp[layed] gu[les] charged on the breast with a bar gemel erm[ine]" (550b). This same description is repeated in the 1892 O'Hart's *Irish Pedigrees* (2: 261). In other words, the arms John Joyce had on his wall are identical to the erroneous blazon in Burke's *General Armory*, which is probably the source of the error.[10]

In a recent essay, Edmund Epstein gives as the "official description of the Joyce arms" the following: "Argent an eagle with two heads displayed gules, charged on the breast with a bar gemel ermine" (Epstein 4). He gives as his sources O'Hart, whose blazon does not give the eagle two heads, and Edward MacLysaght's *Irish Families*, which gives the ermine fess instead of the bar gemel. Epstein seems to have taken the "average" of the two prevalent descriptions. Of the two, MacLysaght's would be considered closest to "official," since his work was written while he was the Chief Herald of Ireland. MacLysaght blazons the Joyce arms: "Argent an eagle with two heads displayed gules, over all a fess ermine" (MacLysaght XVII). For the purposes of this study, however, the "deviant" description from the 1884 Burke's *Armory* is the relevant one, since Joyce's picture of the arms precisely matches it. Curiously enough, Burke's 1884 *Armory* is still available in reprint, and is frequently found behind the counters of

Illustration 3-D Rendering of Joyce Arms owned by James Joyce. Courtesy of Poetry/Rare Books Collection, State University of New York at Buffalo.

Illustration 3-E Arms of Joyce of Galway.

jewelers, stationers, and others who offer to find "your authentic family crest" (meaning, most likely, the coat of arms of somebody else who happens to share your surname). Perhaps John Joyce obtained his rendering from one of these entrepreneurs.

It would appear that James Joyce's reverence for the putative paternal arms was comparable to his father's. In 1909, Joyce wrote to Stanislaus asking him to take the coat of arms out of its frame so that he could bind it into a manuscript of *Chamber Music* that he presented to Nora for Christmas that year (*Letters* 2: 262). His hope that the manuscript, with the family arms and the initials of Joyce and Nora, might become a family legacy, was expressed in Joyce's note to Nora when he sent the gift: "Perhaps this book I send you now will outlive both you and me. Perhaps the fingers of some young man or young girl (our children's children) may turn over its parchment leaves reverently when the two lovers whose initials are interlaced on the cover have long vanished from the earth" (*Letters* 2: 278).

In a letter cited by the Colums (written "some time before she went into the hospital [in Zurich] where she died in 1951"), Nora Joyce expressed concern that she might have to sell the manuscript, and she described it: ". . . it is written on parchment and bound in cream coloured leather with the Joyce crest [sic] on one side of the cover and our initials on the other side" (Colum 238).[11] As Ellmann notes the MS (*JJ* 307–8) is now in the possession of Joyce's grandson, Stephen Joyce.

Mr. Stephen Joyce has kindly provided me some information on the heraldic engraving in *Chamber Music*, along with a facsimile of an *ex libris* plate which he believes is based on that rendering (letter to the author, June 1985). In addition to the coat of arms bound into the manuscript, Joyce had a second rendering of the coat of arms, which remained on the wall of his Paris apartment in the 1930s (Colum 181); this is the rendering now at SUNY-Buffalo. This second armorial rendering is probably the one referred to in a letter Joyce wrote in 1912, which gives an idea of the value that Joyce placed on the coat of arms. When the threat of eviction endangered the belongings in his Trieste apartment, Joyce, in Dublin at the time, expressed his material priorities in another letter to his brother: "Pay great attention to my directions as to my table, desk, MSS, verse-book and crest. All the rest can go damned" (*Letters* 2: 305). In 1935, in a letter to Harriet Shaw Weaver, Joyce quoted the motto on his heraldic rendering in a letter expressing concern over the trouble brewing in Europe: "And perhaps [Europe] is where the gas is really going to be turned on. Well, so be it. The motto under my coat of arms, however, is *Mors aut honorabilis vita. . .*" (*SL* 377).

Finally, in 1939, Paul Léon wrote to Herbert Gorman to enumerate Joyce's objections to the forthcoming authorized biography, and concludes saying, "the idea of printing on the cover the arms of Dublin or those of the Joyce family had better be abandoned at once" (*JJ* 724–25). The gesture of binding his arms into his book, *Chamber Music*, was a gesture that Joyce did not take lightly, and was apparently a prerogative not accruing to his authorized biographer.

Like Sterne and Shakespeare, Joyce was interested in canting devices: for instance, in *Ulysses*, Leopold Bloom tries to get an advertisement printed for Alexander Keyes featuring two crossed keys at the top (*U* 7.142–51 {120.21–33}), and one of the heraldic charges assigned to H. C. Earwicker in *Finnegans Wake* is a "coleopter" (*FW* 546.7): a beetle—an "earwig"—for Earwicker. The Joyce arms are not themselves canting arms, but Joyce is able to approach a canting effect through the sustained association of the Dedalus name and myth with birds of prey, which become emblematic of Stephen's identity. In *Portrait*, Stephen Dedalus contemplates "the hawklike man whose name he bore" (*P* 225), and the hawk serves as Stephen's emblem throughout *A Portrait* and *Ulysses*.

This reference is a part of a complex system of emblematic uses of birds in *A Portrait;* this motif has been the subject of a great deal of Joycean exegesis, and I will not attempt to discuss all of Joyce's bird imagery here. I will, however, point out the close connection between canting devices and the bird emblems in *A Portrait*. In his 1965 essay, "The Correspondence of Birds to Things of Intellect," Ronald Bates notes the four major birds alluded to in *Portrait:* hawk, heron, dove and crane.

Three of these have specific associations with the identities of characters: Stephen, the namesake of the hawklike man, is the hawk.[12] The crane, which in Stephen's beach epiphany is connected with the girl ("her legs were as delicate as a crane's" [*P* 171]), is also connected with Cranly, as his name would suggest. Bates notes the legendary qualities of the crane, especially its supposed vigilant and prophetic character. In heraldry, this is represented by the peculiar convention of having the crane hold a stone in one claw, because, as George Ferguson explains, "should the crane fall asleep, [it] would drop [the] stone on the other foot and so awaken . . ." (14). The crane so depicted is called in heraldry the "crane in its vigilance" (*CG* 247).

A clearer use of a canting bird emblem is that associated with Stephen's rival, Heron, who is as much a heron-like man as Stephen is a hawklike man. It is remarked of Stephen that: "He had often thought it strange that Vincent Heron had a bird's face as well as a bird's name. A shock of pale hair lay on the forehead like a ruffled crest: the forehead was narrow and bony and a thin hooked nose stood out between the closeset prominent eyes which were light and inexpressive" (*P* 76). Bates notes that in *De Occulta Philosophia* of Agrippa, "The *ardea*, or heron, is significant of difficult, or arduous things" (282), and that "Heron and Stephen are explicitly called 'rivals,' and 'the virtual heads of the school' [*P* 84]" (Bates 283).

In this connection, there is an interesting coat of arms recorded in several sources, including Burke's *Armory* (371b), Papworth's *Ordinary* and Gough and Parker's *Glossary:* the arms of Fournier are blazoned, "Az[ure] a hawk volant seizing a heron also volant or" (Papworth 304b). This is interesting not only as an emblematic statement of the iconographic relationship between hawk and heron, but because the tincture of the field and the posture of the hawk are identical to those in a note for "Circe" in the British Museum Notesheets. In the notes designated "Circe 9," what would appear to be a draft for the Dedalus arms contains the blazon: "hawk volant in a field azure" (Herring, *U Notesheets* 315). Whether or not Joyce might have known the blazon of the arms of Fournier is not important; but it is interesting that both Joyce's note and the blazon from Papworth use two terms relatively rare in heraldic references to birds of prey: the "hawk" is usually called a falcon, and the volant posture is rare (though not unheard of) in describing birds of prey. In the final version of "Circe," the blazon of the Dedalus arms retains the volant pose, while incorporating the red eagle and silver field of the Joyce arms. The blazon of the Dedalus arms is slightly contradictory, in that it incorporates "volant" (the attitude of flight) while retaining the word "displayed" from the blazon of the Joyce arms; in "An eagle gules volant in a field argent displayed" (*U* 15.3948–49 {572.16–17}), the last word seems to be used in its common sense rather than the heraldic sense of the spread-eagle. Whether the error properly accrues to the apparition of Simon, to Stephen, to Joyce, or to someone else entirely, I will not speculate.

What the note in the British Museum Notesheet does indicate, however, is that the heraldic device was originally directly connected with the network of bird emblems originating in *Portrait*, especially the idea of the hawklike man. Several references in the British Museum and Buffalo notes for *Ulysses* connect the "Circe" chapter with the hawk emblem.[13] In its final form, the bird motif in "Circe" is expanded to encompass numerous birds of prey and carrion fowl. The interchangeable use of the eagle and hawk is intelligible not only because both birds of prey are considered within the domain of falconry (the subject of the other "subtle and curious jargon" [*P* 180]), but also because Joyce uses the two birds in connection with one another. Stephen's reflections on eagles begin quite early in *A Portrait:* he is taunted by Dante's remark that, if Stephen did not apologize, "the eagles will come and pull out his eyes" (*P* 8). Hugh Kenner suggests a source for this scene: "[There was a] large wooden eagle on the parlour wall of the house where James Joyce lived as a child. Perhaps someone once told little Jim that if he was naughty, the eagle would come down and punish him."[14]

That an eagle on the Joyce's wall might have been an object of fascination and menace to the young James Joyce is very suggestive of how the eagle functions in Stephen Dedalus's imagination. Ellmann remarks that "a dream of [Joyce's] youth was to be a bird, both in its song and in its flight. . . ." (*JJ* 165). Stanislaus Joyce recalls the prominent use of the eagle in his brother's (lost) juvenile Parnell elegy:

> At the end of the piece [James Joyce's juvenile elegy, "Et Tu, Healy"] the dead Chief [Parnell] is likened to an eagle, looking down on the grovelling mass of Irish politicians from
>
> *His quaint-perched aerie on the crags of Time*
> *Where the rude din of this . . . century*
> *Can trouble him no more.* (*MBK* 46)

Stanislaus also recorded one of Joyce's eagle epiphanies:

> What moves upon me from the darkness subtle and murmurous as a flood, passionate and fierce with an indecent movement of the loins? What leaps, crying in answer, out of me, as an eagle to an eagle in mid air, crying to overcome, crying for an iniquitous abandonment? (*MBK* 174–75)

Joyce's eagle emblem embodies several levels of symbolism: it not only recalls the haunting "apologise" motif, but also evokes images of destiny and lofty attainment. The image's suggestiveness in Joyce's works is enhanced by the fact that in addition to conventional eagles Joyce may have seen, and the wooden plaque that Kenner referred to, there was also the red eagle in John Joyce's heraldic eagle. Because the eagle on the wall is equally a symbol of menace and a paternal legacy, it haunts Stephen's imagination at the same time that it reminds him of his destiny.

Throughout *A Portrait,* Stephen contemplates his birdlike identity with specific reference to medieval iconography:

> Was it a quaint device opening a page of some medieval book of prophecies and symbols, a hawklike man flying sunward above the sea, a prophecy of the end he had been born to serve and had been following through the mists of childhood and boyhood, a symbol of the artist forging anew in his workshop out of the sluggish matter of the earth a new soaring impalpable imperishable being? (*P* 169)

Not only has Stephen referred to conventional iconography of the bird, but he has specifically invoked attributes, not of the legendary hawk, but of the eagle. George Ferguson explains: "The eagle may generally be interpreted as a symbol of the Resurrection. This is based upon the early belief that the eagle, unlike other birds, periodically renewed its plumage and its youth by flying near the sun and then plunging into the water" (17).

Thus if Stephen's artistic being is hawklike, then his hawk is, in turn, eagle-like, as is made clear by the image of the bird "flying sunward" and becoming an "imperishable being" (cf. Bloom's reflection on the consequences if one were to "Stare the sun for example like the eagle . . ." [*U* 13.1132–33 {378.6}]). The iconographic equation of the hawk and eagle is reinforced in the next passage, when Stephen longs to "cry aloud, the cry of a hawk or eagle on high . . ." (*P* 169).[15]

Through his allusions to the Joycean eagle *cum* Dedalean hawk in *Portrait,* Joyce paves the way for the Dedalean escutcheon to herald the identity of the hawklike man in a fashion that emulates the rebus quality of the names of Cranly and Heron. Indeed, like the Jesus of Mulligan's song, Stephen can say "My father's a bird," when, in the passage from "Circe" already discussed, he summons him with the calls of a falconer: "*Holà!* Hillyho" (*U* 15:3941 {572.8}; Gifford and Seidman 421). When Simon appears, he *is* a bird that "*swoops uncertainly through the air, wheeling, uttering cries of heartening, on strong ponderous buzzard wings*" (*U* 15.3945–46 {572.12–14}), and that cries the blazon of the Dedalus arms, at the center of which is another bird of prey. The arms differ from the Joyce arms only in the eagle's posture: the "displayed" pose is changed to "volant"—the attitude of flight (Illus. 3-F). Thus the flying bird of prey on the escutcheon parallels the flying "hawklike man" (with buzzard wings) who proclaims it; in this fashion, Joyce makes the heraldic device proclaim its bearer's identity, in a manner similar to the rebuses of Sterne and Shakespeare. The connection between the "eagle gules volant" of the novel, and the "hawk volant" in the British Museum notesheet, suggests that Joyce modified the Joyce arms to serve his thematic purposes; I find this suggestion more consonant with Joyce's use of heraldic emblems than Epstein's reductive assertion that "Joyce prided himself on his knowledge of heraldry, but here he does not report on the family coat of arms fully or in proper form" (Epstein 4).

This heraldic hallucination in "Circe" seems to enact elements of Stephen Dedalus's Shakespeare theories. First, Joyce has hidden his own identity in *Ulysses* by taking the Joycean arms off the wall and writing them into his novel; the gesture is reminiscent of his binding the heraldic emblem into the *Chamber Music* manuscript in 1909. Second, the coat of arms is, by definition, an hereditary legacy. It therefore pertains to the pervasive paternal theme of *Ulysses*—at the center of which is Shakespeare. John Shakespeare received his grant of arms two months after his grandson (William's son, Hamnet) had died. Stephen argues that William Shakespeare's paternal grief over the loss of his son and heir is translated into a mirror image in *Hamlet,* where the son and heir confronts the loss of his father; in turn, this is mirrored by Leopold Bloom's grief for his dead son, Rudy, and by Stephen Dedalus's figurative loss of his estranged father.

Stephen's vision of his father proclaiming the Dedalus arms represents one level of resolution for the theme of thwarted primogeniture. In *A Portrait,* a much younger Stephen had listened to his father's "long and incoherent monologue" when the declining family fortunes forced the first of many relocations: "He felt too that he was being enlisted for the fight, that some duty was being laid upon his shoulders" (65–66). Later in the same chapter of *Portrait,* he thinks, "In the profane world, as he foresaw, a worldly voice would bid him raise up his father's fallen state by his labours . . ." (84). While Stephen has become estranged from his father by the time of *Ulysses,* and does not acknowledge him when their paths cross, in the "Circe" vision he recalls the prophetic challenge of *A Portrait,* and acknowledges his paternal legacy. Moreover, Joyce commemorates the wit and talents of his own father in the character of Simon Dedalus, and he weaves into his fiction the heraldic signature of the presumed Joycean arms, of which both John and James Joyce were so manifestly proud.

Illustration 3-F Arms of Dedalus, as blazoned in the "Circe" chapter of *Ulysses*. Illustration by Dan Brooks.

Thus, like Sterne before him, Joyce converts his art into a medium of hereditary legacy and becomes like Stephen Dedalus's "Rutlandbaconsouthamptonshakespeare, . . . the father of all his race, the father of his own grandfather, the father of his unborn grandson" (*U* 9.866–69 {208.12–17}).

Joyce's and Sterne's heraldic references to themselves in their novels do not merely echo the reflexivity in Shakespeare's punning references to his name; they amplify it. Moreover, the association that Sterne implies between himself and Yorick, as well as that which Joyce implies between himself and Stephen Dedalus, extends beyond each author's granting his presumed coat of arms to his character. Sterne actually wrote his personal letters over the name Yorick and published a volume of his sermons under the same name. In a strikingly parallel gesture, Joyce signed the name "Stephen Daedalus" to a letter to Oliver St. John Gogarty on 3 June 1904 (Bloomsday minus 13; *JJ* 153–54); also, the first publication of "The Sisters" *(Dubliners)* appeared in the *Irish Homestead* of 13 August 1904 under the name Stephen Daedalus. Thus the fictive persona becomes, in itself, a mode of the artist's impressing his identity into his work. In a more pointed fashion, however, the use of the presumed family arms by the respective authors of *A Sentimental Journey* and *Ulysses* is an explicit personal signature, analogous to Shakespeare's punning signatures in the sonnets.

Finally, by using as signature the coat of arms, one of the most compelling traditional emblems of paternal legacy, each novelist emphatically blazons his paternal claim to artistic posterity. Stanislaus Joyce noted the similarity between the paternal concerns in the works of his brother and Sterne:

> There was undoubtedly a vague Hamletic complex both in Sterne and in my brother, but although Sterne, in the loss of his father as the result of a silly duel, suffered in early youth a heavy blow to his deepest affection, and thus might have had reason to cultivate a tragic outlook on life, he refused to do so. He chose to be Yorick, because he did not with to be Hamlet. (*MBK* 32)

Being Yorick was a way of dealing with the Hamletic loss of a father, and the Shakespearean lack of a surviving heir. Sterne's paternal legacy is as effectively thwarted as are Yorick's attempts to complete his account of his travels; both Sterne and Yorick appropriately bear as crest the imprisoned starling that continually cries "I can't get out" (Sterne, *SJ* 96 *et passim*). Yorick/Sterne's filial dilemma brings to mind a pervasive "filiative" theme which Edward Said has remarked upon in modern works, including *Ulysses* and *The Waste Land:*

> One very strong three-part pattern, for example, originates in a large group of late nineteenth- and early twentieth-century writers, in which the failure of the generative impulse—the failure of the capacity to produce or generate children—is portrayed in such a way as to stand for a general condition afflicting society and culture together. . . . (Said 16)

If, in the works of Shakespeare, Sterne, and Joyce, we find a powerful statement of this failure, we also find an aesthetic solution to the failure, through the author's filiative creation of a literary work bearing the author's paternal ensign. Sterne is able to transmit his heraldic legacy to posterity through fictively creating a surviving "heir" in Yorick. Similarly, Joyce follows in the emblematic tradition established by Sterne and Shakespeare when he places his heraldic emblem in *Ulysses.* This distinctive (and quite literal) filiative gesture constitutes a partial resolution of the paternal estrangement pervading Joyce's early life and art.

CHAPTER FOUR

". . . all Irish, all kings' sons": Joycean Heraldry Through *Ulysses*

(*U* 2.280–81 {31.30})

A. Walton Litz called attention to the intensely aural quality of Joyce's later work, saying: "It is a critical commonplace to say that Joyce's later work reflects a growing concern with the possibility of accommodating musical and literary forms. . . . The near-blindness which darkened his later years merely intensified the musical qualities which are evident throughout his early writings" (Litz 62–63).

While there is considerable justification for Litz's contention, this point has often been taken to an extreme, to suggest that Joyce was insensitive to the visual, or, at least, incapable of doing justice to it. Joyce's authorized biographer, Herbert Gorman, twice warns the reader against ascribing visual sensitivity to Joyce: at one point, he notes, ". . . it is demonstrable that Joyce's eye afflictions have shaped his handling of creative literature to a surprising degree" (91). Later, speaking of Joyce in the present (1939), he says: "[When walking] Joyce must pick his way carefully, making sure that it is on stable ground that he plants his foot, and exert other senses to recompense himself for the partial failure of one. The critic would do well to consider this in any exhaustive attempt to analyse the work of Joyce" (331).

In a 1959 article ("Joyce's Visual Imagination"), Robert S. Ryf cited T. S. Eliot, Harry Levin, and Richard M. Kain to the effect that Joyce's imagination and writing were rooted in the aural; Ryf argues convincingly, however, that Joyce's visual imagination was of great significance in his work, and that it bore comparison with certain cinematic techniques. Moreover, one of the earliest commentators on *Ulysses*, Joyce's friend

Frank Budgen, recalled that "In spite of his more than semi-blindness, Joyce had a natural feeling for the visual arts" (361). Finally, Clive Hart has observed that in both *Ulysses* and *Finnegans Wake* "the great bulk of the imagery remains visual." Of the *Wake*, Hart adds: "There never was a book more cluttered with visible symbols; the optical field is constantly crammed with every variety of stage property, from the tiniest trifle to the most megalomaniac object of desire" (Hart, *Structure and Motif* 32).

In this chapter I explore a specific dimension of Joyce's visual imagination—that pertaining to heraldry—as manifested in *Ulysses*. I will subsume within this discussion heraldic allusions in *A Portrait* and early works. In *Ulysses*, Joyce begins to make specific use of heraldic "blazon," a form of language devised to render the visual in unambiguous verbal terms. The manner in which blazon compresses the visual and the verbal is clear in the definitions of the word: according to the *OED*, the noun "blazon" means both the "description or representation, according to the rules of Heraldry, of armorial bearings" and the shield itself, or the "armorial bearings, coat of arms" (*OED* 1: 228). Such an equation of the visual and the verbal is characteristic of Joyce, who frequently transforms the visual into the aural—as when Stephen expands Aquinas's "*Pulcra enim dicuntur ea quae visa placent*" to include "esthetic apprehensions of all kinds, whether through sight or hearing or through any other avenue of apprehension" (*P* 207; see also Scholes and Corcoran 690), and as when the older Stephen of *Ulysses* transforms visual aesthetics in the opening passage of "Proteus": "Ineluctable modality of the visible: at least that if no more, thought through my eyes. Signatures of all things I am here to read, seaspawn and seawrack, the nearing tide, that rusty boot. Snotgreen, bluesilver, rust: coloured signs. . . . Shut your eyes and see" (*U* 3.1–9 {37.1–10}).

Just as, in *Portrait*, Aquinas's "visa" is taken to transcend the literally visual, in *Ulysses* Aristotle's ideas of the visible are apprehended with eyes shut. But this point can be taken too far; Joyce's medium was, after all, the written word, and attempts to reduce the visible to the verbal are in the nature of the beast. In this context, the suggestion that Joyce's rendering of the visual relies on the aural sense is almost tautological. Nevertheless, it might be pointed out that Joyce makes more of the visual aspect of the printed word than do many writers: Karl Beckson has discussed Stephen's notation in his geography book of "himself, his name and where he was" (*P* 15) as a *carmen figuratum* (shaped poem; see Beckson 95–96) poem; similarly, the opening passage of the eighth chapter of *FW* has text shaped like the Greek delta, or ALP's siglum. Other remarkably visual stimuli in

Joyce's texts include the headlines of "Aeolus"; the musical notation in "Scylla and Charybdis," "Ithaca," and *FW* 44 and 272.L2; the running marginalia and footnotes of *FW* II.2, and the drawings at the end of that chapter.[1] Finally, the very cover of the first edition of *Ulysses* is an encoded sign of the author's devisal, and an heraldic one at that: the original cover was based on the colors of Greece, azure and argent.

To consider the genesis of the heraldic emblems of *Ulysses* and earlier works, we can begin with the last chapter's point of departure: Chapter Three documented Joyce's interest in the arms used by his father and showed him taking pains to bind an engraving of the arms in a presentation manuscript of *Chamber Music*. Even earlier than that, Joyce dabbled in matters heraldic: in *Our Friend James Joyce*, Padraic Colum recalls that after meeting Joyce in 1902, "I was not interested in what he was reading, but once when I came to the counter [at the National Library] after he had been there, an attendant said of a book that had been put aside, apparently to be reserved, "For Mr. Joyce." It was a book on heraldry" (18). During the fictional 1902 *(A Portrait)*, Stephen Dedalus was also spending time at the National Library, and thinking about heraldry; first, when he compares his Thomistic aesthetics with the "subtle and curious jargons of heraldry and falconry" (*P* 180), and later, when he offers to document his lineage at the office of arms (*P* 202).

But what book(s) of heraldry might Joyce (or Stephen) have been reading in 1902? My single greatest source of frustration in this study has been the inability to arrive at definite determinations of Joyce's heraldic sources. On the one hand, neither Thomas Connolly's bibliography of Joyce's library (Connolly, *Personal Library of JJ*), nor Ellmann's list of Joyce's books at Trieste (Ellmann, *Consciousness of J* 97–134; see also Gillespie, *Inverted Volumes*), indicates that Joyce owned a single book on the subject of heraldry.[2] On the other hand, given the libraries to which Joyce had access, the possible sources are virtually unlimited. Joyce's 1912 notes for the *Hamlet* lectures in Trieste include references not only to the arms of Shakespeare, but also to those of Oxford University: giving as his source J. S. Rait's *Life in the Medieval University* (Cambridge, 1912), Joyce notes the constitution of the medieval trivium and quadrivium, and then writes what would appear to be a related note, "Arms of Oxford. Book. 7 clasps, 3 crowns" (Quillian 47). References in letters and other accounts indicate that Joyce continually collected heraldic information along with the other odds and ends of which his later works were constituted: Clive Hart cites a note from Paul Léon to Frank Budgen, containing supplementary information for Budgen's book on *Ulysses*, which states that Joyce had written "to prof [Bernhard] Fehr for the arms and motto" of Zurich ("Introduction," Budgen xv); we will see below the use to which that information was put. In the British Museum Notesheets for *Ulysses*, there are references to the heraldic bearings of the Isle of Man ("Three Legs of Man"), which Joyce used in *Ulysses* (15.2179 {507.14}), and those of Gibraltar ("arms . . . castle & key"), which, to my knowledge, he did not use.[3]

As I mentioned in Chapter One, Ruth von Phul's 1971 essay on heraldic language in "Proteus" maintains that Joyce's specific source was Oswald Barron's article in the Eleventh *Encyclopaedia Brittanica.* While it is not unlikely that Joyce did indeed use this source, he apparently used many others: every heraldic term that occurs in "Proteus" could have come from another source,[4] and he uses terms in subsequent chapters that are specifically *not* found in Barron's essay (e.g., the heraldic description of the pelican, used to characterize Bloom: "a very pelican in his piety" [*U* 14.921 {409.24}] in "Oxen").[5]

Finally, the many specific references to personal arms (including his own as blazoned in Burke's *Armory*, those of Bellingham, and the heraldic motto of Sir John Blackwood) would suggest that Joyce had access to a work like Burke's *General Armory.* Most of Joyce's heraldic language could be found in the works of Ruskin (as discussed above, in Chapter One), or in the numerous heraldry books in print during his lifetime, including *Boutell* and Fox-Davies, and, for some specific references, Brewer's *Dictionary of Phrase and Fable.* Nor would his sources be limited to those in print, since heraldic bearings are ubiquitous in Europe, gracing everything from tea tins to headstones. Gorman recalls Joyce's walks past "crumbling armorial bearings in dark stone" (Gorman 338) near his residence at the Rue de Grenelle during the 1920s. In short, the possible sources for Joyce's allusions are so diffuse as to make Joyce's use of heraldic allusion a case of intertextuality in the sense described by Jonathan Culler, taken to "include anonymous discursive practices, codes whose origins are lost, that make possible the signifying practices of later texts" (Culler 103).

A passage in *Giacomo Joyce* shows that Joyce had begun to make use of the heraldic code as a mode of characterization as early as 1914: the passage employs heraldic blazon to characterize the anonymous inamorata (thought to be Amalia Popper [*JJ* 342]): "Unreadiness. A bare apartment. Torbid daylight. A long black piano: coffin of music. Poised on its edge a woman's hat, red-flowered, and umbrella, furled. Her arms: a casque, gules, and blunt spear on a field, sable" (16).[6]

Quillian states that this allusion "connects Amalia Popper to the House of Shakespeare," the arms of which also feature a spear on sable, and concerning which Joyce had already made notes in 1912 (Quillian 46, n.13). Vicky Mahaffey, on the other hand, suggests that Joyce is erecting an heraldic funerary monument to his love:

> Joyce's pictorial epitaph for his "dead" love serves as an image of her "infidelity" as well as of her demise; Joyce emphasizes this by ironically modeling his design on Hawthorne's description of the scarlet letter that marks the common tombstone of Hester Prynne and Arthur Dimmesdale . . . "ON A FIELD, SABLE, THE LETTER A, GULES." (Mahaffey 398)

These two different interpretations of one Joycean blazon illustrate how heraldic intertextuality works in general, and how it will function in Joyce's other works. A single reference to an heraldic charge, tincture, or motto, invokes other heraldic achievements (historical and literary) which feature the same devices. For a reader of a first edition of *Ulysses,* the cover of which featured the white letters on a blue background, the novel's network of heraldic allusion begins before the reader opens the book. Joyce had inquired into the arms and motto of Zurich: Zurich's arms exhibit the simplicity of true medieval arms, consisting of a simple two-colored shield, with a single partition and no charge: "Per bend azure and argent" (Illus. 4-A). Budgen mentions these, the colors of the city in which Joyce wrote much of *Ulysses,* saying that the trams of Zurich were "painted bright cobalt blue and white, colours of the town of Zürich, colours of the Greek flag [Illus. 4-B], colours of the covers of *Ulysses*" (27). Joyce commented on the heraldic character of the cover on several occasions; in a letter (quoted in translation) to Alessandro Francini Bruni of 7 June 1921, he remarks: "The colours of the binding (chosen by me) will be white letters on a blue field—the Greek flag though really of Bavarian origin and imported with the dynasty. Yet in a special way they symbolise the myth well—the white islands scattered over the sea" (*Letters* 3: 46). Later, in a letter to Harriet Shaw Weaver of 26 February 1923, Joyce refers to the Egoist Press edition of *Ulysses* as "the Greco-Bavarian telephone directory" (*Letters* 3: 72–73). Thus, the colors of the cover of *Ulysses* transform it into an heraldic banner bearing the modern colors of Odysseus's homeland, but these colors in turn derive from the Bavarian House of Wittelsbach;[7] moreover, the colors are also those of Zurich.

This type of heraldic symbolism, that of "colors," is as pervasive in *Ulysses* as it continues to be in our societies (e.g., witness the systematic use of emblematic "colors"—this is the actual word used—among American motorcycle and street gangs). In "Ithaca," Leopold Bloom suspects D. B.

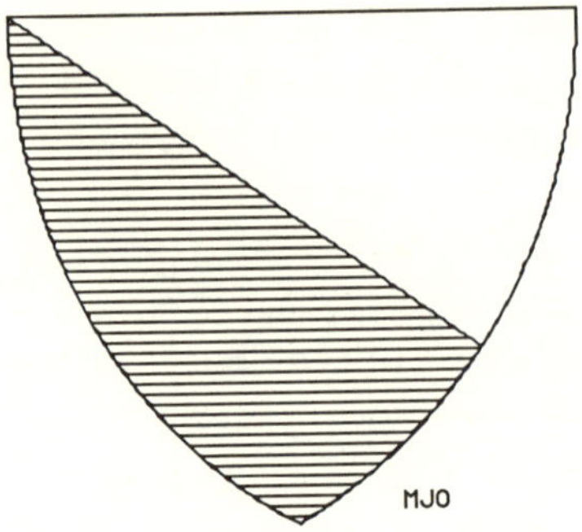

Illustration 4-A Arms of Zurich: Per bend argent and azure.

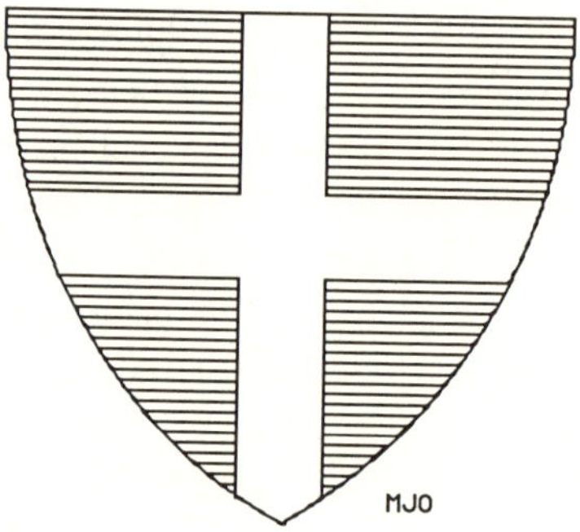

Illustration 4-B Arms of Greece: Azure, a cross argent.

Murphy (the former "W. B." of the Random House edition) of "sailing under false colours" (*U* 16.496 {626.24}). Stephen's imagination is also densely populated with heraldic colors. Just as Stephen's revolt against the Catholic church takes the form of a sacramentally-based aesthetic, so do his respective revolts against father, fatherland, and the church invoke the heraldic tinctures of those entities. There is an ironic twist to Stephen's appeal to the office of arms to demonstrate his Irish lineage in *Portrait:* Davin asks Stephen, "What with your name and your ideas . . . Are you Irish at all?" (*P* 202). Stephen's instinctive reply—challenging Davin to accompany him to the office of arms to inspect the Dedalus lineage—has the effect of documenting his Irishness by appeal to a British authority occupying Dublin Castle (as Ulster King did until 1943). Heraldry in Ireland was for several centuries the emblematic code of a British social order; it consequently stands in the same relation to Stephen's efforts to rid himself of his English Master as his sacramental aesthetic does to his efforts to rid himself of the second of his "two masters" (*U* 1.638 {20.27}), the Italian. Heraldry, a code emblematic of both masters, continues to be prominent in the same imagination in which Stephen "must kill the priest and the king" (15.4437 {589.28–29}).

Stephen's earliest childhood memories in *A Portrait* illustrate his sensitivity to the emblematic colors of faction. It is remarked that: "Dante had two brushes in her press. The brush with the maroon velvet back was for Michael Davitt and the brush with the green velvet back was for Parnell" (*P* 7).[8] Dante's choice of emblematic colors is peculiar; in his annotations for *Dubliners*, Don Gifford notes that Parnell "had a superstitious aversion to green" (Gifford, *J Annotated* 96); nevertheless, for Dante green stands for Parnell as it stands for Ireland. I am at a loss to determine why maroon should stand for Davitt. Maroon is one of those non-heraldic tinctures that one nevertheless finds used, since the English Sovereign has a monopoly on scarlet livery; such so-called "stains" as "murrey" or "sanguine" serve the function of the dark red maroon as a "gules-substitute." In his study of Irish flags, G. A. Hayes-McCoy describes several banners of Davitt's movement, the Land League, none of which is maroon. One banner features Parnell with the allegorical figure of Hibernia kneeling at his feet (Hayes-McCoy remarks, "In similar compositions of Volunteer days it was the Volunteer who knelt to Hibernia; nationality personified had lost something of its mystique in the intervening century" [176]); on the reverse of the same banner is the image of Davitt. Like other Land League banners, this one is green (Hayes-McCoy 175–79).

But for whatever reason, for Dante, green is Parnell, and maroon is Davitt. At first, the two colors peacefully coexist in Stephen's emblematic imagination, until the scandal of Parnell's adultery, which was the catalyst for his political downfall: "[Stephen] wondered which was right, to be for the green or for the maroon, because Dante had ripped the green velvet back off the brush that was for Parnell one day with her scissors and had told him that Parnell was a bad man" (*P* 16). James Carens writes in a recent essay: ". . . through Stephen's reflection, maroon has become identified with the Catholic anti-Parnellites and green with Parnell; and the two forces, Church and State, associated in the prologue to the novel are soon, though dimly, recognized by Stephen to be at war with one another" (300–1). The opposition is further complicated by red's being the color of the royal livery, as well as the tincture of the charge on the Dedalus arms. The opposition between green and red (in its various connotations), stated in nascent form in the Christmas dinner episode of *Portrait,* where the holly and the ivy form the backdrop to the argumentative reenactment of Parnell's fall, continues in *Ulysses,* where red occurs in literal and figurative references to the royal livery as well as to the Church.[9]

In her 1980 study, "Typology and Iconography in *Ulysses,*" Mary Dudley Schueler notes several of these instances of the Irish green in conflict with the royal red in *A Portrait* and *Ulysses.* In addition to noting the above instances of Dante's brushes and the Christmas dinner, she discusses this pattern in *Ulysses,* including the song "The Croppy Boy," where "*Father Green,* the priest to whom 'the croppy boy' goes for confession, turns out to be a *British redcoat* in disguise" (Schueler 116). Other occurrences of the royal color include that in "Aeolus": under the heading "THE WEARER OF THE CROWN," there is the description of "His Majesty's vermilion mailcars, bearing on their sides the royal initials, E.R. . . ." (*U* 7.16–17 {116.17–18}); and the red uniforms of Privates Carr and Compton in "Circe": "*their tunics bloodbright in a lampglow* . . ." [15.60–61 {430.34}]). The repeated references throughout *Ulysses* to the fight between Myler Keogh ("that's the chap sparring out to him with the green sash" [*U* 10.1136 {250.37–38}]) and the British Serjeant-major Percy Bennett ("The redcoat" [12.969 {318.40}]) is one extension of the green/red conflict, as is the confrontation between Stephen and Carr in "Circe": among the bystanders, the "Virago" shouts "Green above the red, says he. Wolfe Tone." The Bawd replies, "The red's as good as the green. And better. Up the soldiers! Up King Edward!" (15.4517–20 {593.4–7}).

A more figurative elaboration of the royal livery occurs in the stag/fox hunt motif. Bloom recalls in "Eumaeus" that "Fox" was one of the aliases used by Parnell (16.1323 [649.30]). For this reason the references to foxes being hunted (e.g., that following Simon Dedalus's appearance as a bird of prey in "Circe" [15.3951–63 {572.20–33}]) refer to the pursuit of Parnell by English and Irish forces, characterized in hunting pinks. Parnell is also represented as a "noble stag," a beast also frequently hunted in *Ulysses.* In his essay, "The Shade of Parnell," Joyce said that, after his fall, Parnell "went from county to county, from city to city, 'like a hunted deer' " (*CW* 227), an image which Ellmann (*JJ* 774, n.7) notes is suggestive of a quotation from Goethe that, according to W. B. Yeats: "ran through the papers ["during the quarrel over Parnell's grave"], describing our Irish jealousy: 'The Irish seem to me like a pack of hounds, always dragging down some noble stag' " (Yeats 211).

Joyce also evidently associated himself with the deer, as a comment to Daniel Hummel indicates (*JJ* 438).[10] He uses the animal as one of Stephen's two emblematic beasts (the second being the hawk) in *A Portrait* and *Ulysses.* Ellmann (*JJ* 145) also notes that the passage in Joyce's broadside poem, "The Holy Office," in which Joyce portrays himself as a deer ("Firm as the mountain-ridges where / I flash my antlers on the air." [*CW* 152]), is an echo of the allusion to the hunted stag in the early essay version of *A Portrait:* "Let the pack of enmities come tumbling and sniffing to the ["my" in *SH*] highlands after their game. There was his ground and he flung them disdain from flashing antlers" (In *P* 259; *SH* 34–35). Stephen becomes a deer once more in "Proteus," where the protean dog is a staghound for a moment, and Stephen the stag: "I just simply stood pale, silent, bayed about" (*U* 3.311 {45.22}).[11]

The heraldic significance of Stephen (and Parnell) as hunted stags is two-fold: first, it relates to the origin of the "hunting pinks" in royal livery, the scarlet of Stephen's English master, and second, it plays upon the rôle of the stag as an heraldic charge. A. C. Fox-Davies explains the first point:

> *A propos* of this it is interesting to note the curious legend that the "pink" of the hunting field is not due to any optical advantage, but to an entirely different reason. Formerly no man might hunt even on his own estate until he had had licence of free warren from the Crown. Consequently he merely hunted by the pleasure of the Crown, taking part in what was exclusively a Royal sport by Royal permission, and for this Royal sport he wore the King's livery of scarlet. (*CG* 73)

This fact connects the references to the hunt in *Ulysses* (Bloom's reflections on "Lady Mountcashel" and the "Ward Union staghounds" [*U* 8.340–41 {160.27–28}]; the hunt in "Circe," [15.3951–63 {572.20–33}]) specifically to the scarlet royal livery which is, in other instances (e.g., Private Carr) the livery of Stephen's, and Ireland's, antagonists.

The second level of this motif's heraldic significance has to do with the traditional crest of Ireland (Illus. 4-C),[12] which featured "*on a wreath or and azure, a tower triple-towered of the first* [or], *from the portal a hart springing argent, attired and hoofed gold*" (*Boutell* 218). This gives special importance to Joyce's characterization of himself, Stephen, and Parnell as stags, since he has chosen not only a beast hounded (literally) by persecutors in the royal livery, but also a beast specifically emblematic of Ireland. The connection between the English Sovereign and the pursuit of the proverbial Irish stag is made more explicit in one of Joyce's notebooks for "Circe" than it was ultimately made in the novel: while Edward VII appears in *Ulysses* in rather curious regalia ("*a white jersey on which an image of the Sacred Heart is stitched with the insignia of Garter and Thistle, Golden Fleece, Elephant of Denmark. . . .*" [15.4449–52 {590.15–18}]), he does little more than sing a few lines from Mulligan's "Ballad of Joking Jesus." In the Buffalo Notebook V.A.19, he engages in the sport of kings by shooting a stag (Herring, *Joyce's Notes* . . . 238).

The royal colors are present (and usually resented) in a number of ways throughout *Ulysses.* In addition to quotations of the royal livery and emblems as incidental detail (as in the postal carriers in "Aeolus," mentioned above, and the royal arms featured on advertisements and labels of merchants holding Royal Warrants), the liveries of the King and others appear in the context of racing colors. Stephen looks at the photographs of race

Illustration 4-C Arms of Leinster, with traditional crest of Ireland: On a wreath or and azure, a tower triple-towered of the first, from the portal a hart springing argent, attired and hoofed gold. From Fox-Davies, *The Book of Public Arms* (1894). Photograph courtesy of the Library of Congress.

horses in Mr. Deasy's office, and "saw their speeds, backing king's colours" (2.303–4 {32.18}).[13] In "Cyclops," Joe Hynes speaks contemptuously of the clergy's deference to the Crown, and remarks: "—And what do you think, says Joe, of the holy boys, the priests and bishops of Ireland doing up his room in Maynooth in His Satanic Majesty's racing colours and sticking up pictures of all the horses his jockeys rode. The earl of Dublin, no less" (12.1402–5 {330.40–331.2}). The last reference is to one of the minor reminders of the royal presence over Dublin: "Earl of Dublin" was one of the lesser titles that Edward VII had held as Albert Edward, Prince of Wales.[14]

To counter the preponderance of allusions to royal English heraldry, *Ulysses* also contains heraldic recognition of Ireland. The most interesting and sustained use of these is in "Cyclops," where the epic atmosphere is enhanced by many learned references to the traditional ensigns of Ireland, most of which emerge from the surprising erudition of the Citizen. Although one of the epic catalogues of the Citizen's emblems connects him with "the first Prince of Wales" (12.192 {297.12}), this allusion is not so much an association with allegiance to the then-styled Earl of Dublin, but rather one in a series of allusions to the idea that all Irishmen, like the Prince of Wales, were "princes, the sons of kings" (12.86 {294.16–17}), because of their descent from the chiefs, or "kings," of the Irish septs. This motif is introduced in connection with the Prince of Wales in "Nestor": Mr. Deasy, who has a picture of Albert Edward over his mantelpiece, remarks, "I have rebel blood in me too. . . . We are all Irish, all kings' sons" (2.278–80 {31.28–30}).

The Citizen demonstrates a degree of heraldic acumen that permits him to distinguish pure Celtic heraldry from the variety contaminated by English rule. With historical precision, he looks forward to Ireland's regaining its former glory, "when the first Irish battleship is seen breasting the waves with our own flag to the fore, none of your Henry Tudor's harps, no, the oldest flag afloat, the flag of the province of Desmond and Thomond, three crowns on a blue field, the three sons of Milesius" (12.1306–10 {328.8–11}).

The Citizen refers to two armorial devices: the first is the harp on the azure field, which remains the Presidential Flag of the Republic of Ireland (Campbell and Evans 20). Although the harp, traditional charge of the province of Leinster (derived from the harp of Brian Boru), was used as a national symbol from the fifteenth century, the Citizen finds it objectionable because of its presence in the third quarter of the royal arms (Illus. 4-D).[15] An image in "Two Gallants" is suggestive of the supposed English debasement of the Irish harp: the description of a harpist, whose "harp too, heedless that her coverings had fallen about her knees, seemed weary alike of the eyes of strangers and of her master's hand" (*D* 54), alludes to the Irish harp ornamented with an undraped maiden, which was an English embellishment on the more traditional plain harp (see Hayes-McCoy 46–47 for a discussion of the "maiden" harp).

Eschewing this anglicized, and hence odious, emblem of Leinster, the Citizen prefers the arms of the province of Munster, legendarily associated with the Milesians (Thornton 282).[16] The antiquity that the Citizen claims for these arms is attested to by a Commission appointed by Edward IV, which "found [the arms of Ireland] to be azure, three ancient crowns in pale or, within a border argent" (Rothery 272). These arms differ from those of Munster in the arrangement of the crowns—"in pale," meaning in a vertical line down the center of the shield, rather than the conventional "two and one" arrangement (see Illus. 4-E, Arms of Munster)—and in having the silver border; but the field, charges, and number of charges are the same. Rothery notes that these arms are (coincidentally) the mythical arms of Saint Edmund; those arms, in turn, are thought to be the origin of the three crowns in the arms of Oxford University.

In his most subtle allusion, the Citizen refers to the ancient cognizance of the O'Neill sept. Weldon Thornton explains that the slogan the Citizen quotes as he lifts his glass—"his tribal slogan *Lamh Dearg Abu*" (12.1211–12 {325.24})—connects him with the family of O'Neill of Tyrone, whose *cri-de-guerre* was "*Lauv-derg-aboo* (the Red Hand to Victory . . .)" (Thornton 279). The red hand of O'Neill is one of the oldest Irish emblems, and is blazoned "a dexter hand couped at the wrist gules" (*Boutell* 248).[17] Thornton notes that the slogan has led to the evolution of the word "dergaboo" as proverbial for any type of fight. Moreover, as Robert Adams explains, the expression is also associated with drinking, "from the fact that the Allsop bottle carries a red hand on its label" (Adams 143).

As noted, the heraldic tincture, gules, represents Stephen's English master, the King; it also stands for his Italian master, the Pope, and the Catholic Church. Joyce employs this association in the only instance in *Ulysses* in which Stephen appears in red: as Simon Stephen Cardinal Dedalus, Primate of All Ireland. Spenser associated red with Catholicism in Book 1 of the *Faerie Queene*, where Duessa is clad in scarlet (as appropriate to her secret identity, the whore of Babylon). The derivation of the color in *Ulysses* is slightly less exotic than in Spenser: Joyce introduces the papal insignia of the crossed keys in the guise of the emblem of the lower legislative house of the Isle of Man, the House of Keys. Harry Levin points out the connection between the crossed keys and the papacy;[18] thus

Illustration 4-D Royal Arms and Badges. From Fox-Davies, *The Book of Public Arms* (1894). Photograph courtesy of the Library of Congress.

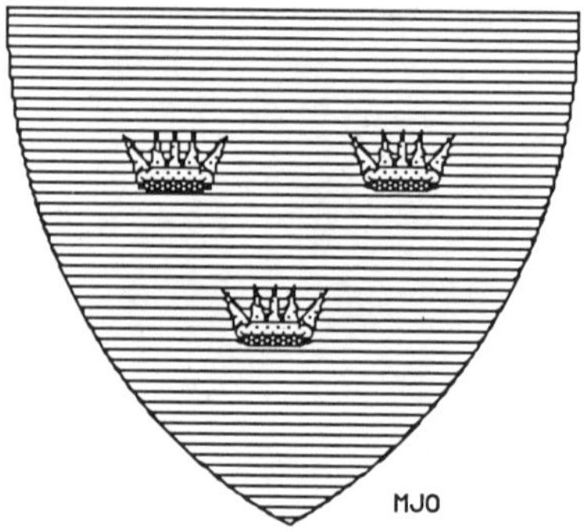

Illustration 4-E Arms of Munster.

Bloom's emblem of home rule ironically emphasizes Ireland's subservience to Stephen's Italian master. This is emphasized in "Circe," when, having been crowned, Bloom receives "The keys of Dublin, crossed on a crimson cushion . . ." (15.1520 {483.25–26}). The image duplicates the papal arms, which feature the crossed keys of the papacy on a field of gules.[19] Thus the Catholic church comes to participate in the red/green duality already discussed in regard to the English monarchy: after receiving the keys on the red cushion, Bloom "shows all that he is wearing green socks" (15.1521 {483.27}).

In Chapter Three, I discussed the arms of Dedalus, which constitute a third instance of the heraldic tincture, gules, dominating Stephen's life. The argent and gules of the Dedalus arms are part of a complex scheme which involves numerous antecedent uses of these colors, including the famous arms variously attributed to Christ, Galahad, and Spenser's Redcrosse (see Chapter 2);[20] the latter is St. George, under whose patronage argent and gules become the heraldic colors of England. Although for all intents and purposes the tricolored, so-called "Union Jack" (the "Union Flag" to the purist) has come into use as the National Flag of the United Kingdom, Fox-Davies (writing at a time when the usage was changing) points out that the Union Flag—featuring a combination of the crosses of St. George (the red cross), St. Andrew (white saltire), and St. Patrick (red saltire; see Illus. 4-F)[21]—was a standard of war, and that the appropriate civil flag of England was the simple argent and gules banner of St. George.

While Tennyson, as the literary embodiment of Stephen's English master, appears in "Circe" wearing the colors of the United Kingdom—"*in Union Jack blazer and cricket flannels* . . ." (15.4396 {588.12–13})—several

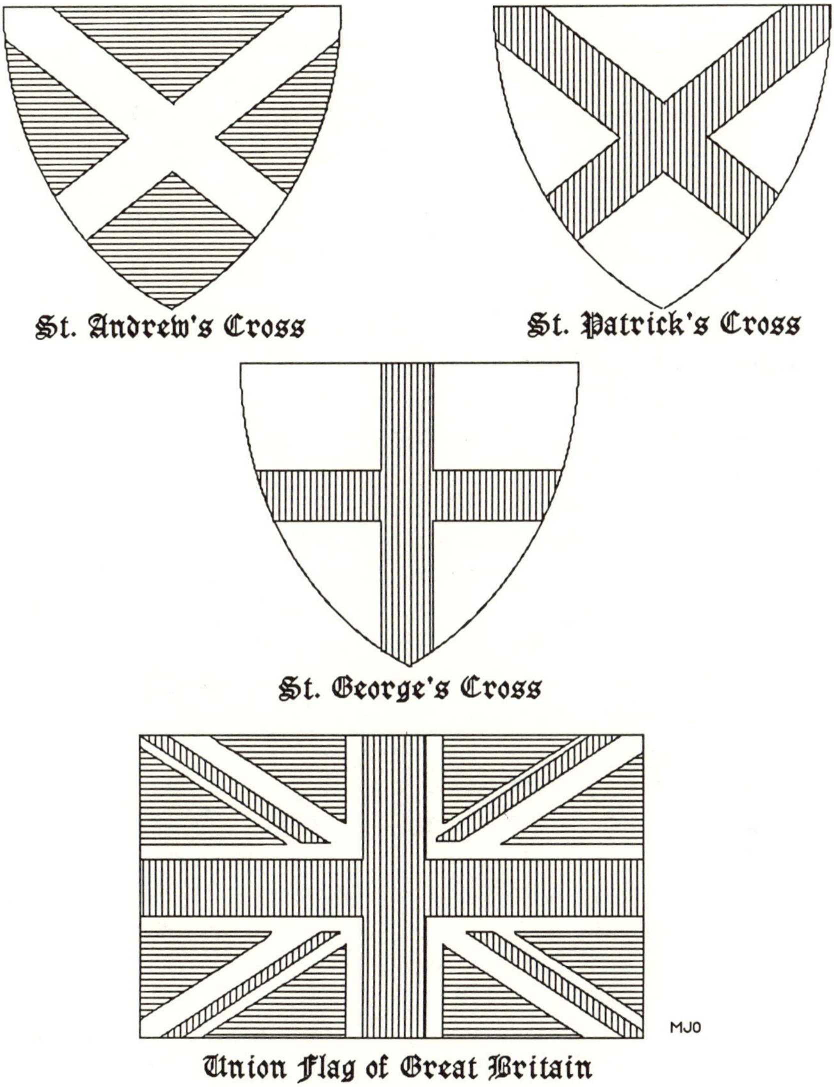

Illustration 4-F

other characters appearing in the argent and gules tinctures participate in the more elaborate heraldic scheme involving the supposed colors of Christ, of England, St. George, and of the Dedalus family (not to mention of Joyce of Galway). The sacrificial connotation of the livery of Christ and St. George is evident in "Lestrygonians," where: "A procession of whitesmocked sandwichmen marched slowly towards him along the gutter, scarlet sashes across their boards. Like that priest they are this morning: we have sinned: we have suffered" (*U* 8.123–25 {154.21–22}).[22]

Similarly, the Dedalus arms are invoked along with those of St. George in "Circe," just prior to Stephen's being struck by Carr, when the confrontation is heralded by a litany of birds of prey (including the eagle, the charge on the Dedalus escutcheon), and Irish heroes fighting after having exchanged "*the pass of knights of the red cross*" (*U* 15.4665–82 {598.17–599.2}). Although there is a clear allusion to masonic ritual here,[23] the simultaneous reference to St. George, the arms of England, and to the paternal colors of Dedalus, should not be ignored.

As I have argued in Chapter Three, the various allusions to the Dedalus arms constitute a recognition on Stephen's part of his hereditary legacy. This recognition is ambiguous for several reasons, including the universal ambiguity of the imagery in "Circe" (i.e., is Simon's heraldic proclamation a function of Stephen's consciousness, a function of narrative, both, or neither?), and the other uses of the Dedalus heraldic colors outlined above. Another reason for the ambiguity of the paternal significance of the Dedalus arms has to do with the use of sable as a tincture connecting Stephen with his figurative father, Bloom. Bloom, who has attended Paddy Dignam's funeral, is dressed in black for the entire 16th of June. In "Cyclops" this attire is converted into heraldic colors, with the nameless "I" 's rhetorical question and reply: "Who comes through Michan's land, bedight in sable armour? O'Bloom, the son of Rory . . ." (12.215–16 {297.39–40}). Like Tristram of Book 9 of *Morte d'Arthur* (see Chapter 2, above), Bloom indirectly faces an armorial antithesis, in the form of: "O'Nolan [John Wyse Nolan], clad in shining armour, [who] low bending made obeisance to the puissant and high and mighty chief of all Erin [the Citizen] . . ." (12.1183–84 {324.32–33}).[24]

Stephen Dedalus is also dressed in black, and this is remarked upon as a sign of connection between him and a symbolic father, Leopold Bloom. In "Circe," as Bloom enters Bella Cohen's, Zoe asks him if he is Stephen's father. Bloom replies, "Not I!" She remarks by way of explanation, "You both in black [sic]" (15.1295 {475.22–27}). The figurative paternal colors are made explicit when Stephen confronts Carr, and, like Bloom in "Cyclops," is seen as wearing sable armour:

BIDDY THE CLAP

Methinks yon sable knight will joust it with the best.

CUNTY KATE

(blushing deeply.) Nay, Madam. The gules doublet and merry Saint George for me! (15.4635–39 {597.12–15})

Thus while the heraldic emblems of "Circe" posit an affirmation of Stephen's hereditary link to Simon, the idea of paternal colors equally imply a link between Stephen and Bloom.

Another possible heraldic connection between Stephen and Bloom's family—more tantalizing than convincing, perhaps—nevertheless deserves mention here: among the many birds with which Stephen associates himself is the lapwing. In "Scylla and Charybdis" he thinks: "Paris and back. Lapwing. Icarus. *Pater, ait.* Seabedabbled, fallen, weltering. Lapwing you are. Lapwing be" (9.953–54 {210.36–38}). Stephen's connection with the lapwing has received much excellent scholarly attention (see Bates; Geckle), and I doubt that my observation will change the contours of this discussion. Stephen's reference to the lapwing, however, also alludes to an heraldic crest that might be found in the Bloom family, not by way of Bloom himself, but rather through his wife, née Marion Tweedy. In his *Complete Guide to Heraldry* Fox-Davies remarks that "*The Lapwing*, under its alternate names of *Peewhit*, *Plover*, and *Tyrwhitt*, will be found in the arms of Downes, Tyrwhitt, and Tweedy" (*CG* 249). In fact, as Fox-Davies's *Armorial Families* (2: 1976–77) indicates, it is not as the "lapwing" that this bird appears as the crest of various Tweedy families, but as the "peewit rising proper."

While Leopold Bloom lacks his figurative heir's penchant for "medieval abstrusiosities" (*U* 3.320 {45.33}), he is not indifferent to heraldic emblems. As an advertising man, for instance, he must be appreciative of the effectiveness of labels and advertisements bearing the royal arms. This practice, of emblazoning products used by members of the royal family with the royal arms or appropriate insignia (e.g., the ostrich feather badge of the heir apparent [Hasler 163–64]), evidently interests Bloom, who in "Lestrygonians" notices a candy advertisement bearing the token of royal appointment: "Lozenge and comfit manufacturer to His Majesty the King" (8.3–4 {151.3–4}).[25]

Perhaps the efficacy of this royal promotional gimmick, and its consequent appeal to Bloom's promotional instincts, is one reason why in "Circe," Bloom is apparently crowned King of England/Ireland. In addition to the overtones of his succeeding Parnell, the uncrowned king, Bloom sports royal regalia ("*a crimson velvet mantle trimmed with ermine, bearing Saint Edward's staff*" 15.1442–43 {481.2–3}), and is attended not only by the Irish officers of arms ("*Athlone poursuivant and Ulster King of*

Arms" 15.1413 {480.11–12}), but also by the Earl Marshal, head of the College of Arms in England, and the Garter King of Arms (15.1437–38 {481.38–39}). One of the ironic dimensions of the hallucinatory coronation, then, is that, as the King of England, Bloom implicitly becomes the authority behind the "By Appointment . . ." labels, one of the most effective advertising schemes in the United Kingdom.

While as King of England, Bloom would clearly be an armiger, he is also associated with armorial emblems on a more modest scale. The narrators in "Cyclops" and "Oxen of the Sun" attribute armorial bearings to him (his sable armour [12.215–16 {297.39–40}] and his "cognisance [of] the flower of quiet, margerain gentle" [14.330–31 {392.23–24}]). Bloom himself appears to be somewhat intrigued by the genteel position represented by a coat of arms: having styled himself "Henry Flower, Esq." in his secret identity (5.62 {72.31} *et passim*), in "Ithaca" he envisions an ideal retirement as a country gentleman, "at the zenith of his career, resident magistrate or justice of the peace with a family crest and coat of arms and appropriate classical motto *(Semper paratus)*,[26] duly recorded in the court directory. . ." (17.1609–12 {715.30–33}).

As a practitioner of the advertising trade, Bloom has a sensitivity to, and appreciation of, effective emblematic devices. This interest is made clear in "Ithaca," where it is stated that his "cogitation" is stimulated by: "the infinite possibilities hitherto unexploited of the modern art of advertisement if condensed in triliteral monoideal symbols, vertically of maximum visibility (divined), horizontally of maximum legibility (deciphered) and of magnetising efficacy to arrest involuntary attention, to interest, to convince, to decide" (17.580–84 {683.25–30}). In this category, he puts his advertisement for Alexander Keyes, for which he appropriates the heraldic emblem of the Manx House of Keys (Gifford and Seidman 104).

Bloom's consciousness of emblems makes him the foremost exponent of the rebus in *Ulysses*. In Chapter Three, I discussed such rebuses as are contained in the Sterne and Shakespeare arms, and those underlying the identities of Heron and Stephen, the hawklike man. The rebus is an underlying principle in *Ulysses*. Names derive from physical objects and traits, so that the on-the-spot etymology of the name of M'intosh (*U* 6.894–95 {112.7–9}) is not fundamentally different from that of the name of Heron in *A Portrait*. Stephen squeezes another rebus out of his name during "Scylla and Charybdis": after his reflections on Shakespeare's puns on "Will," he thinks of the connection between his name and the Greek word for crown: "*Stephanos*, my crown. My sword" (9.947 {210.28});

as if by coincidence, Eglinton immediately remarks, "You make good use of the name."

Bloom's name is likewise a reference to an object: like his *nom de bloom* of Henry Flower, it is an anglicization of his paternal Hungarian name, Virag. His emblematic code (as his floral "cognisance" in "Oxen" suggests) is the language of flowers, which is elaborated into a network of rebuses. As Henry Flower, Esq., he receives a letter from Martha Clifford, which contains "A yellow flower with flattened petals" (5.239 {77.30}). Several lines later, we see Martha's comment. "I often think of the beautiful name you have" (5.248 {77.40–78.1}). Bloom consciously connects Martha's flower and flowery letter with his special emblematic code. To the modern reader, this symbolic code has become approximately as arcane as heraldic symbolism, but Gifford and Seidman point out that this code, which evolved in medieval iconographic and heraldic systems, enjoyed a certain vogue in nineteenth-century greeting cards (69). With the accuracy deriving from a popular knowledge of flower symbolism, Bloom translates Martha's letter: "Language of flowers. They like it because no-one can hear. Or a poison bouquet to strike him down. Then walking slowly forward he read the letter again, murmuring here and there a word. Angry tulips with you darling manflower punish your cactus if you don't please poor forgetmenot how I long violets to dear roses when we soon anemone meet all naughty nightstalk wife Martha's perfume" (5.261–66 {78.14–22}).

Bloom reflects upon, and uses, his floral emblematic code in a variety of ways, including converting his penis into his emblematic cognizance: "[Anticipating his bath, he thinks of] his navel, bud of flesh: and saw the dark tangled curls of his bush floating, floating hair of the stream around the limp father of thousands, a languid floating flower" (5.570–72 {86.39–42}).[27]

While this emblematic code is directly related to heraldry in "Oxen," where the flower is Sir Leopold's charge, Bloom's heraldic rebus is also an issue in "Sirens." There it is made clear that Boylan, the conquering hero, has usurped Bloom's canting emblem, in the fashion of the conquering knights of Malory, who assume the arms of the conquered. When Bloom tries to recall what flower Martha had sent, he thinks, "Means something, language of flow. Was it a daisy? Innocence that is" (11.297–98 {263.35–36}). According to Brewer's (26th ed.) *Dictionary*, the daisy means not only innocence, but infidelity,[28] and, on the page following, flowers become specifically associated with this trait. Molly's infidelity to Bloom is foreshadowed by Boylan's entrance to Lenehan's quotation of the Handelian "See the conquering hero comes" (11.340 {264.40}), which is followed by Bloom's observation that Boylan sports the Bloom cognizance: "(flower in his coat: who gave him?)" (11.366 {265.26}). The relationship between Bloom's bloom and Molly's other lovers is sustained in "Circe," where Boylan appears with "*a red flower in his mouth*" (15.3739 {564.13}), and emphasizes his conquest when "*he hangs his hat smartly on a peg of Bloom's antlered head.*" (15.3763–64 {565.15}). In "Sirens," as Boylan leaves, the flower regains its talismanic significance for Bloom, as "Light sob of breath Bloom sighed on the silent bluehued flowers" (11.457–58 {268.2}), and shortly thereafter he recalls having purchased some music for Molly: "*Blumenlied* [Flower Song] I bought for her" (11.844 {278.32}).

In "Penelope," the Bloom emblem carries the same dual significance, as Bloom's talismanic rebus as well as the emblem usurped by the other suitors of his Penelope, Molly. Her recollections of Mulvey allude to Bloom's emblem: after thinking that she had accidentally anticipated Bloom's name with her invention of "Don Miguel de la Flora . . . flower that bloometh" (18.773–75 {759.35–37}), she recalls that when "I got him excited he crushed all the flowers on my bosom . . ." (18.777–78 {759.40}). Her final affirmation invokes the floral motif: she resolves to wear a "white rose" (18.1553–54 {781.33}), thinks that she would "love to have the whole place swimming in roses" (18.1557–58 {781.38}), and recalls Bloom's courtship of her, when "he said I was a flower of the mountain yes so we are flowers all . . ." (18.1576–77 {782.17–18}).

The occurrence of heraldic flowers in *A Portrait* and *Ulysses* constitutes still another allusion to the royal insignia: in *A Portrait* one of Stephen's childhood memories from Clongowes is of his class's competing in teams designated York and Lancaster, and wearing the floral badges of those historical factions: "The little silk badge with the white rose on it began to flutter." Ultimately, York (Stephen's team) loses to Lancaster, and Father Arnall exclaims, "—Right. Bravo Lancaster! The red rose wins. Come on now, York! Forge ahead!" (*P* 12).[29] Mary Dudley Schueler relates Stephen's personal association with the Yorkist emblem to his litany of pretenders in "Proteus" ("Perkin Warbeck, York's false scion, in breeches of silk of whiterose ivory. . . ." [3.314–15 {45.27}]), concluding that, "Stephen includes himself in the list of pretenders with the admonishment 'live their lives' " (Schueler 84). The rose badges also appear in Bloom's floral preoccupations (in "Circe," Bloom's coronation is marked by "*The ladies* [who] *from their balconies throw down rosepetals*" [15.1446 {481.6–7}]); in the numerous elaborations on Lenehan's "Rose of Castile" riddle, which include the conspicuous red rose in "Sirens" ("A jumping rose on satiny breast of satin, rose of Castile" [11.8 {256.8} *et passim*]); and as one of the Citizen's many emblems in "Cyclops" (12.185 {297.3}).

Bloom's first name also suggests a rebus, one which, like the heraldic flower, connects him to the royal dynasties of England. "Leopold" is a lion, as Mrs. Breen tells him in "Circe": "You were the lion of the night . . ." (15.447 {444.27}). Shortly thereafter, Signor Maffei appears to "bring your lion to heel . . . *Leo ferox* there . . ." (15.711–12 {454.25–26}), and Martha Clifford appears, calling him "Henry! Leopold! Leopold! Lionel . . ." (15.753 {456.13}). In "Penelope," Molly's unconscious wit transforms "Leopold" into "old lion": reflecting on his peculiar manner of sleeping, she thinks: "sure you might as well be in bed with what with a lion God Im sure hed have something better to say for himself an old Lion would . . ." (18.1376–78 {776.30–32}).[30]

Beyond its rôle in characterizing individuals in *A Portrait* and *Ulysses*, heraldry serves as a key to the thematic and aesthetic forms of two chapters, "Proteus" and "Circe." The heraldic allusions in "Proteus" have received the most attention, including a brief mention in Stuart Gilbert's study of *Ulysses* (130–31), and more sustained analysis in Ruth von Phul's 1971 essay in the *Journal of Modern Literature*, as well as some discussion in John Gordon's *James Joyce's Metamorphoses* (7–8). Mary Dudley Schueler also provides an enlightening discussion of the heraldic allusions in "Proteus," noting that "Heraldry, Egyptian hieroglyphics, and Gypsy Cant are all important manifestations of protean philology . . ." (148).

As I have mentioned, von Phul demonstrates the likelihood that Joyce used Oswald Barron's *Encyclopaedia Brittanica* article on heraldry for much of his terminology, and she maintains that much of the allusion is satirizing overly recondite blazon, in the spirit of Barron's purist approach to blazonry. While I would agree that much of the impact of the heraldic jargon is to expose Stephen's pedantry ("We don't want any of your medieval abstrusiosities . . ." [3.319–20 {45.32–33}]), I think Joyce is doing more—and, in a sense, less—than indicting Stephen's pedantry. For instance, while it is true, as von Phul points out, that the blazon of the Dedalus arms in "Circe" (15.3948–49 {572.16–17}) illustrates the syntactic "order [that Oswald] Barron derogates" in his *Encyclopaedia Brittanica* essay (von Phul 400, n.3), it is unlikely that Joyce formulated the Dedalus arms as a satire of awkward blazon. A more likely explanation of the terms used in "Circe" is the language used to blazon the Joyce arms in Burke's *General Armory:* "Ar[gent] an eagle disp[layed] gu[les] . . ." (*Burke's* 550b).

In another instance, von Phul notes that in characterizing the protean dog as "a buck, trippant, proper, unattired" on a field "tenney" (3.337 {46.13}),[31] Stephen has invoked several words from Barron's personal "hit" list (von Phul 401). But what Joyce accomplishes through this use of language is far more intricate than mere parody of the targets of Barron's fury. Why Stephen should transform the dog, by whom he feels threatened, into a deer, is at first confusing, since Stephen himself had been the stag to the mongrel's staghound in a passage almost immediately preceding (3.311 {45.22}). On closer analysis, however, it becomes clear that Stephen has not so much transformed the dog into a stag, as he has transformed Buck Mulligan into a mongrel. Heraldically, a buck, trippant, proper, unattired would be a naturally colored deer, walking (as von Phul explains, "In heraldry, proper = in natural color; attired = with antlers, thus in the context unattired = defenseless" [400]). But Fox-Davies notes that "trippant" is a term which is appropriately applied to heraldic dogs as well as deer (*CG* 204). The connection between the word "buck" and Stephen's erstwhile housemate is apparent; the other terms of the blazon emulate Mulligan's attitudes from "Telemachus": as he shaves, Mulligan speaks of his own name, and remarks that it is "Tripping and sunny like the buck himself" (1.42 {4.5–6}). This conversation is followed by the breakfast and Mulligan's swim, preparatory to which he ostentatiously undresses: "He stood up, gravely ungirdled and disrobed himself of his gown, saying resignedly:—Mulligan is stripped of his garments" (1.508–10 {16.36–38}). In short, Stephen's blazon of the dog, in addition to reflecting his pedantic bent, also constitutes a witty characterization of Mulligan with his "tripping" name, stripped for his swim, as a mongrel "buck, trippant, proper, unattired." The tenney field on which the "buck" is portrayed suggests the Mulligan "livery" (his primrose waistcoat), alluded to at the dog's first appearance: "Dog of my enemy. . . . A primrose doublet, fortune's knave, smiled at my fear" (3.310–12 {45.21–24}).[32]

Beyond this arcane witticism, the heraldic system in "Proteus" serves as a paradigm for the codes of which Stephen's visual aesthetic consists. He transforms the unblemished abdomen of Eve into an heraldic field—"a buckler of taut vellum, no, whiteheaped corn . . ." (3.42–43 {38.8}). Shortly thereafter, he uses heraldic terms to embody the function of the signs of his written art on paper. Writing on a scrap of Deasy's letter, he thinks: "Who ever anywhere will read these written words? Signs on a white field. Somewhere to someone in your flutiest voice. The good bishop of Cloyne took the veil of the temple out of his shovel hat: veil of space with coloured emblems hatched on its field" (3.414–18 {48.24–28}). His use of the term "field" for the locus of the signs, as well as the term "hatched" (which refers to the systems of lines and dots used to render heraldic colors for engravings) makes clear the heraldic context into which Stephen has placed Berkeleyan apprehension of the visible (the bishop of Cloyne is Berkeley).

The thematic use of heraldry described above is facilitated by the network of allusions that begins, not with the opening passages of "Proteus," but with a number of allusions in the previous chapter, "Nestor." Deasy refers to himself both as a descendant of the baronet, Sir John Blackwood, and at the same time as an Irishman, and thereby one of the sons of kings: "We are all Irish, all kings' sons" (*U* 2.279–80 {31.30}). The ambiguity of Deasy's heritage as an Ulsterman is evident in the illustrations in his office, portraying another sort of king's son in "the shapely bulk of a man in tartan filibergs: Albert Edward, prince of Wales" (2.266–67 {31.15–16}), as well as the horses sporting the king's colors. That this heraldically ambiguous situation is one that would demand the services of a herald is emphasized in Stephen's thoughts associating the episode with the heralds' traditional milieu, the tournament. He thinks of the boys' games in the schoolyard as "the joust of life" (2.315 {32.32}), which is echoed by Deasy's remark as they part, that "I like to break a lance with you, old as I am" (2.424–25 {35.37}).

While Deasy's armorial status remains ambiguous—if he is the son of kings, are they Irish or English?—, a solution is implied in the penultimate image of the chapter: Stephen leaves the school, and notices "The lions couchant on the pillars as he passed out through the gate: toothless terrors" (2.428–29 {35.42–36.1}).[33] The ornamental lions, described in the heraldic attitude of repose, constitute a transformation of the traditional lions "passant guardant" of the royal arms into lions in a posture more appropriate to the British Empire after the proverbial sunset. These heraldic lions are recalled in "Proteus," when Stephen adds to the dog's other transformations the "pard, a panther, got in spouse-breach, vulturing the dead" (3.363–64 {47.1–2}). The image evokes a bestiary tradition found not only in Brunetto Latini's *Il Tesoro,* John de Trevisa's *Bartholomeus (de Glanvilla) De Proprietatibus Rerum,* and the *OED* (which quotes from de Trevisa; see Thornton 60), but, as von Phul and Schueler point out, in Barron's *Encyclopaedia Brittanica* (325a) article as well. Schueler notes that the leopards also constitute one further allusion to the royal heraldic insignia (105); Barron explains in his discussion of heraldic leopards that the medieval armorists, blissfully ignorant of the true nature of the leopard, developed an heraldic leopard that was "like the lion at all points" except that its head was turned in the guardant position—facing the viewer, in the fashion of the royal lions.

"Circe" is a chapter which, like "Proteus," is concerned with various visual codes, as is clear from the copious notes that Joyce took on such arcane semiotic systems as the languages of parasols, handkerchiefs, playing cards, fortune-telling, and the rituals of freemasonry.[34] The chapter begins with Stephen's picking up on ideas concerning a "language of gesture": "So that gesture, not music not odour, would be a universal language, the gift of tongues rendering visible not the lay sense but the first entelechy, the structural rhythm" (15.105–7 {432.18–20}).[35]

The uses of heraldry in "Circe" include Stephen's emblematic alignment with his natural father as well as with Bloom, and the definition of his relation to his two masters, the English and the Italian. The montage of emblems also connects Bloom with the Dedalus bird emblems: Bloom's father, Rudolph Virag appears and "*with feeble vulture talons he feels the silent face of Bloom*" (15.259–60 {437.24–25}); Bloom's grandfather, Lipoti Virag, exhibits such avian tendencies in 15.2404 {515.5}, where "*he crows derisively*"; 15.2433–34 {516.2–3}, where "*he gabbles gluttonously with turkey wattles*"; 15.263 {522.18}, where he appears "*sloughing his skins, his multitudinous plumage moulting*"; and so forth, through his departure at 15.2638 {523.8} with a "Quack!" Bloom himself appears as a phoenix ("*in a yellow habit with embroidery of painted flames and high pointed hat*" [15.1927–28 {498.7–12}]). Other characters connected with the Dedalean emblem are Bella, whose "*falcon eyes glitter*" (15.2753 {527.13–14}); Florry, who "*lolls spreadeagle in the sofacorner* . . ." (15.2075 {503.15}; an eagle displayed, as it were), and Don Emile Patrizio Franz Rupert Pope Hennessy, who appears twice "*in medieval hauberk, two wild geese volant on his helm* . . ." 15.1915 {0}; 15.4507 {592.19–20}).

Just before the climax of the heraldic montage, in the confrontation of the red and green (also the red and black), between Stephen and Carr, Stephen and Bloom are joined in one further image relying on the accretion of heraldic emblems throughout the book. As Stephen has been associated with the deer, so is Bloom in "Circe," where Boylan hangs his hat on Bloom's cuckold antlers. Also, Mrs Bellingham accuses Bloom of envying her servant, whose livery features "the Bellingham escutcheon garnished sable, a buck's head couped or" (15.1050–51 {466.26–27}). Actually, the emblem "Mrs" Bellingham has quoted is not the escutcheon, but is rather the crest of Lady Bellingham, given in both *Burke's Peerage* and Burke's *General Armory* in the exact phrase Joyce used. But Stephen, who was a hunted stag in "Proteus," and Bloom, who is a hunted, horned cuckold in "Circe," are joined on the crested escutcheon of the mirror in "Circe": "*(Stephen and Bloom gaze in the mirror. The face of William Shakespeare, beardless, appears there, rigid in facial paralysis, crowned by the reflection of the reindeer antlered hatrack in the hall.)*" (15.3821–24 {567.17–20}).

These heraldic references create a network of emblematic associations which do not form anything as consistent as a schema. As I noted earlier, the heraldic connections between Stephen and Simon, and between Stephen and Bloom, are contradictory, and tend to complicate rather than to resolve the crucial, and ultimately unanswerable, issues of paternal, tribal, and national affiliations raised in *Ulysses*. But the patterns of heraldic allusion originating in *A Portrait* and expanded in *Ulysses* do enrich an understanding of the visual, emblematic dimension of *Ulysses*. Finally, the rich texture of the connections that the emblems of *A Portrait* and *Ulysses* engender (e.g., the relations among Stephen, Bloom, the papacy, the English monarchy, the Irish septs, and so forth) give a slight inkling of the far more complex system of heraldic motifs that Joyce was to create in writing *Finnegans Wake*.

CHAPTER FIVE

"Armigerend everfasting horde": The Heraldry of *Finnegans Wake*

—Finnegan's Wake 476.34

Considering his strategic importance in English letters, the herald is a strangely neglected figure in literary scholarship. Chaucer relies heavily on his heralds, having them identify the fallen knights in "The Knight's Tale"; he finds himself once again in need of their expertise in the "House of Fame." Spenser humbly admits that the description of the feast in *The Faerie Queene*, Book 5, Canto 3, "Were worke fit for an Herauld, not for me . . ." (Stanza 3, l. 6). Even Ian Fleming's ever-resourceful 007 requires an able assist from the College of Arms in *On Her Majesty's Secret Service*, where James Bond tracks down his nemesis, Blofeld, with the aid of one "Sable Basilisk Pursuivant." Learning that Blofeld's Achilles' heel is a lust for arms and a title, Bond is able to pursue the nefarious would-be armiger through research materials at the College of Arms: to supplement his usual arsenal, 007 carries copies of Burke's *General Armory* and the *Extinct and Dormant Baronetage*.[1]

Joyce's heralds may not see as much action as Fleming's, but we have seen that they were put to good use in his first two novels. Stephen Dedalus uses the Ulster King of Arms as a threat in *Portrait*, when he stridently offers to document his Irishness by appealing to the Ulster King's place of work, the Office of Arms in Dublin Castle (*P* 202). Ellmann relates this bit of genealogical bravado to the cry of the Circean Simon Dedalus: "Ulster king-at-arms" (*JJ* 11); also in the "Circe" chapter of *Ulysses*, the heralds perform their typical processional function with an atypical candidate for coronation, Mr. Leopold Bloom.

In addition to their genealogical functions, and their duties at ceremonies of state, the Irish heralds, like their Scottish and English counterparts, had another function, one which does not appear in Joyce's first two novels. In *Intelligible Heraldry*, the Lynch-Robinsons explain:

> In about 1568 [in Ireland] a system of funeral certificates was adopted. It was then usual to conduct funerals with great ceremony and in the case of armigerous persons heraldic banners were displayed. Officers of Arms were required to attend such funerals to see that only authorised arms were thus used and thereafter to lodge a certificate to this effect in the Ulster office. (112)

Here is a clear explanation of why we should find heralds doing their official work at a wake, as we do at *Finnegans Wake.* According to testimony received through Yawn (III.3), among those at the memorial for HCE/Finnegan are heralds: "Ulster Kong and Munster's Herald with Athclee Ensigning and Athlone Poursuivant and his Imperial Catchering . . ." (*FW* 498.11–13). The relationship between these individuals and the Irish Office of Arms is reasonably clear: "Ulster Kong" is easy to identify, and the title of the pursuivant in the Irish Office is given in its correct form: "Athlone Poursuivant." The other two officers in the Dublin Castle office were heralds: the Cork Herald (Cork is in Munster, hence "Munster's Herald"), and the Dublin Herald (Athclee, as McHugh notes, is from the Irish name for Dublin, "Baile Átha Cliath").

HCE himself seems to be a herald or king of arms in two references: first, when he appears wearing the insignia that the heralds share with the Lord Mayor of London, the collar of SS: "his loose Eating S.S. collar" (292.29), and second, when his fall is forecast/recapitulated in the phrase "Then old Hunphydunphyville'll be blasted to bumboards by the youthful herald who would once you were" (*FW* 375.5–7). Moreover, when HCE as tavern keeper is called "Norreys" in II.3, this hints not only at the Norwegian captain, but also to the oldest king of arms in the English College of Arms: Anthony Wagner notes that the earliest records of the Norroy King of Arms (circa 1338) refer to "Andrew Norreys or Norrois, King of Heralds" (Wagner 20–21).

But there seems to be much more of king than king of arms about the ubiquitous HCE; a more suggestive correlation is that between the four Irish officers of arms and the four traditional provinces of Ireland: Ulster King, Dublin [in Leinster] Herald, Cork [in Munster] Herald, and Athlone [in Connacht] Pursuivant.[2] This relationship suggests a further link, that between the four Irish heraldic officers and the four annalists/gospellers of *FW*, Matthew, Mark, Luke, and John (collectively, the "Mamalujo"), who are also connected with the four provinces. Indeed, specific references in the *Wake* link the four with the heraldic bearings of the provinces (Illus. 5-A). "Johnny"/Yawn would seem to be addressing Mark Lyons-as-Munster when, in III.3, he addresses "the three crowns round your draphole (isn't it dram disgusting?)" (*FW* 521.7–8). Here he evokes the provincial/national symbol advocated by the Citizen in "Cyclops" (*U* 12.1308–10 {328.110–12}), the three crowns of Munster. Similarly, Matt Gregory is addressed with a clear reference to the emblem of Ulster, the red hand: "Gently, gently Northern Ire! Love that red hand!" (522.4). There is an allusion to the dimidiated (composed of the halves of two different shields) escutcheon of Connacht in relation to Johnny MacDougal at 482.14–15: "Number four, fix up your spreadeagle and pull your weight!" Connacht bears on the dexter an eagle displayed (to be precise, half an eagle, since the field is dimidiated), and a human arm on the sinister (Illus. 5-A).

Other hints of heraldic identities of "X" include Mark Lyons's name and symbol, which might connect him not only with Saint Mark, whose emblem is the lion, but also with the Scottish King of Arms, known as the Lyon King of Arms (styled "Lord Lyon," preserving an archaic spelling of the Scottish royal symbol); this possibility is reinforced by Mark's appearance with an heraldic line of division at the beginning of III.3: he is seen "trailing the wavy line of his partition footsteps" (*FW* 475.25). A "wavy" line is a type of line used to "partition" (this is also the heraldic term) an heraldic field; perhaps it is also a wavy "lion." Reference to the Norroy King of Arms, earlier linked with HCE, is repeated in connection with the four when they are "them four hoarsemen on their apolkaloops, Norreys, Soothbys, Yates and Welks" (557.1–2). Finally, the siglum that identifies the four, the "X," might also be seen as the saltire, which is the Cross of Saint Patrick, or the Irish component of the Union Jack.

A possible explanation for the association of the four annalists with the heraldic symbols of the provinces, and the correlative officers of the Irish Office of Arms, is that the four historians serve the function of heralds. In general, they seek to identify HCE in his multifarious incarnations; like the officers of arms alluded to in *Portrait*, the annalists engage in genealogical inquiries. In other instances, emulating the heralds of medieval tradition, they serve as officials attempting to identify the participants in a tournament or a combat—both pervasive motifs in *FW*. Finally, like heraldic officers at a funeral, they serve to legitimize the stature of the deceased/slumbering HCE by acknowledging his heraldic bearings.

There seem to be references both to the four's heraldic function, as well as to their connection with the heraldic bearings of the four provinces, when, in their "starchamber quiry" (III.3), they appear "within their

Illustration 5-A Arms of the Irish Genealogical Office (formerly Office of Arms), quartering the arms of the four provinces: Leinster, Connacht, Ulster, and Munster.

quarterings" (476.34; "quarterings" is the word used to refer to the quartered arms of a shield [Lynch-Robinson 35]), and are referred to as "those quartermasters" (477.13; also a nautical term). This suggestion is further substantiated by the annalists' immediate commencement of their inquest of Yawn with genealogical queries: "Friends! First if yu don't mind. Name yur historical grouns" (477.35). They pursue the questioning observing "I take it, you have your letters" (478.1–2), as in letters patent, such as Shaun bears (419.19, 23). They are concerned with genealogical questions in III.4, noting ALP was "tocher [German: "Tochter" = daughter] of davy's, tocher of ivileagh" (557.10–11), and that "You can ken that they [HCE and family] come of a rarely old family by their costumance. . . ."

(560.32–33). In other words, they function as heralds identifying lineage by bearings. On 584.28, the heraldic character of the four's observations is made clear when they identify the family group as "Armigerend everfasting horde" (*FW* 476.34).

It is generally understood that the central questions of *FW* are questions of identity; one traditional approach to such questions addresses them in genealogical terms. In *The Sigla of Finnegans Wake*, Roland McHugh describes the annalists' search for HCE:

> Like God ᗰ [Joyce's manuscript siglum for HCE; see also 110.17, 299.F4] is a goal, a thing sought, a retort to the enigma of creation, a potentially dangerous but obsessively desired power of truth, a thing endowed with sanctity. For the purposes of *FW*, "the inspectors" may be folklore collectors, civic annalists or explorers of the Upper Nile, but they are all seeking . (12)

The first concern of I.2 is ᗰ/HCE's genealogy, and an exploration into the origin of his name ("Naw, yer maggers, aw war jist cotchin on thon bluggy earwuggers" 31.10–11). It is made clear, for instance, that he is not descended of the "Earwickers of Sidlesham" (30.7–8). Amidst the evidence brought to bear on this history is sigillography—a study of the siglum, or seal, that authenticates the documentary evidence related to HCE: "The great fact emerges that after that historic date all holographs so far exhumed initialled by Haromphrey bear the sigla H.C.E. . ." (*FW* 32.12–14).

Genealogical queries become a characteristic ritual throughout the *Wake*, particularly where the four are involved. In addition, in the opening passages of I.7, Shaun demonstrates his flair for genealogical manipulation in denigrating the roots of Shem, notwithstanding the fact that their forebears must (?) be identical:

> A few toughnecks are still getatable who pretend that aboriginally he was of respectable stemming (he was an outlex between the lines of Ragonar Blaubard and Horrild Hairwire and an inlaw to Capt. the Hon. and Rev. Mr Bbyrdwood de Trop Blogg was among his most distant connections) but every honest to goodness man in the land of the space of today knows that his back life will not stand being written about in black and white. (*FW* 169.1–8)

The *Wake* is a book of personal history, but only in the sense that any monarchic or dynastic biography is "personal history." The personal history merges with world history, because of HCE's many identities as warriors, princes, kings, and (as one must say to preserve one's sanity) so forth. Consequently, heraldic references in *FW* are clues both to HCE's identities, and to the historic persons, dynasties, and events in which these personages take part. In *Ulysses*, and particularly in "Nestor" and "Proteus," heraldry evoked images of history as Stephen's "nightmare"; in the *Wake*, the heraldry of the dream yokes the nightmare of history with the personal history and experience of HCE and/or the Dreamer, whoever they are. I do not suggest that heraldic evidence ultimately clarifies the identities of HCE and the Dreamer; rather, the heraldic evidence compounds the ambiguity, and multiplies possibilities. Although it is possible to infer that the Dreamer is someone who knows at least as much about heraldry as Joyce did, Clive Hart (*Structure and Motif* 80) has pointed out that this type of inference breaks down for reasons related to the content of the hallucinations of "Circe": it is inconceivable that Bloom could know all of the trivia (including much royal heraldry) in his hallucination, yet it is virtually inconceivable that the coronation hallucination would be that of anyone but Bloom. Hart quotes Harriet Shaw Weaver's view: "that Mr. Joyce did not intend the book to be looked upon as the dream of any one character, but that he regarded the dream form with its shiftings and changes as a convenient device, . . . suited to a night piece" (Hart 81).

Whoever the Dreamer is, or whoever they are, the heraldic content of the Dream(s) is substantial. One might take the Dreamer of the *Wake* to be the reader—this is my way out of this debate—; then, one could suggest that the herald, or the student of heraldry, might be a good candidate for "that ideal reader suffering from an ideal insomnia" (120.13–14).

In *The Books at the Wake*, James Atherton gives close attention to the number of heraldic motifs in *FW*. He first identifies heraldry as the language of Vico's second, heroic age, and cites Vico's description from the *New Science:* "The second [language] was by heroic blazonings with which arms are made to speak" (Atherton 32). This idea of arms "made to speak" is especially evocative of the canting arms which occupy so prominent a position in Joycean heraldry (cf. the French expression for canting arms, "armes parlantes"). Atherton notes that this "middle tongue" is that referred to in one of the most explicitly historical parts of *FW*, the children's history lesson in II.2, and cites the heraldic terms used in the following passage: "Beware how in that hist subtaile of schlangder lies liaison to tease oreilles! To vert embowed set proper penchant. But learn from that ancient tongue to be middle old modern to the minute" (270.15–18).

Atherton relates this passage to the discussion of the Fall that has preceded, and notes that both "vert" and "proper" are heraldic terms (33), and that both pertain to color, "vert" meaning green (a color that, as will be seen, is almost a constant in heraldic allusions to the Fall and HCE[3]), while "proper" simply means that the charge is depicted in its natural colors. "Embowed" is also used in heraldry, and means slightly bent, or arched. In subsequent discussion, Atherton observes recurrent heraldic elements, including references to the arms and motto of Dublin,[4] the mottoes of the Order of the Garter and of the House of Savoy ("F.E.R.T.," an acronym susceptible to numerous interpretations, both historically and *Wake*-fully), and the red hand of Ulster (Atherton 33–34).

The passage that Atherton quotes to illustrate heraldry as Viconian middle language (270.16–22) is embedded in an historical discussion, and, on close inspection, it becomes clear that heraldry illustrates more than the evolution of Viconian language—although it does this as well. For one thing, heraldic sources make possible the identification of another person and book at the *Wake*. "Vert" and "embowed" (arched) can be used to describe snakes in heraldry (see, for example, the arms of O'Dea, which include "in chief two snakes embowed vert"; MacLysaght, Plate VII). This use of these terms connects the heraldic passage with the description of the garden of Eden on the next page, containing the sentence: "This is the glider that gladdened the girl that list to the wind that lifted the leaves that folded the fruit that hung on the tree that grew in the garden Gough gave" (271.25–29).

The scene is recognizable as the snake ("glider") tempting Eve, but the identity of Gough, and why he should "give" a garden has been a mystery. Glasheen (108) suggests that it might be a reference to Sir Hugh Gough, the subject of a statue in Phoenix Park, but adds "I do not understand the references to him." Although the Gough that gave the garden might be the Gough in Phoenix Park, it seems more likely that the reference is to Henry Gough, the author of the *A Glossary of Terms Used in British Heraldry* (1847). Gough's revised glossary (1894) "gives" (heraldic jargon for blazoning) not one, but two gardens under "Paradise": the arms of Macklean of Scotland, and of the Company of Fruiterers, London (Gough [1894] 442; Illus. 5-B). Both coats of arms depict the serpent tempting Eve ("the glider that gladdened the girl") in the garden of Eden. These armorial achievements are reminiscent of one that Dominic Manganiello identifies as being associated with HCE, the arms of the O'Reillys of East Breffny (Manganiello 30–31): these arms feature a snake descending from a tree (cf. "To vert embowed set proper penchant"). If HCE, alias "Persse O'Reilly," displays these arms at home, then one can make sense of Issy's annotation to "the garden Gough gave": "Tho' I have one just like that to home, deadleaf brown with quicksilver appliques, would whollymost applissiate a nice shiny sleekysilk out of that slippering snake charmeuse" (271.F5). Issy likely has seen at her house a rendering of the O'Reilly coat of arms, and likens it to the arms of the Company of Fruiterers: "Tho' I have one just like that to home."

This instance of heraldic allusion illustrates three points: first, like many of the heraldic allusions in the *Wake*, it is very deeply embedded. Second, like many of these allusions, it provides a graphic encapsulation of the Fall of Man, or the Fall of HCE. Third, it relates HCE and his family to historical personages. In the discussion that follows, I will point out how armorial bearings in *FW* connect HCE and his family with several Irish "septs" (Celtic tribal groups, roughly the Irish equivalent of Scottish clans), with English gentry and aristocracy, and ultimately with the Royal Family of England; how these armorial bearings identify HCE with cities, nations, and empires, and finally, how heraldry serves the themes of history and the fall in *FW*.

The matter of legitimate heraldic bearings warrants attention quite early in the *Wake*, and our attention is immediately directed to the name and arms borne by HCE's august forebear, whose identity emerges from a background of chivalric battles: "Assiegates [lances] and boomeringstroms. . . . Arms appeal with larms, appalling" (4.6–7). The description of "Bygmester Finnegan of the Stuttering Hand" (4.18)[5] culminates in the first passage (if one starts at page 3) of Wakean blazon: "Of the first was he to bare arms and a name: Wassaily Booslaeugh of Riesengeborg. His crest of huroldry, in vert with ancillars, troublant, argent, a hegoak, poursuivant, horrid, horned. His scutschum fessed, with archers strung, helio, of the second" (5.5–8).

Illustration 5-B Arms of the Company of Fruiterers. Illustration by Dan Brooks.

By way of Shakespeare (*Hamlet*, 5: 1, l. 31: Adam was "the first that ever bore arms"), the bearer shares with Adam not only armorial bearings, but a Fall—to which the arms allude. McHugh and others have glossed the "ancillars" as referring to maidens (Latin: "ancilla" = handmaiden), and hence alluding to the "Maggies" of HCE's alleged indiscretion. The *OED* points to another root—an armorial one—in "ancile," a sacred shield of the Romans (from "ancilia"—a small oval shield); in his discussion of shields, Randle Holme (*Academy of Armory*, 1688) includes "*Ancile*, a shield without corners" (1: 5). Atherton has also observed that "antlers" is another reading of "ancillars," with an allusion to cuckoldry (33). This reading, along with the "vert" (green) of the crest, is particularly compatible with the rumors of HCE's "first offence in vert or venison" (34.25). The "hegoak" has been glossed by Campbell and Robinson as a "he-goat" (39; "he-goat" was an epithet applied to Joyce by Virginia Woolf[6]), i.e., the "hegoak, poursuivant" is a satyr chasing the "ancillars." This sense of "poursuivant"—chasing, or in pursuit—is more likely here than its other heraldic meaning (a sub-officer of the College of Arms) mentioned by McHugh. Since these are arms of the Fall, however, the possibility that the hegoak might be a tree (of Life, Knowledge, or both) should not be overlooked. This allusion connects the arms of "Booslaeugh of Riesengeborg" to HCE's O'Reilly arms, which feature a snake descending an oak. The remainder of the blazon describes the "scutschum [escutcheon, as distinct from the crest] fessed," which would be a shield with a horizontal band, or "fess," crossing its field (see Illus. 1-E). In the fess is the escutcheon's charge, the archers.

This coat of arms differs from others related to HCE in many respects, but it shares some elements with them. One is its use of "vert" in connection with the Fall. The term repeats throughout the book's armorial descriptions, including the "fidd of Verdor" (99.29), Finn MacCool's motto of "F.E.R.T." (127.10), the "vert embowed" (270.16), and the various plays on the Middle English (another middle tongue) pronunciation of "vert," which in our day is spelled "fart."[7] The "vert" motif also connects with the Fall, since the Viconian thunder is often a "fart," as in "By Dad, youd not heed that fert? Fulgitudes ejist rowdownan tonuout [F.E.R.T.]" (258.3–4).

Another heraldic motif sustained from the page 5 blazoning is the fess; the principal charge of HCE's arms on 546 is "partifesswise," and the Festy King's crime includes "flying cushats out of his ouveralls and making fesses immodst his forces on the field" (85.29–31). It is perhaps merely coincidence that this heraldic ordinary, which is so frequently used in *FW*, is found in the arms of Joyce of Galway as recorded in the Irish Genealogical

Office; as I pointed out in Chapter 3, none of Joyce's own renderings of the Joyce arms make use of the fess. Nevertheless, it is interesting that the Festy King, whose "crimes" frequently resemble recriminations (real and imagined) levelled against Joyce, should share an heraldic ordinary with the Joyces of Galway. Perhaps by using heraldic bearings, the Festy King, like Joyce, becomes guilty of social pretension: "therinunder proudly showing off the blink pitch to his britgits to prove himself (an't plase yous!) a rael genteel" (*FW* 93.4–5).[8]

Dominic Manganiello has demonstrated that many of the heraldic allusions in *FW* are linked to the armorial bearings of Irish septs (Manganiello 30–31). Manganiello researched a series of articles published in the [Dublin] *Weekly Irish Times* in the 1930s, and located relevant items in back issues that Joyce had requested from Constantine Curran (*Letters* 3: 403). Glasheen notes that H. C. Earwicker's name suggests "earwig" and is consequently rendered "Persse O'Reilly" (from the French "perce–oreille": earwig) in "The Ballad of Persse O'Reilly" (Glasheen 217), and Manganiello points out that the characterization of HCE's murder by "the MacMahon chaps" is described in terms that derive from the arms of the O'Reilly sept. The altercation is described: "On the fidd of Verdor the rampart combatants had left him lion with his dexter handcoup wresterected in a pureede paumee bloody proper" (*FW* 99.29–31).[9]

This is very close to the blazon of the arms of the O'Reilly sept as given in Burke's (761a) and in the *Weekly Irish Times* of 21 January 1933: "Vert two lions rampant combatant or supporting a dexter hand couped at the wrist erect and apaumee bloody proper" (4; see Illus. 5-C). Manganiello also observes the connection between the description of the aftermath of HCE's "murder" and the arms of O'Reilly of East Breffny. The events after the murder (the election of a new pope, and so forth) are said to follow "aslike as asnake comes sliduant down that oaktree" (*FW* 100.11). Manganiello observes that this phrase resembles one of the O'Reilly crests: "An oak tree with a snake descendant proper issuing out of a ducal coronet or" (Manganiello 31). This is also the device found in the second and third quarters of the East Breffny O'Reillys: as Illus. 5-D shows, the first and fourth quarters are identical to the sept arms described above (Illus. 5-C), and the second and third quarters bear "Argent, on a mount an oak with a snake descending its trunk proper" (Fox-Davies, *Armorial Families* 2: 1471). I take the blazon from Fox-Davies's *Armorial Families* because the description in the *Weekly Irish Times* is somewhat confusing, seeming to place the O'Reilly supporters in the second and third quarters:

The O'Reillys of County Down have made a combination of the above arms and crest which gives the arms of this branch as follows:—Quarterly first and fourth, the same as given for the O'Reillys of East Breffny [actually the sept arms; the arms being described are those of O'Reilly of East Breffny] second and third argent on a mount an oak tree, a snake descending the trunk all proper supported by two lions rampant gules. Their crest is the same, but in addition a second crest is used: An arm in armour mailed, couped at the elbow, the gauntlet grasping a dagger all proper. The motto is the same in both cases. (4)

Illustration 5-C Arms of O'Reilly. Illustration by Dan Brooks.

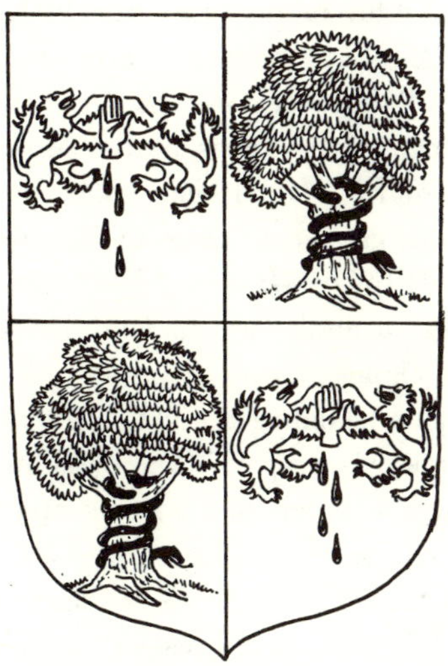

Illustration 5-D Arms of O'Reilly of East Breffny. Illustration by Dan Brooks.

I might mention here that the heraldic information in the *Weekly Irish Times* "Irish Family Names" series was comparable in quality to that often found in popular publications in the United States: the series seems to have been predicated upon the assumption of arms by "right of name," an idea not endorsed by the Ulster King, who continued to be the Irish heraldic authority until 1943; nor is it endorsed by the Chief Herald of Ireland, whose office considers grants of arms to descend in the direct male line. Clearly the "Irish Family Names" series was designed to sell papers: each masthead bore a message directing the attention of all persons bearing the name discussed that week to look at page four. The information in the series seems to be largely from O'Hart's *Irish Pedigrees*, and consequently the editors perpetuated some heraldic errors from O'Hart's work, as well as adding some of their own. One type of error is that in the description of the quartered O'Reilly arms, which seems to position the lions in the pose of supporting the oak tree; the lions are actually heraldic supporters, occupying the same position in relation to the escutcheon as the lion and unicorn on the Royal Arms of England, or the two women in the arms of Dublin. The quarterly arms were those of Myles George O'Reilly, "The O'Reilly" (see "Myles the Slasher" [99.24–25], Glasheen 217), whose use of supporters would be in right of his sept chieftaincy, a right not recognized by the Ulster King (Fox-Davies 421).

Another type of error in the *Times* series is evocative of the kind of expedient and "enthusiastic" genealogical research which in early 1984 caused Burke's Peerage Ltd. to proclaim Ronald Reagan's lineal descent from Brian Boru. In their haste to assign arms to the Finnegan families of Ireland, the editors of the *Weekly Irish Times* became responsible for the prominent appearance of the arms of the Molloy sept in *Finnegans Wake*. In my readings of *FW*, I had been unable to find specific allusions to the arms of the Finnegan sept, even though there is a resemblance between these and the O'Reilly arms of *FW* 99.29: both feature lions in the "rampant combatant" attitude (two rampant beasts facing one another). MacLysaght blazons the Finnegan arms, "Gules two lions rampant combatant supporting a sword in pale [standing upright] blade wavy [with a somewhat serrated blade] point upwards proper" (MacLysaght, Plate XI). But aside from the tenuous relation between the O'Reilly and the O'Finnegan lions, I do not believe this coat of arms appears in *FW*.

I am indebted to Manganiello's research, however, for making it possible for me to understand why the Finnegans of the *Wake* bear the arms of the Molloy sept. Manganiello identified Joyce's use of material from the *Weekly Irish Times* of 18 July 1936, which featured "Irish Family Names:

Finnegan." Taking the *Times* at its word, Manganiello states: "Joyce also incorporated into his work some of the material on Irish family names about Finnegan. The arms of the family, argent a lion rampant sable between three trefoils slipped gules, is transformed into 'the liofant . . . mid trefoils slipped the sable rampant' (599.06)" (Manganiello 31). Manganiello identifies what must have been Joyce's source, and one can infer that as far as Joyce knew, this coat of arms was indeed the Finnegan coat of arms. So in a sense, for the reader of *FW*, these are the Finnegan arms. For the historical record, however, these are the arms of the Molloy sept (Illus. 5-E).

To understand how this came about, one need only read on in the *Times* article: among a number of crests allegedly used by Finnegans is "A greyhound courant in front of a tree (this is the Crest given in O'Hart's *Irish Pedigrees*)" (*Times*, 18 July 1936, 4). With this clue, it is possible to determine that the editors of the *Times* looked in the index of O'Hart's *Irish Pedigrees* under "Finnegan." O'Hart does not give the Finnegan arms, but there are two page references under "Finnegan" in O'Hart's index (1: 870), one of which leads to the early descendants of "O'-Maoluaidh," a.k.a. "The Molloy." The Molloy is said to have a descendant named (but certainly not surnamed) "Fiongan," which O'Hart explains was anglicized "Finnegan" (O'Hart 1: 590). In other words, on the strength of there having been a Molloy named Fiongan, the *Times* concludes that the Finnegans "are more directly descended from the powerful family of Molloy. . . ." Having made this leap into genealogical absurdity, the editors sanguinely—and silently—granted the Molloy arms to Finnegan. Under any other circumstances, such a journalistic grant of arms would have

Illustration 5-E Arms of O'Molloy. Illustration by Dan Brooks.

been as ephemeral as the tabloid containing it; by a series of accidents, however, the *Times* became one of Joyce's heraldic sources, so the Molloy arms are eternally attributed to the Finnegans in *Finnegans Wake.* I have no reason to suspect that Joyce was aware of any of this, but I think it is interesting that an heraldic "ghost" in an Irish newspaper should make Joyce's Finnegan a pedigreed kinsman of Beckett's *Molloy.*

The leaved plants surrounding the lion in the Molloy arms, the trefoils, are heraldic plants with three leaves, and are generally similar to shamrocks; indeed, the trefoil was one of the royal badges used in connection with Ireland (see Illus. 4-D). There is another hint of the Molloy/Finnegan coat of arms earlier in *FW,* in II.1, when the reference to the "evangelion, sabre accusant" occurs in a passage also referring to trefoils: "Et would proffer to his delected one the his trifle [trefoil or shamrock] from the grass" (*FW* 223.19–22). In context, there is not only a suggestion of the lion of St. Mark ("evangelion"), but the sable ("sabre") heraldic lion of Finnegan, surrounded by trefoils.

Manganiello also traced Joyce's use of emblems that have actually been used by Finnegans, identified in the same number of the *Weekly Irish Times.* Before reading Manganiello's note, these emblems had entirely eluded me in my readings; I am in good company in this respect, however, for in regard to the passage in Book IV, "A hand from the cloud emerges, holding a chart expanded" (*FW* 593.19), William York Tindall remarked, "The hand emerging from the cloud with a chart, serving no high purpose, is the hand of a gargoyle or a decoration on time's map" (Tindall 307). Yet Manganiello notes the precise high purpose of this emblem: it is based on a crest used by some members of the Finnegan family (Manganiello 31): ". . . out of a cloud a hand erect holding a book expanded proper" (*Times* 4). Still another crest used by the Finnegans appears in Book IV: the Finnegan "vinebranch leaved vert and fructed proper" appears as "The vinebranch of Heremonheber on Bregia's plane where Teffia lies in leaved invert and fructed proper. . ." (604.3–5). In *Fairbairn's Crests,* "A vinebranch, leaved, vert, fructed, proper [the misleading placement of commas after "leaved" and "fructed" are in *Fairbairn's*]" is identified as belonging to the family of "FINNCANE" (*Fairbairn's* 1: 181b; 2: P1.89, Cr. 1).

The other numbers of the *Weekly Irish Times* that Joyce requested were 7 January 1933 ("Irish Family Names: MacGuinness or Guinness"), 25 February 1933 ("Irish Family Names: O'Connell), 14 October 1933 ("Irish Family Names: O'Gorman"), 27 January 1934 ("Irish Family Names: O'Shea"), 29 August 1936 ("Irish Family Names: Lennon"), and a particularly interesting number of which he requested four copies: 1 August

1936, featuring one of the twelve tribes of Galway, by the name of Joyce.[10] The blazon given is identical to that in Burke's and O'Hart's *Irish Pedigrees* (the latter being the newspaper's likely source), and hence was identical to the armorial painting Joyce had on his wall, and which he had already commemorated in print in *Ulysses.* Manganiello does not mention the occurrence of these arms in *FW;* McHugh finds a connection between the "eagle gules volant" in *Ulysses* and the "raaven geulant" of *FW* 136.13. This last seems a bit strenuous; I am willing to entertain virtually any possibility, but I am most convinced by the connection Adaline Glasheen finds between the Joyce arms and the "Phoenix" references in *FW* (Glasheen 233). There is likely a connection between the legends of the eagle's rejuvenating itself by flying into the sun, and the phoenix's similarly pyrotechnic resurrection. Certainly a red eagle, as the Joyces bore, resembles a phoenix more closely than it resembles the eagle of nature. Finnegan would seem to bear the Joyce emblem on an heraldic surcoat, which the speakers of 24.29 refer to as his "bloodeagle waistcoat." Moreover, just as the earwig (perce-orielle) is a rebus for Persse O'Reilly, so is the Joycean eagle: according to McHugh, "orel" is the Pan-Slavonic word for eagle. Thus such references as *"Prszss Orel"* (105.10–11) and the description of HCE as "hunter's pink of face, an orel orieled" (310.26–27) become allusions to the arms of Joyce of Galway, while simultaneously converting the eagle into a rebus for O'Reilly.

Another Irish sept identification made possible through knowledge of heraldic emblems is another of the Galway tribes, O'Kirwan. McHugh glosses the reference to Butt's target (replaying the Buckley story), "the frustate fourstar Russkakruscam, Dom Allaf O'Khorwan, connundurumchuff" (352.33–34), as referring to "Daniel O'Connell, commander-in-chief." While recognizing this distinct possibility, I suggest that another reading would be O'Kirwan. Not only does "O'Khorwan" resemble O'Kirwan, but there is an important heraldic clue in "connundurumchuff." Taking the word to mean a conundrum, or a riddle (see McCarthy, *Riddles* 18) involving a "chuff," the answer to the conundrum-chuff might be a Cornish chough (a black bird common in heraldry) borne as an emblem—as it is in the arms of the "O'Kirwan" sept: "Argent a chevron sable between three Cornish choughs proper" (MacLysaght 203–4; Plate XVIII; see Illus. 5-F). A likely candidate for Butt's victim from among the O'Kirwan sept might be Owen Kirwan, who was executed in 1803 with Robert Emmet.

One more sept emblem the occurs in the *Wake* also appears as a provincial insignia: the Red Hand of Ulster, which is traced to the red hand on the O'Neill coat of arms. MacLysaght blazons these arms: "Argent

Illustration 5-F Arms of O'Kirwan. Illustration by Dan Brooks.

two lions rampant combatant gules supporting a dexter hand couped at the wrist of the last [gules], in chief three estoiles [stars] of the second, in base waves of the sea therein naiant a salmon all proper" (MacLysaght, Plate XXIII). The legend behind this emblem is discussed in Chapter 4, in connection with the Citizen's invocation of the O'Neill *cri-de-guerre*, *Lamh dearg abu* (Up the red hand). Nathan Halper discussed this emblem's occurrence at 522.4 (Halper, "Of the Stuttering Hand" 7–8), and 23.3–4, where Jarl van Hoother "clopped his rude hand to his eacy hitch"; it also appears in connection with HCE before the Festy King trial, when HCE appears on the Butt Bridge, "his alpenstuck in his redhand" (85.11–12). The red hand appears not only in token of his guilt (as in caught redhanded), but of the province of Ulster, and of the O'Neill sept; the red hand also figures prominently in heraldic achievements of other septs linked to the O'Neills, such as those of MacGuinness or Guinness (from the *Weekly Irish Times:* "Vert a lion rampant, [sic] or on a chief argent a dexter hand erect couped at the wrist gules").

HCE shares with the O'Neill sept not only the red hand emblem, but also the salmon in the base of the O'Neill coat of arms. In a *JJQ* essay, Patricia A. Morley discusses the relation of Finn MacCool's *salmon of knowledge* to Earwicker and Shem (Morley 268), and Glasheen traces numerous allusions to salmon in *FW* (253–54). Aside from these well-documented allusions outside of an heraldic context, HCE bears a fish for crest when he explicitly declares his coat of arms toward the close of III.3. Having established his many historical accomplishments, HCE (like Simon and Stephen Dedalus before him) proclaims his gentility by claiming armorial bearings:

These be my genteelican arms. At the crest, two young frish, etoiled, flappant, devoiled of their habiliments, vested sable, withdrewers argent. For the boss a coleopter, pondant, partifesswise, blazoned sinister, at the slough, proper. In the lower field a terce of lanciers, shaking unsheathed shafts, their arms crossed in saltire, embusked, sinople. Motto, in letters portent: *Hery Crass Evohodie.* (*FW* 546.5–11)

Glasheen identifies the two "frish" as versions of the two girls in the park, as well as those supporting the Dublin arms (Glasheen 294), and the image of fishy girls has some curious antecedents in Joyce's life and writings: Ellmann refers to Lucia Joyce's last dance performance on 28 May 1929, for which "she appeared in a shimmering silver fish costume she had designed herself. . . ." (*JJ* 612); years earlier, in *Giacomo Joyce,* the lover describes his beloved's form as "a little smooth naked body shimmering with silver scales" (*GJ* 7).

Bernard Benstock elaborates on the connection between the two girls and the "frish," interpreting HCE's arms as a version of the arms of Dublin:

Joyce takes as his blueprint the Dublin city arms, depicting two women in Grecian attire at either side of the shield bearing the images of three castles. . . . (The Dublin maidens are the *two young frish* and the castles are seen as a *terce of lanciers.*) Dublin wit has it that the women's gowns are raised above their feet so that they may step across the omnipresent mud puddles. . . . but Joycean wit goes one better, assuming that the puddles were caused by the girls having urinated and from this basic joke the park incident evolves. (Benstock, "Every Telling . . ." 5)

The other elements in HCE's arms incorporate familiar aspects of Joyce's other heraldic allusions: the "boss" (usually a structural protrusion from the center of a buckler, but here seemingly a charge) is a "coleopter"—a beetle, or earwig, punning on Earwicker as Shakespeare's shaking spear puns on his name. Vincent John Cheng observes in his recent study of Shakespeare in *FW* that Shakespeare's arms are also present in this armorial display; I agree, but I am not sure his argument is the same as mine. Cheng sees "a verbal resemblance" between the blazon of Shakespeare's arms and the blazon contained in lines 5–7 on 546 (Cheng 181; also 196). I think that the Shakespearean allusion is in lines 9–10, where there is a "terce of lanciers, shaking unsheathed shafts," thus duplicating the canting gesture of Shakespeare's falcon crest.

HCE's heraldic pun is anticipated in the story of the origin of his name (*FW* 30–31), where the earwig is the actual source of his name, and in such statements as HCE's reference in the tavern to his "gay giftname of insectarian" (358.7–8). Gough's *Glossary* indicates that beetles are exceediingly rare in the heraldic bestiary; the arms of one Muschamps family feature "three beetles proper," but it is noted that this blazon is "possibly . . . an error of some writer, who has mistaken *flies* for beetles (as the name of the bearer suggests), however, the *stag beetles* (*lucanidae* of naturalists) occur" (Gough [1894] 51). If, however, as McHugh suggests, Randle Holme's *Academy of Armory* was a source for *FW* (McHugh finds the carving terms of *FW* 569.21–23 in the *Academy* 3: 78), then it is worth noting that Holme identifies a person named "Earwigg" who has canting arms: "He beareth Argent, an *Earwig erected* proper. 3 such is born by the name of *Earwigg.* It is naturally the Feet and Body yellowish, the Head and Tail reddish brown, with two black horns at the end of the Tail" (2: 471).

The beetle is one of two canting emblems connected with HCE in the *Wake.* The other is found among the epithets directed at HCE from outside the gate: he is called "*Wheatears*" (71.11), which McHugh (*Sigla* 15) indicates is a rebus on the funerary monument of William Earwicker of Sidlesham (cf. references in HCE's speech at the end of "Yawn" [III.3] to "wheatears" [550.26], and "Good wheat!" [616.10]).

Thus far, the elements in HCE's specific armorial bearings on 546, and those in many emblems alluded to in connection with him, assert his rank as a gentleman, and connect him with the O'Reilly, Finnegan, Joyce, and O'Neill septs. But the Irish armorial allusions lack an heraldic element found in other references to HCE's arms: supporters, or figures flanking the armorial achievement (e.g., the women on either side of the Dublin arms; the lion and unicorn of England). While HCE shares emblems from the O'Reilly arms, and while Myles O'Reilly and his sons apparently used supporters (lions rampant or), HCE does not use supporters of any of the sept chieftains.[11] He does, however, have armorial supporters in two instances. In his appearance as "HUMP" in the "Mime" chapter (II.1), he appears as Hamlet's father ("Armèd at point exactly, cap-a-pe" [*Hamlet* 1: 2, 1. 200]) with complete armorial bearings: "cap-a-pipe with watch and topper, coat, crest and supporters" (*FW* 220.26–27).[12] Later, in the "Tavern" episode (II.3), after HCE has asserted his aristocratic rank ("confessedly in my baron gentilhomme to the manhor bourne. . . ." [365.4–51]), the exodus of the patrons becomes both a reprise of the prankquean riddle, and a grant of supporters:

And they [the patrons] all pour forth. Sans butly Tuppeter Sowyer, the rouged engenerand, a barttler of the beauyne, still our benjamin liefest, sometime frankling to thise citye, whereas bigrented him a piers half subporters for his arms, Josiah Pipkin, Amos Love, Raoul Le Febber, Blaize Taboutout, Jeremy Yopp, Francist de Loomis, Hardy Smith and Sequin Pettit followed by the snug saloon seanad of our Café Béranger. The scenictuturs. (372.5–12)

Supporters conventionally occur in pairs; HCE has a generous supply of them, numbering at least eight. McHugh identifies the names as early settlers of Dublin, Georgia, as is the granter of the arms (Tuppeter Sowyer, from Jonathan Sawyer, the founder of Dublin, Georgia). Fox-Davies explains the significance of supporters in English heraldry:

In England the right to bear supporters is confined to those to whom they have been granted or recorded, but such grant or record is very rigidly confined to peers, to Knights of the Garter, Thistle, and St. Patrick, and to Knights Grand Cross, or Knights Grand Commanders (as the case may be) of other Orders. [. . .] As by an unwritten but nowadays invariably accepted law, the Orders of Garter, Thistle, and St. Patrick are confined to members of the peerage, those entitled to claim (upon their petitioning) a grant of supporters in England are in practice limited to peers and Knights Grand Cross or Knights Grand Commanders. (*CG* 419)

In strict English practice, then, HCE's supporters might make him either a knight or a peer; of the two, only a peer is normally granted *hereditary* supporters, a knight's grant generally being effective only within that knight's lifetime. The phrase "piers half subporters for his arms" suggests (in addition to the prankquean riddle) that he has received either half of a peer's supporters, or the supporters appertaining to half a peer—or both. There are a number of reasons why HCE should be a peer; if we associate him with the subject of the first riddle of I.6, the clues to his identity include "hold as an earl, he counts" (*FW* 128.5–6; an English earl is the equivalent of the continental "count": an earl's wife is a countess). Another factor linking HCE to the peerage has not so much to do with his social rank, but rather pertains to a version of his crime in the park: if his exposure occurs in his act of relieving himself, then he is a "peer," or one who "pees" (perhaps three "e"s are required).

The ample references to HCE's aristocratic connections provide, among other things, some additional books at the *Wake*. Among the epithets directed at him in I.3 is "*Purged out of Burke's*" (71.29–30), which could refer to any of the commonly available books—Burke's *Landed Gentry*, *Peerage*, or the *General Armory*, all of which list armigers of varying ranks, with blazons of armorial bearings. In this connection, McHugh also says that the initials "B.L.G." (131.3) in the first riddle of I.6 stand for "Burke's *Landed Gentry* (cf. Chuff's aspirations in II.1 "I shall reside with our obeisant servants among Burke's mobility" [235.12–13]).

If HCE is not always a peer, he is almost certainly of the higher echelons of the gentry, with the "E" of "HCE" often standing for variants of "Esquire," as in "Humme the Cheapner, Esc" (*FW* 29.18–19), "Handiman the Chomp, Esquoro" (102.16), "Her Chuff Exsquire" (205.22), "Hocus Crocus, Esquilocus" (254.20), and "Hemself and Co, Esquara" (557.1). But equally prevalent are references such as the "piers subporters" that link him to the aristocracy. In his identity as the Duke of Wellington, he would also be a Knight of the Garter, who sports the garter of that order amidst his other regalia: "his magnate's garters" (8.19; cf. "so buckely hosiered from the Royal Leg" [536.15]). HCE, whether as Wellington or another peer, or a member of the Royal Family, is probably a Knight of the Garter, an honor which is also suggested by the prevalence of variations throughout *FW* of the Garter motto, "Honi soit qui mal y pense": for example, "Honey swarms where mellisponds" (*FW* 238.33–34), and "O'Neill saw Queen Molly's pants" (495.27–28).

An important *leitmotiv* related to HCE's armigerous status has to do with "letters patent," which would be the documentary device whereby a grant of arms or other hereditary honor might be conveyed from the Sovereign through the Earl Marshal (who heads the College of Arms). The famous "letter" of *FW* takes the form of letters patent in III.1, when Shaun is carrying it and is questioned as to its content: asked if he is able to read "those shemletters patent for His Christian's Em?", Shaun replies "I'm as afterdusk nobly Roman as pope and water could christen me. . . . I am, thing Sing Larynx, letter potent to play the same backwards. . ." (*FW* 419.19–24). Thus, on one level, Shaun bears documents that might certify his heritage through HCE, who, as ALP testifies, is "liable to succumb when served with letters potent below the belch" (492.35–36), and whose heraldic motto appears on his armorial achievement in "letters portent" (546.10).

An issue connected to HCE's armigerous status is that of his family; heraldry dictates the proper marshaling of arms by heirs and spouses of armigers, but rules are not certain to be strictly applied in the *Wake*. For instance, if ALP is Mrs. or Lady HCE (see Benstock, *Joyce-Again's Wake* 7–8), she would not bear HCE's arms in her own right while he lived; the paternal arms of HCE's wife would be marshaled (arranged for display) either on an inescutcheon (small shield) in his coat of arms if she is an heiress, or "impaled" (occupying the sinister half of the escutcheon) if she is not (i.e., if she has a living brother). On the other hand, if she were either HCE's heiress or his widow, she would bear the family arms, but not on the conventional shield: she would bear them on a lozenge shaped field (Franklyn 13).

There seems to be an allusion to a woman's armorial display in the "solution" to the geometry problem (293). Among the other interpretations made of ALP's genitalia/vortex/*Vesica Piscis*, etc., "Kev" (Shaun) ultimately sees the rhombus at the center of the figure as the heraldic field of a widow or heiress—a lozenge: "And be the powers of Moll Kelly, neighbour topsowyer, it will be a lozenge to me all my lauffe" (299.27–29). This passage has, naturally, been glossed as "a lesson to me all my life" by most readers from Campbell and Robinson through McHugh, but there is also the heraldic meaning of the lozenge, reinforced by the presence of "topsowyer," which on 372.6 is "Tuppeter Sowyer," who serves as the officer who grants HCE his armorial supporters. Also, the footnote appended to Kevin's exclamation (299.F4) provides the "Doodles family" sigla for HCE, ALP, Issy, the four annalists, *FW*, Shaun, and Shem. These sigla figure in the heraldry of *Finnegans Wake:* the significance of "X" as St. Patrick's Cross has been discussed, and ALP's siglum (△) is the top half of her armorial lozenge on 293. In the aftermath of a *Wake*, ALP as a widow would indeed bear HCE's arms on a lozenge, as did Lady Southdown of *Vanity Fair* (Illus. 2-F). This would also be the field on which an unmarried heiress would bear the arms of her father.

But there is little evidence with which to answer the question of ALP's heraldic or social privileges in right of HCE; like Molly Bloom in "Circe," she is often relegated to the status of a dispossessed woman of social rank unequal to her husband. When the triumphant Bloom has been (hallucinogenically) crowned King and Pope, "*The former morganatic spouse of Bloom is hastily removed* (*U* 15.1508 {483.13}). Brewer's (26th ed., 593) defines a "morganatic marriage" as one "in which the wife does not take the husband's rank, because legally or according to court bye-laws [sic] the marriage is not recognized." Presumably, in such an arrangement, the children by the woman would not inherit rank or privilege either; such an arrangement was considered in the case of Edward VIII and Mrs. Simpson, but English law does not recognize such a marriage. Wakean law does, however, and HCE's self-defense in III.3 refers to his "morgenattics litt" (545.27; morganatic marriage bed).

If HCE resembles the erstwhile King of England and late Duke of Windsor in his preference of marital arrangement, he also shares with English monarchs the same heir apparent: the Prince of Wales. This family legacy derives, in part, from one of the lesser titles of Albert Edward (Edward VII), Earl of Dublin—a title subjected to some derision in "Cyclops"

(*U* 12.1404–5 {331.1}). In 1934, Frank Budgen observed, "In *Work in Progress* Ireland figures only as the estate of the Lord of Dublin and is populated with his quarrelsome and troublesome tenants" (154). The status of the actual Prince of Wales as Earl of Dublin was obsolete by the time *Work in Progress* came into being as *Finnegans Wake*, but the Earldom remains intact in the pages of *FW.* Finn MacCool was characterized as an earl in the first riddle of I.6 (128.5), and Shaun dresses as an earl in his appearance at the beginning of Book III ("dressed like an earl in just the correct wear" [404.16–17]).

HCE is connected with the Prince of Wales by an allusion to the motto of the Prince of Wales, references to the Black Prince, and by allusions to the "Peace, perfect peace" motif from *Ulysses*, which perpetuates a derisive connection between Albert Edward's reputation as the "peace-maker," and a hymn.[13] HCE's word "selvischdischdienence" (*FW* 357.25) contains the motto of the Prince of Wales, "Ich dien" ("I serve").[14] HCE is connected with Edward, the Black Prince, by Johnny MacDougal, who recalls his drowning on the "princest day, when Fair Margrate waited Swede Villem, and Lally in the rain, with the black prints, now extincts. . ." (*FW* 387.19–20). Finally, as HCE's litany of his accomplishments and good deeds draws to a conclusion in III.4, he seems to equate himself simultaneously with Christ and with Albert Edward through his references to "the prince of pacis" (549.7) and "peace, perfect peace" (549.12).

These references are most significant in relation to emblems used by Shem and Shaun, which assert their paternal legacy of Prince of Wales and Earl of Dublin. The most prominent device is the recurrence of the badge of the heir apparent, commonly called "the Prince of Wales' crest" or "the Prince of Wales' feathers." Neither of these expressions is precisely correct, since the badge (which is not a crest) is borne by the heir apparent to the throne, who happens to be the Prince of Wales. Fox-Davies explains: "The badge of the eldest son of the Sovereign, as such, and not as the Prince of Wales, is the plume of three ostrich feathers, enfiled with the circlet from his coronet" (*CG* 458; see Illus. 5-G).

This emblem would have been quite familiar both in Great Britain and on the continent in Joyce's day, since it was displayed by merchants enjoying the patronage of the Prince, and who, by virtue of that patronage, had Royal Warrant to use his emblem.[15] During Joyce's lifetime, the badge was displayed as part of the armorial achievement of the Prince of Wales (see Illus. 1-H), as it is now; the change that seems to have taken place in practice, however, is that while the badge was formerly displayed above the coat of arms, adjacent to the actual crest of the Prince of Wales

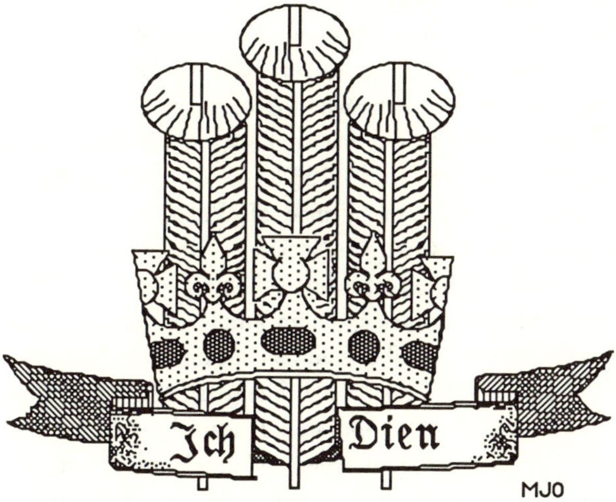

Illustration 5-G Badge of the Heir Apparent.

(which is the lion statant guardant, differenced by a label of three points), it now appears beneath the arms in what is called the "compartment" (area between the escutcheon and the motto scroll).[16] The display of the badge next to the crest led to the common reference to the badge as a crest, which is reflected in the emblem's use as a crest at *FW* 485.2 ("tripenniferry cresta"). The emblem derives from the so-called "Shield of Peace" of the Black Prince (*Sable, three ostrich feathers, their quills passing through escrolls bearing the words Ich Dien* [*Boutell* 77]).

The first appearances of this emblem in *FW* are in connection with Shem rather than Shaun. In I.7, Shem is described as sporting "trinity plumes on the right handle side of his amarellous head" (180.9–10), and amidst the debris in his house "O'Shame" are "borrowed plumes" (183.32). In these and the following instances, Shem's plumes serve both as the heir apparent's badge and the literary artist's quill pen. In the "Mime" of II.1, Glugg/Shem the artist envisions himself a king among artists "eagelly plumed. . ." (231.13), and later he makes his last attempt at guessing the heliotrope riddle after "leaving codhead's mitre and the heron's plumes sinistrant to the server of servants and rex of regums" (233.16–17). That the "heron plumes" allude to the ostrich plumes of the Prince of Wales is clear from the next phrase, "server of servants," which suggests the Prince's motto, "Ich dien" (I serve). Finally, Shaun introduces Shem/Dave the Dancekerl with reference to two distinctively Welsh emblems: alluding to a Welsh emblem used in Shakespeare's *Henry V*, Shaun remarks that he recognizes Shem/Dave because "I smelt the garlic leek!" (462.29–30: Gaelic [Welsh] leek, and Gaelic League). Immediately thereafter, he notes that "He's not too timtom well ashamed to carry out onaglibtograbakelly in his showman's sinister the testymonicals he gave his twenty annis orf, showing the three white feathers. . ." (463.1–4). Once again, Shem sports the badge of the heir apparent, the Prince of Wales.

Why this emblem is so frequently associated with Shem is a puzzle to me since, in the crucial question of who is heir apparent to HCE, most evidence points to Shaun. As Padraic Colum amply documents, Joyce uses the term "cad" with pointed emphasis on its meaning as "younger son": cadet.[17] In *FW*, Shaun is "Primus" and Shem is "Caddy": Shaun, the elder, would be the heir apparent, and would bear the badge of the heir. Indeed, he apparently does just that when he proclaims his coat of arms in III.3: responding to the annalists' suspicion that Yawn is Shem ("The gist is the gist of Shaum but the hand is the hand of Sameas. Shan — Shim — Schung. There is a strong suspicion on counterfeit Kevin. . . ." [483.3–5]), Yawn declares that he is of elevated social class: "My ruridecanal caste is a cut above you peregrines" (484.28–29), and declares a right to arms: "Sagart can selt laud nilobstant to Lowman Catlick's patrician morning coat of arms with my High tripenniferry cresta and caudal mottams: Itch dean" (485.1–3). The allusion to the three feathers ("tripenniferry cresta") and the motto of the Prince of Wales is perhaps clear to the reader, but the skeptical questioners hear the motto as a fish: "Ichthyan!" (485.10). According to Barbara DiBernard, the passage containing the annalists' query ("The gist is the gist of Shaum. . .") identifies "Shaun as the false alchemist who tries to claim the work of Shem as his own" (98), and W. Y. Tindall stated that Yawn's claiming the emblem of the Prince of Wales means, "As Prince of Wales, Yawn is heir apparent of 'Yod' or 'Bog,' the royal (and divine) father" (260).

The boasting, priestly Yawn (McHugh identifies "Sagart" as Irish for "priest"; cf. clue in I.6, Riddle 1: like the "priestridden Godforsaken race" of *P* 37, the subject of the riddle "swarms with saggarts" [*FW* 135.36]) is certainly a Shaun-like speaker, but he seems to bear Shem's emblem. On the other hand, the motto "Ich dien" seems a direct antithesis of Stephen Dedalus's "Non serviam" (*P* 117, 239), and thus is appropriate to the obsequious priest/public servant aspect of Shaun *versus* the artistic autonomy of Shem. I have entertained two possibilities with regard to Yawn's identity at this point: first, that Shaun is usurping the emblem used in other instances by Shem, thus heraldically posing as Shem in a manner analogous to his claiming Shem's writing (noted by DiBernard); or, second, it is Shem rather than Shaun who speaks through Yawn in this instance; by this theory, Shem is recognizable by the feathers that have, in all other occurrences in the *Wake*, been his peculiar insignia. In other words, Shem, usually relegated to the rôle of cad, becomes heir, through a combination of the emblem of the heir apparent, and a pose through the person of Yawn. Perhaps a more plausible suggestion than this second theory would be that the brothers merge once again in Yawn.

To cast further doubt on the Yawn-as-Shem theory, while it is true that Shem has been consistently associated with the plumes of the heir apparent, it is Shaun who has consistently pretended to the status of armiger throughout the *Wake*. The first references to Shaun's armigerous station are somewhat oblique, but are nevertheless significant. At the very outset of Book III (one working title of which was "Shaun the Post"; *Letters* 3: 90), Shaun's attire is a montage of banners, including the American flag ("a starspangled zephyr" 404.27), and the flag of the Republic of Ireland, represented in the green, white, and gold of "in peas, rice, and yeggyyolk, Or for royal" (404.29–30); his clothes feature not only the heraldic "Or," but also include a "crinklydoodle front with his motto. . ." (404.28). Shaun nevertheless shows some reticence with respect to his rank, and is protestiing that he is "unwordy" when he reveals that he is "the principot of Candia, no legs and a title" (408.11–12): like another famous Dubliner at the Wake, the paraplegic strangler Billy-in-the-Bowl (referred to on 135.13; see "bowlbeggar," Glasheen 36), Shaun may lack legs, but we ultimately learn that he is the owner of some famous "arms." His advice to his sister in Chapter 14 includes the reference "If I've proved to your sallysfashion how I'm a man of Armor" (446.5–6). This allusion also connects Shaun to Tristan, in its echo of "Armorica" (3.5), according to McHugh; and, as Patrick McCarthy has pointed out to me, one of many armor/condom references in the *Wake*.

The armorial allusions, which become increasingly specific, culminate in the revelation of Yawn's "Lowman Catlick's patrician morning coat of arms" (485.1–2), with the badge and motto of the Prince of Wales. The "Lowman Catlick's patrician arms" connect Yawn's bearings with HCE's "Roman Catholic arms" observed by the annalists in II.4 (389.26), and possibly suggest an heraldic link between the family and the papacy, or with the "Breast Plate of Saint Patrick" (the prayer which Glasheen has observed is the basis for 500.14–16 [Glasheen 226]), or both.[18] A further heraldic connection with Christianity is made when the hard-of-hearing annalists transform "Itch dean" to "Icthyan!" in the succeeding paragraph, linking Yawn's crest to HCE's crest of "two young frish," an emblem that links HCE and his heir(s) to an even more distinguished forebear than the Prince of Wales: the earlier Prince of Peace, Jesus Christ.

From its earliest appearances in *FW*, there has been something fishy about the three-plumed badge: in the "Mime" it appears with "codhead's mitre" (233.16). Indeed, the confusion of "Itch dean" and "Icthyan" finds proximate authority in Brewer's *Dictionary* (one of Joyce's well-documented sources; according to Glasheen, "one of *the* source-books of *FW*" [her italics; 38]): the entry explaining the origin of "Ich dien" is on the same page as that explaining "Ichthus": "*Ichthus* for *I*e'sous, *CH*ristos, *TH*eou *U*ios, *S*oter [Jesus, Christ, Son of God, Savior]. This notarica is found on many seals, rings, urns, and tombstones, belonging to the early times of Christianity, and was supposed to be a 'charm' of mystical efficacy" (26th ed., 432).[19] The current edition of *Brewer's* adds, for the benefit of the unlettered, that "ichthus" is Greek for fish; this makes the word fish a combination rebus/acronym for Christ's name, and his identity as fisher of men.

The annalists' mistake (if mistake it is) connects Yawn's crest with the fish icon, and thus relates the crest of the heir apparent with that of HCE: "At the crest, two young frish, etoiled, flappant. . ." (546.5–6). The fish as a family emblem has been established through repeated associations between HCE and Finn MacCool's salmon of knowledge, and Yawn's response to the query that ends, "Perhaps you can explain, sagobean? The Mod needs a rebus" (523.19–20). Yawn's lengthy piscatorial speech (523.21–525.5) alludes to the rebus/acronym for Christ, and to the family emblem found in his own crest, and that of HCE. The connection of the fish emblem with the badge of the English heir apparent establishes the status of Yawn (whether consisting of Shaun, Shem, or both) as the heir apparent to HCE in both his monarchic and divine incarnations. This connection is reinforced by the implicit connection between the etymology that Brewer's *Dictionary* (26th ed., 432) suggests for the motto "Ich Dien" ("Eich dyn"—Behold the man), and the same phrase in Latin ("Ecce homo"), from the Vulgate (John 19: 5), which has come to be the conventional title for works of art representing the presentation of Christ, in robe and crown of thorns, to Pilate (One such painting by Munkacsy was the subject of an essay by Joyce in 1899: "Ecce Homo" [*CW* 31–37]; cf. Shaun's "Eccolo me" [462.27]).

Whether or not identification with the Prince of Wales can be restricted to Shem or Shaun (which I doubt), an interesting biographical link between the "Shaun"-temperament and the Prince of Wales is provided by Joyce:

like Shaun, who consistently denigrates the efforts of Shem (James) the artist ("his usylessly unreadable Blue Book of Eccles" [179.26–27], or *Ulysses*), the historical Prince of Wales (Edward VIII) apparently took exception to the self-same Blue Book, only in its white cover. Joyce explains in a letter to John Quinn of 5 February 1924:

> *[Ulysses]* is selling well here, though, I believe, the Prince of Wales (who was here incognito as Earl of Chester and, of course, recognized by everybody) complained to a Paris bookseller when he saw the volume (which is half the size of the first edition and bound in white with blue lettering—the Greek flag upside down this time) in the window. The reply of Mr Pierre Paul Petitépatant to H.R.H.'s equerry varies according to the hour of the day and the person who tells the tale. (*Letters* 1: 210)

The identification of HCE and his heir(s) with the Prince of Wales leads to a logical association with the King of England, a condition to which Bloom seemed to rise in his "Circe" hallucination. One ramification of this is the casting of Shem in the rôle of the sinister supporter of the royal arms. Always identified with things sinister (i.e., even when his annotations in II.2 shift from the left margins to the right, they shift to the heraldic "sinister"—the viewer's right), Shem is twice referred to as the unicorn, which is the sinister supporter in the royal armorial achievement. The first such allusion is in the argument between the Mookse and the Gripes in I.6, where the epithet "—Unuchorn!" is followed by "—Ungulant!" (157.3–4). "Unguled" is an heraldic term used to differentiate the tincture of an animal's hooves from its essential color; the most famous example of a unicorn so described is the Royal unicorn: "a unicorn argent, armed [horned], unguled [hooved] and crined [maned] or" (*Boutell* 214). Shem is again a unicorn when he is introduced as Dave the Dancekerl in III.2: Shaun observes that "he would be the unicorn of his kind" (462.20).

Another emblem connecting HCE with the Royal Arms is the "White Horse of Hanover," which appeared in the armorial achievements of the eighteenth-century House of Hanover (see Illus. 5-H). In this context, Willingdone's "white harse" (8.17, 10.2, 10.11, etc.) connects him with the Georges of Hanover as well as with Wellington. Other warrior figures associated both with HCE and the horse emblem in *FW* are William of Orange and William IV ("kingbilly whitehorsed" [75.15–16]), and "Lapoleon, the equestrian, on his whuite hourse of Hunover" (388.16–17). In the "Tavern," Butt recalls "a white horsday where the midril met the bulg" (347.1).

When HCE speaks in his own self-defense in III.3, much of his litany of benevolent actions is based on his royal authority; the consistent proof

Illustration 5-H Arms of the House of Hanover, borne by George I, George II, and George III until 1803. The so-called "Horse of Hanover" is in the base of the fourth quarter.

of this is his use of the monarch's Great Seal, a symbol which from the eleventh century, according to medievalist V. H. Galbraith, has been tantamount to the royal identity: ". . . both the royal bounty and the royal commands were associated in the minds of [the King's] subjects, mostly illiterate, with the Great Seal" (Galbraith 39). HCE invokes royal authority when he grants a city charter as "Enwreak us wrecks" (545.23; Henricus, Rex): "Wherfor I will and firmly command, as I willed and firmly commanded, upon my royal word and cause the great seal now to be affixed . . ." (545.14–16). Tindall notes the similarity between the instrument sealed by HCE[20] and the charter under authority of Henry II granting Dublin to the subjects of Bristol (Tindall 281). HCE's involvement with official seals extends to the studies of I.2, where "all holographs . . . bear the sigla H.C.E." (32.13–14); Clive Hart suggests that ALP's "Lps."

(628.15) might also mean "Lord Privy Seal," the seal used from the thirteenth century in right of the sovereign for matters not sufficiently consequential to warrant the Great Seal (Hart, *Structure and Motif* 205). In the "Tavern" chapter, HCE's protestations of innocence are interspersed with references to his seal as an instrument of truth and foreplay: ". . . but for my sealring is none to hand I swear, she is highly catatheristic and there is another which I have fombly fongered freequuntly and, when my signet is on sign again I swear, she is deeply sangnificant" (357.12–15).

Having considered how HCE's arms, and those used by his heirs, connect him with all levels of armigerous persons, from gentlemen (including Adam, the first who "bore arms"), through knights and peers, to the Prince of Wales, the King of England, and even Jesus Christ, we have not exhausted the possible identifications deriving from the heraldic evidence. HCE's supporters, for example, might qualify him as a knight, peer, prince, or monarch; but Fox-Davies mentions other armigerous entities entitled to supporters: corporations, including cities and counties (*CG* 429). HCE is probably the only "character" in literature to qualify for supporters under these terms: his supporters in the "Tavern," as the original settlers of Dublin, Georgia, are "Dublin supporters," as are the two women flanking the shield of Dublin, Ireland (Illus. 5-I). W. Y. Tindall, Bernard Benstock, Anthony Burgess, Margot Norris, Patrick McCarthy, and others, have discussed the various rôles played by the elements of the Dublin coat of arms—"Azure, three castles argent, flammant proper" supported "on either side [by] a female figure proper, vested gules, lined or. . ." (Fox-Davies, *Public Arms* [1915] 246).[21] The extent of Joyce's interest in the Dublin arms, and their significance in *FW*, are such that Joyce apparently considered using his wood carving of the Dublin arms as the cover for an installment of *Work in Progress*.[22]

In general, it is understood that the three castles and the two women are turned into a graphic version of the park incident, with its three soldiers and two girls. Because the central figure of the incident is HCE, the Dublin arms are most frequently associated with him. Bernard Benstock relates the "two young frish" and the "terce of lanciers" in HCE's arms (546.5–9) to the two supporters and the three castles. Having blazoned these arms, HCE refers to the Dublin arms more explicitly when he mentions "three surtouts wripped up in itchother's, two twin pritticoaxes lived as one, troubled in trine or dubildin too" (546.15–17). In the first riddle of I.6, the subject shows "two remarkable piscines [fish; also, as Bernard Benstock suggests, women who have urinated] and three wellworthseeing ambries" (127.35–36), and is said to have "shot two queans and shook

Illustration 5-1 Arms of Dublin. From Fox-Davies, *The Book of Public Arms* (1915).

three caskles" (128.17). I suspect the supporters appear among the litigants in the Festy King's trial ("egged on by their supporters in the shape of betterwomen. . ." [87.27]), and Benstock related them to the "*Pair of Sloppy Sluts plainly Showing all the Unmentionability*" in I.5 (*FW* 107.6–7; Benstock, *Joyce-Again's Wake* 265; 273). Apart from the graphics on the arms, Clive Hart catalogues twelve variations on the Dublin motto, "Obedientia civium urbis felicitas" (*Structure and Motif* 236), including the answer to the third riddle in I.6: "Thine obesity, O civilian, hits the felicitude of our orb"; the Dublin arms are the central subject of the entire riddle (139.29–140.7).

A corporate coat of arms resembling the Dublin arms is the achievement of Newcastle-on-Tyne, which features three triple-towered castles on a red field. Passages adding these arms to those already collected by HCE include the dialogue between Jute and Mutt, which mentions "O'c'stle, n'wc'stle, tr'c'stle, crumbling" (18.6–7),[23] relating Newcastle and its three castles ("tr'c'stle") to those of Dublin; cf. 555.13: "esker, newcsle, saggard, crumlin."

One more corporate armorial achievement connected with HCE is already familiar from its appearance in *Ulysses:* the arms of the Isle of Man, or the famous "legs of Man." In the "Tavern," HCE is described as "this ale of man . . . our hubuljoynted" (310.30–31), implying the presumably "double-jointed" conjoined legs on the Arms of Man; the emblem is mentioned at least three times in this chapter, recurring in "The threelegged man" (331.8); and in Butt's mention of "the calves of Man!" (339.27).

To consider HCE's accomplishments as a genteel, aristocratic, princely, royal, or even corporte armiger, however, is merely to skim the surface. His most ambitious armorial legacy is yet to be considered: HCE as empire. The assumption of the royal devices of England has already associated him with one empire. HCE is also related to the Napoleonic empire by several allusions. One interesting parallel is entomological: like HCE, whose heraldic emblem is an insect, Napoleon adopted for his royal mantling "Azure, semé of bees"—in other words, his armorial achievement featured mantling that was blue, covered with (semé of) bees, just as the traditional royal field and mantling of France was azure, semé of fleurs-de-lis. But HCE also shares with Napoleon the imperial eagle, an emblem that connects him with other empires, starting with Rome under the Caesars.

Margot Norris has written of the connection between individual acts of invasion and imperialism in Joyce's writings. Describing mythic structures underlying the *Wake*, she says:

> Imperialism or invasion is a literal act of trespass, as in the military campaign of Napoleon or the missionary conquest of St. Patrick. Stealing the birthright in the Jacob and Esau story, looking at forbidden parts as in the voyeurism of the sons of Noah, and loving the "wrong" sex, as in the life of Oscar Wilde, all provide other instances. (37)

Norris notes the manner in which family conflicts of the *Wake* are linked with international conflicts of history; the use of heraldic emblems is one device that makes this equation possible in *FW.* Using examples from *Ulysses* and *A Portrait,* Norris observes: "Like little Tommy and Jacky Caffrey battling over the sand castle in *Ulysses,* or young Stephen competing in math class under the silk badges of York or Lancaster, military disputes are motivated in Joyce's works by a desire for dominance both stronger and more complex than the mere desire for possession" (49). The Wars of the Roses, fought by Stephen at Clongowes in *A Portrait,* and contemplated again by Stephen on the beach in "Proteus," continue to be waged by characters in *FW:* HCE is thought to be "behind the war of the two roses" (94.35–36), and on 96.1, "The rose is white in the darik!"

In *Ulysses,* we have seen that the emblematic red and green transforms the fight between Bennett and Keogh into a reenactment of the centuries of English conquest of Ireland; the individual blow struck by Private Carr undergoes the same transformation, again through the use of heraldic colors (cf. the clue in the first riddle of *FW* I.6: "we strike hands over his bloodied warsheet but we are pledged entirely to his green mantle" [131.20–21]). In *FW,* the rivalry of Shem and Shaun becomes an imperial struggle through the allusion to the estate of the Prince of Wales/Earl of Dublin, and the incident in the park is transformed through HCE's marshaling of the arms and mottoes of numerous empires. In addition to the English royal arms and the arms of Napoleon (Finnegan's "bloodeagle waistcoat" [24.29] becomes HCE's "elbaroom surtout" [52.25]), HCE's eagle (a descendant of Joyce's) connects him with Imperial Rome, which bore an eagle facing dexter. Fox-Davies asserts that Charlemagne bore an eagle as his emblem (*CG* 233); the Holy Roman Empire subsequently bore a two-headed eagle. The Byzantine imperial double eagle descended, in turn, to the Romanovs, Czars of Russia, as well as to the ruling houses of Prussia (*"Prszss Orel"* 105.10–11).

Throughout the *Wake,* individual actions are cloaked in heraldic colors that make personal history a microcosm of world history. The three soldiers are enraged by the debasement of the Irish/Napoleonic token when Willingdone picks up "the half of the threefoiled [trefoil = heraldic shamrock] hat of lipoleums" (*FW* 10.8) and places it on the tail of "his big white harse" (Wellington's horse, Copenhagen, is transformed into the Hanoverian cognizance). Glugg's tantrum in II.1 seems to pit him not only against the seven sacraments, but also against Scottish clans identified by their Tartans: he begins by diving "his head into Wat Murrey, gave Stewart Ryall a puck on the plexus. . . till a Tartaran tastarin toothsome tarrascone tourtoun. . ." (227.29–35).[24] In I.8, ALP appears arrayed in clothing that not only images the terrain through which the Liffey passes, but also evokes heraldic colors: she sports "her bloodorange bockknickers" and "her blackstripe tan joseph" (208.15–17), both allying her with British and Protestant colors. Shem and Shaun sport various flags in their attire, most frequently featuring the tricolor of the Irish Republic (a flag which dates back to the mid-nineteenth century [Hayes-McCoy 144]): in the "Mime," Chuff is hailed as a great Irish hero: "Of all the green heroes everwore coton brieches, the whitemost, the goldenest!" (234.8–10); in the "Tavern," Butt *"changecors induniforums as he is lefting the gat out of his big:*

his face glows green, his hair greys white, his bleyes bcome broon to suite his cultic twalette [celtic twilight, or toilet]" (344.10–12).

Shem wears a national emblem in III.2, when Shaun observes "And, whoa! do you twig the schamlooking leaf greeping ghastly down his blousyfrock? Our national unbloom! Areesh!" (467.10–11). In two instances, the brothers use the red saltire on argent known as St. Patrick's Cross: one of two combatants in the Park appears with "the white ground of his face all covered with diagonally redcrossed nonfatal mammalian blood" (84.19–20), and Shem's "coat macfarlane" (180.10), if taken to represent the arms of the MacFarlane clan, also features the red saltire.

Another Irish emblem from *FW* that I have not seen identified as such is the black raven. Among other emblems, the subject of the first riddle of I.6 "bears a raaven geulant on a fjeld duiv" (136.12–13). McHugh connects this with the Dedalus arms from *U* 15.3948–49 {572.16–17} (cf. "geulant" and "gules volant"), and with Danish pirates who invaded Ireland bearing a raven flag (see the response to the queries of the annalists in III.3: "Her raven flag was out" [480.1; McHugh, *Sigla* 46]). According to G. A. Hayes-McCoy, however, this is also an old banner used in Ireland from the time of the Norman invasions; moreover, after 1913 the Dublin County unit of the Irish volunteers bore "a black raven on a white field" (Hayes-McCoy 200). This insignia is now found in the arms of County Dublin, and can be added to the heraldic bearings that have connected HCE with Dublin, as Lord of Dublin and as the embodiment of the corporate entity.

Finally, the use of heraldic mottoes connects HCE with empires and ruling factions. The Garter motto has already been noted as one associated with the British Empire; James Atherton discusses this motto, and other frequently cited mottoes, including the "F.E.R.T." of the House of Savoy (33–34). He states "Heraldic mottoes are frequently quoted in the *Wake*, where they are probably intended to supply examples of Vico's 'middle language.' " This is no doubt a valid, if somewhat reductive, point. The mottoes also associate HCE's history, lineage, and actions with the imperialist motives observed by Margot Norris. This is true of the many allusions to "S.P.Q.R." (Senatus Populusque Romanus), which Joyce undoubtedly knew as well as did Stephen's classmates (*P* 53). As a Roman bank employee, he would have known the arms of the city, which feature those letters in gold in bend (diagonally) on a red field; it is used freely in the *Wake* (see Hart, *Structure and Motif* 242).

Clearly the heraldic motifs in *FW* accentuate the rich and complex textures of this book. But beyond this statement of the obvious, I hope I have demonstrated that using heraldic information, as a herald or historian might, gives the reader additional clues to HCE's history and lineage. The heraldic allusions in the *Wake* also inform the process whereby Joyce has yoked personal family history with global history, and has equated personal conflict with martial confrontations. Heraldry is at the heart of these themes, as it is at the heart of the crucial question of descent and inheritance in the *Wake*. The cyclical advent and aftermath of HCE's wake, and the framework of human history upon which it is mounted, are full of allusions to the possible heirs to the Earwicker legacy. The marginal annotations and footnotes in II.2 provide an apt summary of this genealogical concern, placed in the context of the children's history lesson: Shaun inscribes, "FROM CENOGENETIC DICHOTOMY THROUGH DIAGONISTIC CONCILIANCE TO DYNASTIC CONTINUITY" (275.R1); Issy's sixth note on the same page alludes not only to Dolphin's Barn, Dublin, but also to the Dauphin, erstwhile heir to the French throne: "Traduced into jinglish janglange for the nusances of dolphins born" (275.F6). On the following page, Shem annotates the lesson "*For all us kids under his aegis*" (276.L3). The reference to the aegis—literally, the shield of Athena; figuratively, the emblem or colors of any authority—suggests the numerous historical legacies inherent in HCE's universal character. Furthermore, in a note following the geometry problem, Shaun writes: "*Primanouriture and Ultimogeniture*" (300.L1), suggesting the legacies appertaining to the elder (Primus) and younger (Caddy) sons under two different systems, Primo- and Ultimogeniture.

The events and forces of history represented by heraldic bearings can also be represented in the image of a chivalric tournament; this image is an important one in *FW*. Much of the heraldic allusion in III.4 is justified by the context, which from 562.65 takes on the appearance of such a tournament: the parents remark of Kevin/Shaun that "By goregous [St George], that boy will blare some knight when he will take his dane's pledges. . ." (562.29–30); subsequent references seem to equate the field of battle with the heraldic field, such as "He will be quite within the pale" (both the region around Dublin, and the vertical third at the center of an heraldic shield), and "With pale blake I write tintingface. . ." 563.15–16; and "I will leave a my copperwise blessing between the pair of them [Shaun and Shem], for rosengorge, for greenafang. Blech and tin soldies. . ." 563.29–30: equating the sons with English red (for St. "gorge," or George) and Irish green, respectively, and with the British black and tan uniforms.

Human history, like the tournament in III.4, and like the *Wake* as a whole, is a tapestry woven of the emblems and colors of invaders and conquered, heirs and disinherited. Heraldry is an essential code for reading the pattern.

CHAPTER SIX

Joyce's Heraldic "Collideorscape"

There is in Joyce's work a thematic and stylistic progression in his use of heraldry, from the vague and probably misleading "bannerets" in "Watching the Needleboats at San Sabba" (*CP* 48), to the elaborate manifestations of the Union Jack in *Finnegans Wake;* from the simple act of binding the Joyce arms in a manuscript of *Chamber Music*, through the more subtle appearances of the "eagle displayed, gules," in *Ulysses* and *Finnegans Wake.* Joyce's increasingly elaborate use of heraldic blazon belies the old commonplace suggestion that Joyce was indifferent to the visual dimension; indeed, it is probable that his eye trouble intensified his interest in the colors and visual code of heraldry. I make this connection because Joyce himself linked blindness with heraldic banners in a letter to Harriet Shaw Weaver in 1928:

> The complete eclipse of my seeing faculties . . . I am warding off by dressing in the three colours of successive stages of cecity as the Germans divide them, namely: green Starr, that is, green blindness, or glaucoma; grey Starr, that is, cataract; and black Starr, that is, dissolution of the retina. This therefore forms a nocturnal tri-colour connected by one common colour, green, with Shaun's national flag of peas, rice, egg yolk, the grey of evening balancing the gold of morning and the black of something balancing the white of something else, the egg probably. (*Letters* 1: 269)

Thus among the state flags paraded through the *Wake* is that of the state of blindness: Shaun instructs the girls in III.2 to "Haul Seton's down, black, green, and grey, and hoist Mikealy's whey and sawdust" (441.4–5). The same banner serves both Republican nationalists and blindmen (perhaps equating the two?) on 503.23–24, where "the grianblanchk sun of gan greyne Eireann" is "A tricolour ribbon that spells a caution."

Much of Joyce's heraldry is, in part, incidental detail appropriate to the encyclopedic human comedies that are *Ulysses* and *Finnegans Wake.* Joyce wrote to Carlo Linati in 1920 that *Ulysses* "is also a sort of encyclopedia" (*Letters* 1: 146), and Ruth von Phul has demonstrated that he likely was inserting heraldic information found in the eleventh *Britannica.* As Atherton has observed, heraldry is "that ancient tongue" from which we learn "to be middle old modern to the minute" (Atherton 32; *FW* 270.17–18). The inclusion of heraldry among the component codes of Joyce's two major works is a technique that is both ancient and "modern to the minute." Margot Norris describes Joyce's technique as "*bricolage,*" using Levi-Strauss's term for the "practice of using bits and pieces of heterogeneous materials without regard to their specific function" (Norris 130). The process is both ancient—being the genetic process underlying "mythical thought and mythical activity"—and modern. Norris sees Joyce's accretion of codes in the *Wake*, including "the semiotics of colors, flowers, clothing, and scents—codes found in Church liturgy, romantic lore, and at the base of children's games and riddles" (135) as the type of "breaking up of the old structures and recombination of the bits and pieces" suggested by Eliot's "These fragments I have shored against my ruins [*The Waste Land,* l. 431]" (Norris 138). On the "middle old modern" side, we have Umberto Eco's assertion that the encyclopedic character of *FW* is peculiarly medieval: "Above all, the cultural syncretism is medieval, the propensity to accept all existing knowledge and to exhibit it as its own encyclopedia, more with a fabulous taste for the collection than a preoccupation with critical verification. The *Wake* displays before the reader the entire treasure of human culture without overdue respect for the actual limits of each system . . ." (Eco 81).

Thus heraldry, like alchemy, the Catholic liturgy, music, children's games, and other systems undergirding the encyclopedic breadth of *Ulysses* and *Finnegans Wake,* is one of many systems of incidental details that simultaneously evoke and break the patterns of civilization. To be more precise, heraldic bearings have been crucial emblems of traditional authorities of western civilization: originating in military and paternal structures, armorial emblems came to represent, in particular, the country, church, and father from which Joyce exiled himself. Eco writes of *Ulysses:* "In the moment in which he renounces family, country and church, Stephen knows he is renouncing the Cosmos in order to participate in the business of contemporary man: to rearrange the world according to the measure of his own situation" (45). Just as the Stephen of *A Portrait* renounces Catholicism in peculiarly Catholic terms—by becoming "a priest of eternal imagination, transmuting the daily bread of experience" (*P* 221), Joyce "rearranges" the codes of traditional authorities to suit his own universe. Among these codes is heraldry, which he converts into a peculiarly Joycean code in *Finnegans Wake,* where his blazonings transcend the limits both of heraldic jargon and the visual field.

What I suggest is that Joyce's heraldry comes into its own in the *Wake,* and is a crucial component of an intensely visual experience. Tindall, Atherton, Hart, and others have suggested that heraldry serves as Vico's pre-language, and I believe that this is both true and significant. Furthermore, I have suggested that the heraldry of the *Wake* brings HCE, his heirs, assigns, aliases, and adversaries into traditional patterns of personal, mythical, and national history. I find an intriguing metaphor for the historical, heraldic patterns of the *Wake* in a textile "Work in Progress" that Joyce described in a letter to Harriet Shaw Weaver, dated 20 September 1928: "Mrs. Bécat is making a wonderful carpet for me representing the Liffey flowing through Dublin into the Irish Sea with the arms of Norway, Dublin, Ireland and my own woven into the scheme" (*Letters* 1: 268).

But Joycean heraldry transcends Viconian and conventional history, and in *FW* heraldry becomes one of the codes which, like the iconography of the *Book of Kells,* is a medium of the "most rare epiphanic vision" that Father Boyle finds at the center of the *Wake* (Boyle x–xi). Father Boyle's exegesis of this vision that resists description relies upon a text of St. Paul: "But as it is written, Eye hath not seen, nor ear heard, neither have entered into the heart of man, the things which God hath prepared for them that love him" (1 Corinthians 2: 9). In Joyce's rendering, cited by Father Boyle, the visual and the verbal become intertwined: "What can't be coded can be decorded if an ear aye seize what no eye ere grieved for" (*FW* 482).

The rôle played by Wakean heraldry in this scheme of things has to do with the conflation of verb and vision possible in heraldry, especially in the rebus of canting arms. The rebus, or physical object standing for a name, lies behind Joyce's remark to Frank Budgen that "The Holy Roman Catholic Apostolic Church was built on a pun" (*JJ* 546); vernacular translations of the New Testament might do better to call Simon Peter "Rocky" in order better to represent the sacred pun on the name of the apostolic successor. In another jest, Joyce staged a visual pun on the name of his father's ancestral town: Frank O'Connor recalled Joyce's placing a picture of Cork in a cork frame, so that one answer would serve for queries as to either the subject of the picture, or the composition of its frame (*JJ* 551). This sense for the comic impact of a rebus constantly finds its way into Joyce's works, from the man-in-the-macintosh's being identified as M'Intosh in *Ulysses,* through the earwig and ear-of-wheat rebuses of HCE in *FW;* it is a sense which is very much at home in the canting images of heraldry.

We find another paradigm for, and an elaboration of, the canting dimension of Joyce's visual imagery, in the iconography of the *Book of Kells,* especially in the so-called "Tunc" and "Quoniam" pages so often called upon in the *Wake.* The "Tunc" page (f. 124r) represents the crucifixion of Christ, not only in the text—"Tunc crucifixebant XPI cum eo duos latrones"—but also in the enlarged "X" which is simultaneously the "X" of the text (the cipher of Christ) and the cross of Christ's death—with supplementary ornamentation of men and monsters, witnesses and participants in the cosmic drama of salvation. At the same time as the icons corroborate and amplify the Christian text, they also dispute it, by allusion to Irish emblems and traditions that predate Christianity; this multivalence of the relation between sign and referent is characteristic of the *Wake.* Beryl Schlossman has discussed the cultural multivalence typical of the *Book of Kells* and *FW:*

> Outside the boundaries of the *lex romana,* Irish symbolism preserves its medieval character because of the juxtaposition of the sacred and obscene. The persistence of Irish paganism within the Catholic position produces Irish heterogeneity, or the sacred comic doubling. . . . Irish illumination is an important model for the new style, the "irish stew" of *Finnegans Wake.* Already in *Ulysses,* the Book of Kells is mentioned in the context of the infinitization and dissolution of fictional characters in Joycean discourse. (183–84)

In addition to the cultural fusion embodied in the *Kells* illuminations, there is also the persistent use of the rebus, as in the Tunc and Quoniam pages. In a discussion of the more elaborate pun in the Quoniam page (f. 188r), Seán Golden observes that "one inherent structural device in Irish art which Joyce shares with the illustrators of the Book of Kells, is the fact that the figures embody a literal and visual pun" (Golden 85). The illuminators of the *Book of Kells* devise ingenious constructs wherein word and visual sign cooperate to an iconographic vision; this cooperation of word and sign is implicit in the underlying system of heraldry. Heraldry is unique in its literal equation of the verbal sign with the visual sign: the verb used to denote the act of rendering an armorial achievement—to "blazon"—applies equally to the formula of a coat of arms and to the visual achievement that the formula describes.[1] As Gerard Brault observes in *Early Blazon,* the peculiar formulaic quality of blazon derives both from the need to render the visual in a form as unambiguously intelligible to one artist as to another, and the probable oral transmission of early blazon, which demanded a system with the mnemonic features which a formulaic structure affords (Brault 8). I can think of few parallels for this system; perhaps blazon might be compared to the formulas used in descriptive bibliography. A more accessible comparison would be the stilted, telegraphic language used in the stage directions of a play; indeed, these two systems, blazon and stage directions, seem to merge in *FW* III.4, in the description of the bedroom of HCE/ALP: "Man's corduory surcoat with tabrets and taces, seapan nacre buttons on nail. Woman's gown on ditto. Over mantelpiece picture of Michael, lance, slaying, Satan, dragon with smoke" (559.9–12).

The *OED* defines a surcoat as a garment "worn by people of rank . . . often worn by men over their armour, and having the heraldic arms depicted on it" (in other words, a literal "coat" of arms); HCE's surcoat is of royal fabric, if the etymology of "corduroy" is taken seriously ("cor du roi"). The heraldic coat bears a charge of a woman's gown, under a crest (over the "mantelpiece," which has overtones of "mantling," a stylized surcoat) depicting the angelic fall of apocryphal scripture. This formulaic description transforms the bedroom into an armorial field, portraying (like many other coats of arms in *Finnegans Wake*) a Fall (in this case, Satan's).

While Wakean blazon does not aspire to the unambiguous clarity of heraldic blazon, it does attempt to equate what is seen with what is heard, after the fashion of blazon. Heraldry provides a key to the "earsighted view of old hopeinhaven" (143.9–10) to which, as Father Boyle has observed, the many echoes of 1 Corinthians 2: 9 throughout the *Wake* point. Another sustained figure compressing the word and the sign, which is more directly significant to heraldry, is the series of variations on "hue and cry." Clive Hart catalogues seventeen of these references (Hart, *Structure and Motif* 227), including ALP's *"He's Hue to Me Cry"* in Chapter 5 (106.2), and the washerwoman's seven crutches, each of which "had its seven hues. And each hue had a differing cry" (215.17). The pun, based on the identity of sound (French: "huer"—to shout) and color in the word "hue," parallels the capacity of heraldic blazon to equate the word "vert" with the color on the visual field. This capacity of heraldry is heightened in *FW*, both through the use of canting arms, which create an identity between the visual rebus and the verbal name of the bearer; and through such devices as casting "vert" both as the armorial "hue" of the Fall, and the "cry" of the Viconian thunder "vert" (pronounced "fart"). Thus, heraldry in *Finnegans Wake* points to a multidimensional system of word and sign which is a paradigm for the novel's central process of semiotic transformation.

The way in which Wakean blazon falls short of (or transcends, depending on one's point of view) its historical counterpart, is in the impossibility of its full visual realization. The reader has perhaps noticed the absence among the illustrations herein of those armorial emblems that especially cry out for a visual aid: those "blazoned" on 5.6–8, 485.1–3, and 546.5–11. I have not attempted to illustrate these because these blazons incorporate an ambiguous aspect which is essential to the character of blazon in *FW*—indeed, of all language at the *Wake*. The visual memory is so impressionable that, just as the Joseph Strick film of *Ulysses* has ensured that (in my mind's eye) Leopold Bloom will forever have Milo O'Shea's face, while other readers (those closer to Broadway) see Zero Mostel, I fear that if I were to have a crest drawn for 5.7 featuring a "horrid horned" he-goat (for "hegoak," after the *Skeleton Key*), I would have forever biased some reader/viewer's mind's eye against seeing the "oak" that also resides in the same word. Contrary to the blazon of "real heraldry," which insists that the language describe one charge, in one position, tinctured in one unambiguous way, the blazon of the *Wake* crowds multiple charges over one another in the same space.

Heraldic bearings at the *Wake* are the corollary of the "charictures in the drame" (302.32): we permit ourselves, for sanity's sake, the convenience of speaking of HCE, ALP, Shem, Shaun, Issy, and so forth, when deep inside we know this is unpardonably reductive. Just as there can be no definitive name for m, △, □, ∧, or ⊥, there can be no collation of the various arms used by the "Doodles family" (299.F4); nor should there be a single visual rendering of each of the arms at the *Wake*. One can see the limiting effect of illustration in the rendering of the Dublin arms from Fox-Davies's 1915 *Book of Public Arms:* in this rendering, which Bernard Benstock used in *Joyce-Again's Wake* (Benstock, *Joyce-Again's Wake* 265), there is ample warrant for the accusation that the girls are raising their skirts. And, since Fox-Davies's book has been a readily available work with something like a definitive character, a work which Atherton even suggested was one of Joyce's sources, this rendering can have some relevance to a reading of the *Wake*. But it must also be noted that the verbal blazon does not insist on scanty drapes; indeed, the supporters in the illustration used in *Intelligible Heraldry*—written by two Irishmen, and with an introduction by the Chief Herald of Ireland—wear extravagantly modest, floor-length gowns (Illus. 6–A).

Illustration 6-A Arms of Dublin. From Lynch-Robinson, *Intelligible Heraldry*.

Thus, the fact that Shaun's arms, as variously described (485.1–3) conflict with earlier family crests, shields, charges, and mottoes attributed to HCE, is not merely a puzzle. It is, rather, an essential characteristic of heraldry at the *Wake.* In like fashion, HCE's own arms conflict with and contradict one another. Put another way, what has been blazoned verbally cannot be blazoned visually: the arms cannot be drawn, since (for example) the "frish" in the crest could not simultaneously be fish and girls (unless one were to blazon them as mermaids). More basic, however, is the conflict between the charges and ordinaries of the field. If the coleopter is on a "boss," it would likely be on a disc projecting from the center of the shield. Yet the beetle is "partifesswise"—a term that partially cancels itself out, as it has the charge crossing the entire field at the fess point (horizontally, across the central third of the field: fesswise), while also horizontally splitting the field in half (party per fess). Moreover, it is difficult to imagine how a terce of lanciers could cross in saltire, since a saltire (diagonal cross) is a figure divisible by two, but not by three. These contradictions will not surprise most readers of *Finnegans Wake,* since they represent the extension to heraldic language of the decentering transformation that Joyce brings to bear on all language in the book. The effect is akin to that resulting from the description in Chapter 17 of (among other things) ALP's siglum, her lozenge, her delta, her genitalia, vortex, and so forth: "A kind of thinglike all traylogged then pubably it resymbles a pelvic or some kvind then props an acutebacked quadrangle with aslant off ohahnthenth a wenchyoumaycuddler, lying with her royalirish uppershoes among the theekleaves" (608.22–26).

What is it? The reader is invited to inspect a fixed object, only to find that it is far from fixed; and it changes shape, perspective, and identity before the viewer's eyes. This ubiquity of flux is central to the heraldic imagery in *FW,* in which "Signs are on of a mere by token that wills still to be becoming this there once a here was world" (608.26–28). Joyce makes use of heraldry's built-in obfuscation, where dexter is "apparently" left, and sinister is right: in I.8, "Reeve Gootch was right and Reeve Drughad was sinistrous!" (*FW* 197.1), and Tristan displays "his sinister dexterity, light and rufthandling, vicemversem" (384.26–27).

The blazon at the *Wake* brings us back to the extremely involved shields in classical literature, such as those of the *Seven Against Thebes:* the arms at the *Wake* do not merely contain emblems, but names and stories as well. The Festy King's "fess" provides a clue to his alleged indiscretion in heraldic terms, and canting terms at that: he is thought to have been "flying cushats out of his ouveralls and making fesses immodst the forces on the field." Not only does the blazon point to a crime of exposure/defecation (making "feces") and/or making "faces," but it also gives him an escutcheon with a "fess," or horizontal band, alluding to his name, whether Festy King or his alias of "Crowbar" (86.8).

A more suggestive antecedent for Wakean blazon than the seven of Aeschylus is the shield of Achilles in the *Iliad.* After Patroclus has been killed while wearing Achilles' armor, Thetis has Hephaistos fashion new arms, the shield of which is described in a passage of more than 125 lines at the end of Book Eighteen. Below are some excerpts of the shield's description, from Richmond Lattimore's translation:

> There were five folds composing the shield itself, and upon it [Hephaistos] elaborated many things. . . . He made the earth upon it, and the sky, and the sea's water, and the tireless sun and the moon. . . .
>
> . . . .
>
> On it he wrought . . . two cities of mortal men. And there were marriages in one, and festivals. . . .
>
> . . . .
>
> But around the other city were lying two forces of armed men shining in war gear. . . .
>
> . . . .
>
> But apart from these were sitting two men to watch for the rest of them and waiting until they could see the sheep and shambling cattle, . . . and two herdsmen . . . playing happily on pipes. . . .
>
> . . . .
>
> He made upon it a soft field, the pride of the tilled land, wide and triple-ploughed, with many ploughmen upon it. . . .
>
> . . . .
>
> He made upon it the precinct of a king . . .
>
> . . . .
>
> He made on it a great vineyard heavy with clusters. . . .
>
> . . . .
>
> He made upon it a herd of horn-straight oxen.
>
> . . . .
>
> And the renowned smith of the strong arms made on it a meadow large and a lovely valley for the glimmering sheepflocks, . . .
>
> And the renowned smith of the strong arms made elaborate on it a dancing floor. . . . And there were young men on it and young girls, sought for their beauty with gifts of oxen, dancing and holding hands at the wrist.
>
> He made on it the great strength of the Ocean River which ran around the outermost rim of the shield's strong structure. (18: 481–607)

The reader will recognize that I have ruthlessly abridged this passage; the full description is far more elaborate. One begins to suspect hyperbole, or at least to wonder how any measure of aesthetic balance can be maintained in the finished shield. The answer comes in line 13 of Book Nineteen, when Thetis puts the shield down before Achilles, and the poet remarks that "all its elaboration clashed loudly." Like the intricate shields of Aeschylus' *Seven Against Thebes,* these arms are not likely to be seen on the battlefield: these are epic arms. Clearly there can be no thought of emblazoning a shield with so many different elaborate designs. Rather, the shield ceases to be a shield, and becomes instead not only a metaphor for the cosmos, but also an encapsulation of the *Iliad* itself: a sprawling panorama of the heavens and earth; a tale of two cities; and a representation of the many pursuits of man—war, peace, agriculture, arts, love, and death.

One might ask in regard to such a panorama (or, to get to the question, "panaroma"):

> if a human being duly fatigued by his dayety in the sooty, having plenxty off time on his gouty hands and vacants of space at his sleepish feet and as hapless behind the dreams of accuracy as any camelot prince of dinmurk, . . . then *what* would that fargazer seem to seemself to seem seeming, dimm it all? Answer: A collideorscape! (*FW* 143.3–28)

The idea of the "collideorscape," combining a kaleidoscope, with its continual flux, and the colliding of many objects on a single landscape, seems particularly apt for the armorial bearings of the *Wake.* HCE bears coats of arms linking him to Adam, Christ, Vasilii Busalev, Finn MacCool, Wellington, Napoleon, various kings of England, Shakespeare, The O'Neill, The O'Reilly, Lord Fitzgerald, The Molloy (masquerading as The Finnegan), Dublin, and an empire or two, while his sons are Princes of Wales, France, and the Church. At the same time, any individual shield bears mutually exclusive charges jockeying for space. The "terce of lanciers" at 546.8–9 can simultaneously be the soldiers in the Park, or the castles on the Dublin arms; their arms can be in "saltire," as in the St. Patrick Cross, or the lanciers may be like the "puny farting little solitires" at 567.34. By virtue of this plurality of aural/oral/visual signs, to see and hear the heraldry at the *Wake* is like "reading" the icons of the *Book of Kells,* the scratches and punctures of the hen's letter in *FW,* or the words of the *Wake* itself.

An heraldic reading of Joyce's works, culminating in the *Wake,* thus becomes not a process of limiting the possibilities to particular heraldic achievements and traditions, but rather a process of expanding the heraldic field to accommodate numerous fields, and innumerable bearings. If such a reading were simply the application of a finite system of conventional symbols, then John Lehmann's assessment of *FW* as a "wanton surrender to the crossword puzzle part of the mind" might be valid;[2] but it is the expansion of the capacities of heraldry and similar semiotic systems "for the greeter glossary of code" (*FW* 324.21), and ultimately Joyce's thorough transformation of these relics of human civilization, that make *Finnegans Wake* the illuminated and illuminating experience that it is.

BIBLIOGRAPHY AND WORKS CITED

Adams, Robert Martin. *Surface and Symbol: The Consistency of James Joyce's* **Ulysses.** New York: Oxford Univ. Press, 1962.

Aeschylus. *Seven Against Thebes.* Trans. Anthony Hecht and Helen H. Bacon. New York: Oxford Univ. Press, 1973.

Armstrong, Edward A. *The Life and Lore of the Bird in Nature, Art, Myth, and Literature.* New York: Crown, 1975.

Atherton, James S. *The Books at the Wake: A Study of Literary Allusions in James Joyce's* **Finnegans Wake.** Carbondale: Southern Illinois Univ. Press, 1959.

Barraclough, E. M. C. *Flags of the World.* London: Frederick Warne, 1965.

Barron, Oswald. "Heraldry." *The Encyclopaedia Brittanica.* Eleventh Edition. Cambridge: University Press, 1910. 13: 311–30.

Bates, Ronald. "The Correspondence of Birds to Things of Intellect." *JJQ* 2 (1965): 281–90.

Beckett, Samuel. "Dante . . . Bruno. Vico. . Joyce." In *Our Exagmination Round His Factification for Incamination of Work in Progress.* 1929; rpt. New York: New Directions, 1972.

Beckson, Karl. "Stephen Dedalus and the Emblematic Cosmos." *JJQ* 6 (1968): 95–96.

Benstock, Bernard. "Every Telling Has a Taling: A Reading of the Narrative of *Finnegans Wake.*" *Modern Fiction Studies* 15 (1969): 3–25.

———. *Joyce-Again's Wake: An Analysis of* **Finnegans Wake.** Seattle: Univ. of Washington Press, 1965.

Benstock, Shari, and Bernard Benstock. *Who's He When He's At Home: A James Joyce Directory.* Urbana: Univ. of Illinois Press, 1980.

Book of Kells. Reproductions from the Manuscript in Trinity College, Dublin. Annot. Françoise Henry. New York: Alfred A. Knopf, 1974.

Boutell's Heraldry. Rev. J. P. Brooke-Little. London: Frederick Warne, 1978.

Boyle, Robert, S. J. *James Joyce's Pauline Vision: A Catholic Expositon.* Carbondale: Southern Illinois Univ. Press, 1978.

Brault, Gerard J. *Early Blazon.* Oxford: Oxford Univ. Press, 1972.

Brewer, E. Cobham. *Dictionary of Phrase and Fable.* 26th ed. New York: Cassell, n.d. [ca. 1890?].

Brewer's Dictionary of Phrase and Fable. Centenary Edition, Revised. Ed. Ivor H. Evans. New York: Harper and Row, 1981.

Brown, Norman O. *Closing Time.* New York: Random House, 1973.

Brown, Peter, ed. *The Book of Kells.* New York: Alfred A. Knopf, 1980.

Budgen, Frank. *James Joyce and the Making of* **Ulysses,** *and Other Writings.* London: Oxford Univ. Press, 1972.

Burgess, Anthony. *Joysprick.* New York: Harcourt Brace Jovanovich, 1973.

———. *Nothing Like the Sun.* Harmondsworth, U. K.: Penguin, 1973.

Burke, Sir Bernard. *Genealogical and Heraldic History of the Landed Gentry of Ireland.* 9th ed. London: Harrison & Sons, 1899.

———. *The General Armory of England, Scotland, Ireland, and Wales.* 1884; rpt. London: Heraldry Today, 1984.

Campbell, Gordon and I. O. Evans. *The Book of Flags.* London: Oxford Univ. Press, 1960.

Campbell, Joseph, and Henry Morton Robinson. *A Skeleton Key to* **Finnegans Wake.** 1944; rpt. New York: Viking, 1961.

Carens, James F. "*A Portrait of the Artist as a Young Man.*" In *A Companion to Joyce Studies.* Ed. Zack Bowen and James F. Carens. Westport, CT.: Greenwood, 1984, 255–359.

Cervantes Saavedra, Miguel de. *The Adventures of Don Quixote.* Trans. J. M. Cohen. Harmondsworth (U.K.): Penguin, 1950.

Chaucer, Geoffrey. *The Works of Geoffrey Chaucer.* 2nd ed. The New Cambridge Edition. Ed. F. N. Robinson. Boston: Houghton Mifflin, 1961.

Cheng, Vincent John. *Shakespeare and Joyce: A Study of* **Finnegans Wake.** University Park: Pennsylvania State Univ. Press, 1984.

Cirlot, J. E. *A Dictionary of Symbols.* 2nd ed. Trans. Jack Sage. New York: Philosophical Library, 1971.

C[okayne]., G. E. *The Complete Peerage of England, Scotland, Ireland, and Wales.* Rev. ed. 12 vols. London: St. Catherine Press, 1916.

Colum, Mary and Padraic. *Our Friend James Joyce.* London: Victor Gollancz, 1959.

Connolly, Thomas E. *The Personal Library of James Joyce: A Descriptive Bibliography.* 1955, rpt. Buffalo: Univ. of Buffalo, 1957.

——— ed. *James Joyce's Scribbledehobble: The Ur-Workbook for* **Finnegans Wake.** Evanston: Northwestern Univ. Press, 1961.

Crow, Martin M. and Clair C. Olson, eds. *Chaucer Life-Records.* Austin: Univ. of Texas Press, 1966.

Culler, Jonathan. *The Pursuit of Signs: Semiotics, Literature, Deconstruction.* Ithaca: Cornell Univ. Press, 1981.

Curran, Constantine. *James Joyce Remembered.* New York: Oxford Univ. Press, 1968.

DiBernard, Barbara. *Alchemy and* **Finnegans Wake.** Albany: State Univ. of New York Press, 1980.

Eco, Umberto. *The Aesthetics of Chaosmos: The Middle Ages of James Joyce.* Univ. of Tulsa Monograph Series, no. 18. Tulsa, OK: Univ. of Tulsa, 1982.

Ellmann, Richard. *The Consciousness of Joyce.* New York: Oxford Univ. Press, 1977.

———. *James Joyce.* New and rev. ed. New York: Oxford Univ. Press, 1982.

Epstein, Edmund L. "James Augustine Aloysius Joyce." In *A Companion to Joyce Studies.* Ed. Zack Bowen and James F. Carens. Westport, CT.: Greenwood, 1984, 3–37.

Fairbairn, James. *Fairbairn's Crests of the Families of Great Britain and Ireland.* Rev. Laurence Butters. 2 vols. in 1. Rutland, VT.: Charles E. Tuttle, 1968.

Ferguson, George. *Signs & Symbols in Christian Art.* London: Oxford Univ. Press, 1961.

Feshbach, Sidney. "Joyce Read Ruskin." *JJQ* 10 (1973): 333–36.

Fox-Davies, A. C. ed. *Armorial Families: A Directory of Gentlemen of Coat-Armour.* 2 vols. 1929; rpt. Rutland, Vt.: Charles E. Tuttle, 1970.

———. *The Book of Public Arms.* Edinburgh: T.C. & E.C. Jack, 1894.

———. *The Book of Public Arms.* New ed. Edinburgh: T. C. & E. C. Jack, 1915.

———. *A Complete Guide to Heraldry.* 1909; rpt. New York: Bonanza Books, 1978.

Franklyn, Julian. *Shield and Crest.* London: McGibbon & Kee, 1967.

Frye, Northrop. *Anatomy of Criticism.* Princeton: Princeton Univ. Press, 1957.

Füger, Wilhelm. "Ravens and Doves." *AWN* N.S. 14 (1977): 91–95.

Galbraith, V. H. *The Historian at Work.* London: BBC, 1962.

Garvin, John. *James Joyce's Disunited Kingdom and the Irish Dimension.* Dublin: Gill and Macmillan, 1976.

Geckle, George L. "Stephen Dedalus as Lapwing: A Symbolic Center of *Ulysses.*" *JJQ* 6 (1968): 104–14.

Gifford, Don. *Joyce Annotated: Notes for* **Dubliners** *and* **A Portrait of the Artist as a Young Man.** 2nd ed. Berkeley: Univ. of California Press, 1982.

——— and Robert J. Seidman. *Notes for Joyce: An Annotation of James Joyce's* **Ulysses.** New York: E. P. Dutton, 1974.

Gillespie, Michael Patrick. *Inverted Volumes Improperly Arranged: James Joyce and His Trieste Library.* Studies in Modern Literature, no. 10. Ann Arbor: UMI Research Press, 1983.

Glasheen, Adeline. *Third Census of* **Finnegans Wake.** Berkeley: Univ. of California Press, 1977.

Golden, Seán V. "The Quoniam Page from the Book of Kells." *AWN* N.S. 11 (1974): 85–86.

Gordon, John. *James Joyce's Metamorphoses.* Dublin: Gill and Macmillan, 1981.

Gorman, Herbert. *James Joyce.* New York: Farrar & Rhinehart, 1939.

Gough, Henry. *A Glossary of Terms Used in British Heraldry.* Oxford: John Henry Parker, 1847.

———, and James Parker. *A Glossary of Terms Used in Heraldry.* 1894; rpt. n.p.: Gale Research Company, 1966.

Grandgent, C. H. *Companion to* **The Divine Comedy.** Ed. Charles S. Singleton. Cambridge: Harvard Univ. Press, 1975.

Grierson, Sir Herbert. *Sir Walter Scott, Bart.* London: Constable & Co., 1938.

Guillim, John. *A Display of Heraldry.* 6th Ed. London, 1724.

Hall, James. *Dictionary of Subjects and Symbols in Art.* Rev. ed. New York: Harper and Row, 1974.

Halper, Nathan. "Note on 'The Hawklike Man'." *JJQ* 17 (1980): 312.

———. "Of the Stuttering Hand." *AWN* N.S. 12 (1975): 7–9.

———. "Red Hand Continued." *AWN* N.S. 12 (1975): 82.

Hart, Clive. *A Concordance to* **Finnegans Wake.** Minneapolis: Univ. of Minnesota Press, 1963.

———. *Structure and Motif in* **Finnegans Wake.** Northwestern Univ. Press, 1962.

——— and Fritz Senn, eds. *A Wake Digest.* Sydney: Sydney Univ. Press, 1968.

Hartley, Lodwick. " 'Swiftly-Sterneward': The Question of Sterne's Influence on Joyce." *Studies in the Literary Imagination* 3 (1970): 37–47.

———. " 'Tis a Picture of Myself': The Author in *Tristram Shandy.*" *Southern Humanities Review* 4 (1970): 301–13.

Hasler, Charles. *The Royal Arms: Its Graphic and Decorative Development.* London: Jupiter Books, 1980.

Hayes-McCoy, G. A. *A History of Irish Flags From Earliest Times.* Boston: G. K. Hall, 1979.

Hayman, David, ed. *A First-Draft Version of* **Finnegans Wake.** Austin: Univ. of Texas Press, 1963.

Heim, Bruno Bernard. *Heraldry in the Catholic Church: Its Origins, Customs and Laws.* Gerards Cross [U.K.]: Van Duren, 1978.

Herring, Philip F. *Joyce's Notes and Early Drafts from* **Ulysses:** *Selections from the Buffalo Collection.* Charlottesville: Univ. Press of Virginia, 1977.

———. *Joyce's* **Ulysses** *Notesheets in the British Museum.* Charlottesville: Univ. Press of Virginia, 1972.

Holme, Randle. *Academy of Armory, or a Storehouse of Armory and Blazon.* Facsimile rpt. English Linguistics: 1500–1800, No. 295. 1688; rpt. Menston, Yorkshire: The Scolar Press, 1972.

Homer. *The Iliad of Homer.* Trans. Richmond Lattimore. Chicago: Univ. of Chicago Press, 1961.

"Irish Family Names: Finnegan." *The [Dublin] Weekly Irish Times* Vol. 62, No. 3299. 18 July 1936, p. 4.

"———: Joyce." *Weekly Irish Times.* Vol. 62, No. 3301. 1 August 1936, p. 4.

"———: MacGuinness or Guiness." *Weekly Irish Times.* Vol. 59, No. 3125. 7 January 1933, p. 4.

"———: O'Connell." *Weekly Irish Times.* Vol. 59, No. 3132. 25 February 1933, p. 4.

"———: O'Gorman." *Weekly Irish Times.* Vol. 59, No. 3165. 14 October 1933, p. 4.

"———: O'Reilly." *Weekly Irish Times.* Vol. 59, No. 3127. 21 January 1933, p. 4.

"———: O'Shea." *Weekly Irish Times* Vol. 60, No. 3180, 27 January 1934, p. 4.

Jonson, Ben. *Every Man Out of His Humour.* In *Ben Jonson.* Ed. C. H. Herford and Percy Simpson. Oxford: Oxford Univ. Press, 1927, 3: 405–598.

Joyce, James. *Collected Poems.* New York: Viking, 1957.

———. *Critical Writings.* Ed. Ellsworth Mason and Richard Ellmann. London: Faber and Faber, 1959.

———. **Dubliners:** *Text, Criticism, and Notes.* Viking Critical Library. Ed. Robert Scholes and A. Walton Litz. New York: Viking, 1969.

———. *Finnegans Wake.* 1939, 1945 with corrections; rpt. New York: Viking, 1982.

———. *Giacomo Joyce.* Ed. Richard Ellmann. New York: Viking, 1968.

———. *Letters of James Joyce.* Vol. 1 ed. Stuart Gilbert. New York: Viking, 1966. Vol. 2 and 3, ed. Richard Ellmann. New York: Viking, 1966.

———. **A Portrait of the Artist as a Young Man:** *Text, Criticism, and Notes.* Viking Critical Library. Ed. Chester G. Anderson. New York: Viking, 1968.

———. *Selected Letters of James Joyce.* Ed. Richard Ellmann. New York: Viking, 1975.

———. *Stephen Hero.* Ed. Theodore Spencer. New York: New Directions, 1963.

———. *Ulysses.* New York: Random House, 1961.

———. *Ulysses.* Critical and Synoptic Edition. Ed. Hans Walter Gabler, Wolfhard Steppe, and Claus Melchior. 3 vols. New York: Garland Publishing, 1984.

Joyce, Stanislaus. *My Brother's Keeper: James Joyce's Early Years.* Ed. Richard Ellmann. New York: Viking, 1958.

———. *The Complete Dublin Diary of Stanislaus Joyce.* Ed. George Healy. Ithaca: Cornell Univ. Press, 1962.

Kenner, Hugh. "James Joyce: A Portrait in Sound." (Audio Tape) Washington, D. C.: National Public Radio, 1980.

Lacey, Robert. *Majesty: Elizabeth II and the House of Windsor.* New York: Harcourt Brace Jovanovich, 1977.

Latini, Brunetto. *Petit Bestiaire.* Paris: Guy Lévis Mano, 1967.

Leach, Mark Carter. "The Literary and Emblematic Activity of Herman Hugo, S. J. (1588–1629)." Diss. Univ. of Delaware 1979.

Lee, Brian North. *British Bookplates.* London: David & Charles, 1979.

Levin, Harry. *James Joyce: A Critical Introduction.* Norfolk, Ct.: New Directions, 1941.

Litz, A. Walton. *The Art of James Joyce: Method and Design in* **Ulysses** *and* **Finnegans Wake.** 1964; rpt. New York: Oxford Univ. Press, 1968.

Lynch-Robinson, Christopher, and Adrian Lynch-Robinson. *Intelligible Heraldry.* 1948; rpt. Baltimore: Heraldic Book Company, 1967.

McCarthy, Patrick A. *The Riddles of* **Finnegans Wake.** Rutherford, N.J.: Fairleigh Dickinson Univ. Press, 1980.

———. "Structures and Meanings of *Finnegans Wake*." In *A Companion to Joyce Studies*. Ed. Zack Bowen and James F. Carens. Westport, CT.: Greenwood, 1984, 559–632.

McHugh, Roland. *Annotations to* **Finnegans Wake.** Baltimore: Johns Hopkins Univ. Press, 1980.

———. *The* **Finnegans Wake** *Experience*. Berkeley: Univ. of California Press, 1981.

———. *The Sigla of* **Finnegans Wake.** Austin: Univ. of Texas Press, 1976.

MacKinnon, Charles. *The Observer's Book of Heraldry*. London: Frederick Warne, 1966.

Maclagan, Michael, and Jirí Louda. *Heraldry of the Royal Families of Europe*. New York: Clarkson N. Potter, 1981.

MacLysaght, Edward. *Irish Families: Their Names, Arms and Origins*. Dublin: Hodges Figgis & Co., 1957.

Mahaffey, Vicki. "*Giacomo Joyce*." In *A Companion to Joyce Studies*. Ed. Zack Bowen and James F. Carens, Westport, Ct.: Greenwood Press, 1984, 387–420.

Malory, Sir Thomas. *Le Morte D'Arthur*. Ed. Janet Cowen. 2 vols. Harmondsworth (U.K.): Penguin, 1969.

Manganiello, Dominic. "Irish Family Names in *Finnegans Wake*." *AWN* N.S. 16 (1979): 30–31.

Morley, Patricia A. "Fish Symbolism in Chapter Seven of *Finnegans Wake*: The Hidden Defense of Shem The Penman." *JJQ* 6 (1969): 267–70.

Morse, J. Mitchell. "Phoenicians and Phoenixes." *AWN* N.S. 14 (1977): 100.

Murphy, Jim. "More from the Book of Kells." *AWN* N.S. 6 (1969): 73.

Nabokov, Vladimir. "Introduction," *Bend Sinister*. 1963; rpt. New York: McGraw-Hill, 1974.

Nason, Arthur H. *Heralds and Heraldry in Ben Jonson's Plays, Masques and Entertainments*. 1907; rpt. New York: Gordian, 1968.

Neubecker, Ottfried. *Heraldry: Sources, Symbols and Meaning*. New York: McGraw-Hill, 1976.

Norris, Margot. *The Decentered Universe of* **Finnegans Wake:** *A Structuralist Analysis*. Baltimore: Johns Hopkins Univ. Press, 1976.

Oxford English Dictionary. Compact Edition. 2 vols. New York: Oxford Univ. Press, 1971.

O'Hart, John. *Irish Pedigrees*, 5th ed. 2 vols. 1892; rpt. Baltimore: Genealogical Publishing Company, 1976.

Olmert, Michael. "Hail to heraldry . . ." *Smithsonian* 15, 2 (May 1984): 86–95.

O'Kearney, Nicholas. *The Prophecies of SS. Columbkille, Maelamlacht, Ultan, Seadhne, Coireall, Bearcan, Malachy, &c.* New York: D. & J. Sadlier, 1857.

O'Shea, Michael J. "Armorial Bearings in *Idylls of the King.*" *Victorian Poetry* 21 (1983): 393–402.

Panaitescu, Emilio Allessandro, ed. *Dante Alighieri: La Divina Commedia:* "Inferno." 2 vols. Milano: Fratelli Fabbri Editori, 1963.

Papworth, John W. *Ordinary of British Armorials.* Ed. Alfred W. Morant. 1874; rpt. London: Tabard Publications, 1961.

Pinches, J. H. and R. V. *The Royal Heraldry of England.* Rutland, VT.: Charles E. Tuttle, 1974.

Quillian, William H. "Shakespeare in Trieste: Joyce's 1912 *Hamlet* Lectures." *JJQ* 12 (1974): 7–63.

Roby, Kinley. "King Edward in Nighttown." *JJQ* 13 (1975): 112–13.

Rose, Danis, ed. *James Joyce's The Index Manuscript:* **Finnegans Wake** *Holograph Workbook VI. B. 46.* Colchester: A Wake Newslitter Press, 1978.

Rothery, G. C. *A B C of Heraldry.* Boston: Cornhill, n.d. [ca. 1910].

Ruskin, John. *The Works of John Ruskin.* 39 vols. London: George Allen, 1906.

Ryf, Robert. "Joyce's Visual Imagination." *TSLL* 1 (1959): 30–43.

Said, Edward. *The World, the Text, and the Critic.* Cambridge: Harvard Univ. Press, 1983.

Schlossman, Beryl. *Joyce's Catholic Comedy of Language.* Madison: Univ. of Wisconsin Press, 1985.

Schneider, Ulrich. "Freemasonic Signs and Passwords in the 'Circe' Episode." *JJQ* 5 (1968): 303–11.

Scholes, Robert. *Semiotics and Interpretation.* New Haven: Yale Univ. Press, 1982.

——— and Marlena G. Corcoran. "The Aesthetic Theory and Critical Writings." In *A Companion to Joyce Studies.* Ed. Zack Bowen and James F. Carens. Westport, CT: Greenwood Press, 1984, pp. 689–705.

Schueler, Mary Dudley. "Typology and Iconography in *Ulysses:* A Study of Joyce's Use of Irish Geography and History as Imagistic Correspondents of Occultist Doctrines." Diss. Univ. of Tulsa 1980.

Scott-Giles, C. W. *Shakespeare's Heraldry.* 1950; rpt. London: Heraldry Today, 1971.

Shakespeare, William. *William Shakespeare: The Complete Works.* The Pelican Text Revised. Gen. ed. Alfred Harbage. Baltimore: Penguin, 1969.

Shinagel, Michael. *Daniel Defoe and Middle-Class Gentility.* Cambridge: Harvard Univ. Press, 1968.

Skrabanek, Petr. "Wassaily Booslaeugh of Reisengeborg." *AWN* N.S. 10 (1973): 42.

Slocum, John J., and Herbert Cahoon. *A Bibliography of James Joyce.* New Haven: Yale Univ. Press, 1953.

Spenser, Edmund. *The Faerie Qveene.* Ed. A. C. Hamilton. Longman Annotated English Poets. London: Longman, 1977.

Sterne, Laurence. *A Sentimental Journey Through France and Italy.* Ed. Graham Petrie. Harmondsworth (U.K.): Penguin, 1967.

———. *Tristram Shandy.* Norton Critical Edition. Ed. Howard Anderson. New York: Norton, 1980.

Stout, Gardner D., Jr. ed. *A Sentimental Journey Through France and Italy by Mr. Yorick,* by Laurence Sterne. Berkeley: Univ. of California Press, 1967.

Swartzlander, Susan. "Multiple Meaning and Misunderstanding: The Mis-Trial of the Festy King." James Joyce Conference. Philadelphia, 15 June 1985.

Thackeray, W. M. *The Book of Snobs* [1848]. Ed. John Sutherland. New York: St. Martin's Press, 1978.

———. *Vanity Fair.* Riverside Edition. Ed. Geoffrey and Kathleen Tillotson. Boston: Houghton Mifflin, 1963.

Thornton, Weldon. *Allusions in* **Ulysses:** *An Annotated List.* Chapel Hill: Univ. of North Carolina Press, 1968.

Tindall, William York. *A Reader's Guide to* **Finnegans Wake.** London: Thames and Hudson, 1969.

Vico, Giambattista. *The Autobiography of Giambattista Vico.* Trans. M. H. Fisch and T. G. Bergin. Ithaca: Cornell Univ. Press, 1944.

———. *The New Science of Giambattista Vico.* Trans. T. G. Bergin and M. H. Fisch. Ithaca: Cornell Univ. Press, 1968.

Virgil. *The Aeneid.* Trans. Robert Fitzgerald. New York: Random House, 1981.

von Phul, Ruth. "The Boast of Heraldry in the 'Proteus' Episode of *Ulysses.*" *Journal of Modern Literature* 1 (1971): 399–405.

von Volborth, Carl Alexander. *Heraldry: Customs, Rules and Styles.* Poole: Blandford, 1981.

Wagner, Sir Anthony. *Heralds of England: A History of the Office and College of Arms.* London: HMSO, 1967.

White, Patrick. "The Key in *Ulysses.*" *JJQ* 9 (1971): 10–25.

White, T. H., trans. *The Book of Beasts.* 1954; rpt. New York: Dover, 1984.

Wilson, Angus. *The World of Charles Dickens.* New York: Viking, 1970.

Woolf, Virginia. *A Writer's Diary.* Ed. Leonard Woolf. New York: Harcourt Brace Jovanovich, 1954.

Yeats, William Butler. *The Autobiography of William Butler Yeats.* New York: Collier Books, 1965.

APPENDIX

The Joyce General Armory: A Glossary of Arms, Heraldic Terms, Charges, Ordinaries and Mottoes Used in Joyce's Works and This Study

The following is an alphabetical arrangement of some of the "subtle and curious jargon" relevant to Joyce's heraldry, and to this study. I have tried to collect all explicit references to coats of arms, heralds, heraldic mottoes, or heraldic language in Joyce's published works. Undoubtedly many of Joyce's allusions to heraldry (especially in *Finnegans Wake*) are missing from the glossary; I can make no claim to furnishing a comprehensive "Joycean Armory," but I hope that this listing provides some assistance to those seeking an introduction to this corner of Joyce's lexicon.

I have tried to be selective in including references to terms that have a common as well as an heraldic meaning; for example, the term "engrailed" from "Cyclops" (*U* 12.1734 {340.25}) is not glossed, because, although it has an heraldic meaning (a type of line of partition), that is not its sense in this usage; it is used as an architectural term. In general, I have excluded terms clearly being used in a nonheraldic context (e.g., "engrailed" above; also, while I have an entry for *azure,* I do not include the reference on *P* 166, which is out of heraldic context), but where there is room for argument, I have included the terms in question, in the hope that this argument might take place. Finally, I have included some terms and concepts that are not exclusively heraldic in character, but that I judged relevant to this study, and to heraldry in general (e.g., see **sigillography; flowers, language of; morganatic marriage**).

Terms that are used in discussing one entry which are themselves defined under a separate entry in this appendix are in bold face, as are the entry headings.

A.E.I.O.U. When Stephen thinks to himself "A.E.I.O.U." (*U* 9.213 {190.3}), he is alluding to his debt to A.E. (George Russell); but the roster of vowels also suggests an heraldic motto or two. Thornton notes that:

> these letters were also stamped on coins and medals and inscribed on public buildings by Frederick III, Emperor of the Holy Roman Empire (1415–93). The motto these letters stood for is variously given, usually as 'Archidux Electus Imperator Optime Vivat'. (Thornton 165)

Perhaps a more pertinent meaning is one given by Fox-Davies (*CG* 452): "Aquila Electa Iuste Omnia Vincit" (The chosen eagle vanquishes all by right). This is particularly apt, given Stephen's personal emblem of an eagle in flight in the Dedalus arms (*U* 15.3948–49 {572.16–17}), and the very next statement following "A.E.I.O.U." in this chapter: Eglinton asks, "Do you mean to fly in the face of the tradition of three centuries?"

accident. In its heraldic sense, a generic term for marks of **difference.** It is used at *FW* 269.14, in a sentence with **proper** and **difference.**

achievement. A full armorial display (shield, **helm, crest, mantling,** etc.).

annulet. A small ring, used as a mark of cadency for a fifth son. See **cadency;** Illus. 1-A, 2-C.

apaumée. Of a hand, meaning with palm faced forward, as single hands are almost invariably portrayed in heraldry. This term can be used to describe the red hand of Ulster and of the O'Neill sept, and describes the hand in the O'Reilly arms. The O'Reilly blazon is the source of the term's use in *FW* 99.31.

argent. One of the two heraldic metals: Silver; also equivalent to white. See **tinctures.** Argent is the tincture of the Dedalus field: *U* 15.3949 {572.17}. The "ancillars" of *FW* 5.7 are argent, and HCE's crest at 546.6–7 features "withdrewers argent."

armiger. One entitled to a coat of arms; traditionally, of at least the rank of gentleman. An armiger is said to be "armigerous." Shakespeare was an armiger, as is remarked in "Scylla and Charybdis":

> He was a rich country gentleman, Stephen said, with a coat of arms and landed estate at Stratford and a house in Ireland yard, a capitalist shareholder, a bill promoter, a tithefarmer. (*U* 9.710–12 {203.34–37})

Bloom has fantasies of being an armiger in "Ithaca" (*U* 17.1609–12 {715.30–33}). See *FW* 584.28, where the HCE family group is an "Armigerend everfasting horde."

Athlone Pursuivant. Junior officer of the old Irish Office of Arms. See **herald.** Appears in "Circe" in the procession accompanying Bloom's coronation with Ulster King: *U* 15.1413 {480.11–12}. See also *FW* 498.11–13.

attired. Term used to describe the horns of an heraldic beast when their tincture differs from that of the beast (i.e., the argent unicorn supporting the royal arms is "attired or"). Stephen stretches the term's usefulness by making "unattired" mean a hornless buck: *U* 3.337 {46.13}.

banneret. A small, squared-off flag. In "Watching the Needleboats at San Sabba" (*CP* 48): "O hearts, O sighing grasses, / Vainly your loveblown bannerets mourn!" The context of the reference suggests to me that Joyce really means a "pennon" (an elongated, sometimes swallow-tailed ensign), since true bannerets do not resemble grasses.

bar. One of the heraldic **ordinaries;** a horizontal charge like the **fess,** but of lesser depth. If, as is conventionally supposed, the fess is approximately one-third of the height of the field, then the bar would be approximately one-fifth. The most important thing to know about heraldic bars is that, being horizontal, they can tend neither dexter nor sinister; there are no bar sinisters in the English-speaking world. The confusion comes from "barre sinistre," French for "bend sinister." See **bend.**

bars gemel. Pairs of bars or "barrulets" (diminutive of bars); from "gemelli" (twins). See **Joyce;** Illus. 3-C.

basilisk. An heraldic beast, featuring a cock's head and feet on a dragon's body. Identical to the cockatrice, although the basilisk is sometimes distinguished from the cockatrice by its having an extra head extending from its tail (Gough and Parker 123). In "Proteus," Stephen imagines himself as a priest, "clutching a monstrance, basiliskeyed" (*U* 3.115–16 {40.3–4}); in "Scylla and Chraybdis," "Stephen withstood the band of miscreant eyes glinting stern under wrinkled brows. A basilisk" (*U* 9.373–74 {194.20–21}); in "Circe," Bella is pictured "*with a hard basilisk stare*" (*U* 15.2835 {530.17}). See also *GJ* 14; *FW* 577.2.

baton. A bendlet terminated within the field, used as a mark of difference.

bear. A canting charge in the arms of the canton of Berne, Switzerland, and those of Berlin, the bear seems to occur as an heraldic charge in the "Tavern" (II.3), where Butt says:

> Come alleyou jupes of Wymmingtown thaat graze the calves of Man! A bear raigning in his heavenspawn consomation robes. Rent, outraged, yewleaved, grained, ballooned, hindergored and voluant! Erminia's capecloaked hoodoodman! (*FW* 339.26–30)

Cf. 340.20–21: "Bruinoboroff, the hooneymoonger, and the grizzliest manmichal in Meideveide!" I cannot connect a bear with Wellington (Wymmingtown), heraldically or otherwise, but in the latter reference it seems to be a canting charge for Brian Boru.

bearing. Any individual **charge** or heraldic emblem.

Bellingham. In "Circe," Mrs Bellingham accuses Bloom of envying her servant when he stood "behind my chair wearing my livery and the armorial bearings of the Bellingham escutcheon garnished sable, a buck's head couped or" (*U* 15.1049–51 {466.24–27}). Joyce has placed the crest on the escutcheon: *Burke's Peerage and Baronetage* (London: Burke's, 1976) gives the arms as "Arg., three bugle horns, sa., stringed and garnished, or. *Crest*—A buck's head, couped, or" (240).

bend. One of the heraldic **ordinaries;** a wide, diagonal band crossing the heraldic field. Unless specified to be a "bend sinister," the bend is depicted as a "bend dexter" (running from the top left to the lower right of the field as viewed). A narrow bend is a "bendlet." See Illus. 1-E.

bezant. See **roundel.**

billet. An upright rectangular charge.

Black Prince. See **Edward, the Black Prince.**

blazon. The formulaic language used by the heralds to describe coats of arms and related devices. The language of blazon abounds in Joyce's works, but some of the more conspicuous instances are the Dedalus arms (*U* 15.3948–49 {572.16–17}), those of Wassaily Booselaeugh of Riesengeborg (*FW* 5.6–8), and those of HCE (*FW* 546.5–11). See also **O'Reilly, Finnegan.**

Bluemantle. One of the four **pursuivants** of the College of Arms; named for the mantle of a Knight of the Garter. See **Garter, Order of.** As "blushmantle" in *FW* 24.9.

bordure. A border at the edge of the field, approximately one-fifth of the shield's width. Often a mark of **difference;** in Scotland, a mark of **cadency.**

boss. A structural rather than an heraldic feature, a boss is a round, metal protrusion from the center of a shield. It figures in the blazon of HCE's arms, however, where the coleopter is said to serve "For the boss" (*FW* 546.7).

buck. The traditional crest of Ireland is a hart springing from a tower (Illus. 4-C). See **Ireland.** In "Proteus," Stephen watches a dog, and blazons its postures: "He turned, bounded back, came nearer, trotted on twinkling shanks. On a field tenney a buck, trippant, proper, unattired"

(*U* 3.335–37 {46.11–13}). The mongrel has likely been transformed into a canting charge for Mulligan, who sees his name as "Tripping and sunny like the buck himself" (*U* 1.42 {4.5–6}).

Burke. A renowned family name (notorious?) in heraldic and genealogical circles; Sir Bernard Burke, the son of the founder of *Burke's Peerage,* was the Ulster King of Arms at the time of Joyce's birth. It would seem that there is at least one book of Burke's at the *Wake,* but I am not certain which one(s). His 1884 *General Armory,* for all of its inaccuracies, is a basic tool of heraldic research, and is the *sine qua non* of the stationers and jewelers determined to find "your authentic family crest." Because of its limitations, the *General Armory* would not be a reliable source for a *bona fide* pedigree, but Burke's *Landed Gentry* might be.

As a **peer,** HCE might be in Burke's *Peerage.* Among the epithets directed at HCE is "*Purged out of Burke's*" (*FW* 71.29–30), which could refer to any one of the three books. McHugh suggests that the initials "B.L.G." (131.3) in Riddle No. 1 of I.6 stand for "Burke's *Landed Gentry.*" In *FW* II.1, the triumphant Chuff predicts that "I shall reside with our obeisant servants among Burke's mobility" (235.12–13); presumably meaning he would be listed in the *Peerage.*

cad. While sometimes used in the common sense of a "ne'er do well," this word is used pointedly by Joyce, in its strict sense of a "cadet," a younger son (the expression derives from the need of straitened younger sons to enlist in the military without commission). In *U,* Simon Dedalus refers to Mulligan as a cad in "Hades" (*U* 6.49 [88.15]); Bloom, reproaching himself for his lust in "Nausicaa" thinks "An utter cad he had been" (*U* 13.747 {367.12–13}); in "Circe," Philip Beaufoy calls Bloom a "low cad" (15.852 {459.30}); Molly uses the word (18.892 {763.3}). In *FW* 14.12, Shem and Shaun appear as "Caddy and Primas": younger son (cadet) and oldest (heir). Cf. 101.35: "O me and O ye! cadet and prim. . . ."

cadency. A system used to distinguish arms of different branches of a single family. In England, the arms of the oldest son are differentiated from the father's by a "label of three points" (which looks, as a matter of fact, like HCE's siglum), and other marks exist to differentiate the arms of younger sons (a crescent for the second son, a mullet [star] for the third, and so forth). In Scotland, "bordures" are used to distinguish the arms of the heir (oldest son) and cadets (younger sons) from those of the father, and from one another's.

canting arms. Also "allusive" arms; arms that refer by visual pun (rebus) to the name of the **armiger.** Examples: the spear in Shakespeare's arms; the olive branch in those of Oliver St. John Gogarty (a rare instance of a pun on a given name; most canting arms allude to the surname); the Festy King's "fesses" (*FW* 85.30), the earwig ("coleopter") on HCE's arms (*FW* 546.7), and so forth. Randle Holme's *Academy of Armory* (1688) gives an instance of earwigs in canting arms for "Earwigg" (2: 471). In "Oxen of the Sun" Bloom is "the good sir Leopold that had for his cognisance the flower of quiet, margerain gentle" (14.330–31 {392.23–24}). As often as Joyce uses canting emblems and arms (the keys of Keyes), I have not detected any use of the expression "canting arms." While I find no etymological connection between the idea of canting ("singing") arms and the verses from *The Canting Academy* alluded to in *U* and *FW* ("*White thy fambles, red thy gan* [*U* 3.381 {47.23}]), I think it possible that heraldic jargon and "cant" are connected in Stephen's imagination in "Proteus"; moreover, there is an occasional coincidence of heraldic blazon and cant in *FW*, as in "but you must have the proper sort of accident to meet that kind of being with a difference. Flame at his fumbles but freeze on his fist" (269.14–16).

canton. One of the heraldic **ordinaries;** a square portion of either side of the chief, smaller than a quarter (a distinction recognized by nearly every heraldic writer except Barron [Barron 320b]). See Illus. 1-E.

cartouche. An oblong escutcheon used primarily in ecclesiastical heraldry.

casque. A term for a helmet sometimes used in blazon. See *GJ* 16: "Her arms: a casque, gules, and blunt spear on a field, sable." Cf. *U* 9.296 {192.16}: Stephen looks at his hat and his ashplant, and thinks, "My casque and sword"; also, *U* 15.4611 [596.20].

castle. See Dublin, Newcastle.

charge. Generally speaking, anything depicted on a coat of arms. Some writers distinguish a charge from an **ordinary;** Barron writes of "ordinary charges" (317b).

chevron. One of the heraldic **ordinaries;** shaped like an inverted "V" (and, therefore, like Shaun's siglum). Used as military insignia: *U* 15.4614 {596.23}. See Illus. 1-E.

chief. One of the heraldic **ordinaries;** the top third of the shield.

cipher. In royal heraldry, the monarch's insignia, consisting of the initials (e.g.: "VR" = "Victoria Regina") and other emblems (e.g., Royal badges, crowns, etc.). "His Majesty's vermilion mailcars, bearing on their sides the royal initials, E.R." (*U* 7.16–17 {116.17–19}).

colors. In heraldry, the "colors"—azure (blue), sable (black), gules (red), purpur (purple), and vert (green)—are distinct from the metals—or (gold) and argent (silver). The term to describe both "color" and "metal" is **tincture.**

Cor ad cor loquitur. Cardinal Newman's heraldic motto, which appears in numerous contexts in *P* and *U.* In *P* 116, Stephen fantasizes about receiving forgiveness from the Blessed Virgin, hand in hand with Emma; the virgin says, "It is one heart that loves another heart. Take hands together, my dear children, and you will be happy together and your hearts will love each other." Father Boyle links this passage to "Cor ad cor loquitur" (87). In *U,* the motto is echoed in the cliché "Heart to heart talks" (*U* 8.7 {151.9}). The cliché retains the syntax of the Latin motto, "cor ad cor loquitur," and would seem to be one of several echoes of this motto in *P* and *U.* In "Oxen of the Sun," the phrase appears again in Bloom's reveries: "Did heart leap to heart?" (14.1070–71 {413.36}).

Cork Herald. One of two heralds in the old Irish Office of Arms. I take "Munster's Herald" (*FW* 498.11) to refer to this herald, since Cork is in Munster.

coronet. Crown found in arms of Princes and peers. See **ducal coronet.**

Cornish chough. A black bird with red beak and feet; common as a charge in heraldry (in the arms of Cardinal Wolsey, for example, and based on those arms, in the bearings of Christ Church, Oxford). The Cornish chough is also the charge on the arms of O'Kirwan, one of the twelve tribes of Galway (with Joyce); in this context, the chough occurs in *FW* 352.34. See **O'Kirwan;** Illus. 5-F.

couchant. Used to describe an heraldic beast (especially a lion) in an attitude of repose, but not slumber (i.e., the lion's head is up when it is "couchant," but not when "dormant"). As Stephen leaves the school in "Nestor," he notes "The lions couchant on the pillars as he passed out through the gate: toothless terrors" (*U* 2.428–30 {35.42–36.1}); Illus. 2-E.

couped. Of a hand or other limb, portrayed as if severed. See **O'Neill, Red Hand.**

crest. Not, as many people think, a synonym for coat of arms, but rather an heraldic ornament found atop the helm of an armorial achievement. Joyce uses "crest" as distinct from "escutcheon" in *U* 17.1610 {715.31}; *FW* 5.6, 220.27, and 546.5. Also, see *U* 12.1873–74: in Hans Walter Gabler's edition, the umbrella of Frederick Falkiner bears his "engraved initials, crest, coat of arms and house number"; the crest is omitted in the Random House edition {344.21–22}, as is Stephen's reference to Shakespeare's crest (9.925 {209.2–3}).

Crivelli. Family name of Pope Urban III; according to John Garvin, the Pope's canting arms had as a charge a seive (Italian "crivello" = sieve; it is also an idiom meaning "riddle"), and had sows as supporters. Garvin notes references to these arms in *FW* 155.112–13 (Garvin 173).

Crom abu. Cri de guerre of the Fitzgeralds, also used as their heraldic motto. Cf. "crow cru cramwells Downaboo!" (*FW* 53.36–54.1) and "Crum abu! Cromwell to victory!" (500.6).

Crux upon crux. Bogus motto attributed to Pius IX by Martin Cunningham in "Grace" (*D* 167); the source is a prophetic motto attributed to the 101st pope (O'Kearney 106). Cf. "crucycrooks" (*FW* 155.17); see **Union Jack.**

Dauphin. The canting title of the heir apparent to the French throne (his heraldic charge was a dolphin), used in connection with one of HCE's heirs apparent in the "sleepingchambers" of III.4, the sons are "daulphin and deevlin" (*FW* 566.20).

David, Star of. See Solomon, Seal of.

Dedalus. The Dedalus arms, suspiciously like those of Joyce of Galway, are blazoned in "Circe" (15.3948–49 {572.16–17}). "Keep our flag flying! An eagle gules volant in a field argent displayed. Ulster king at arms!" (Illus. 3-F).

dexter. The right side of an heraldic shield *from the standpoint of the bearer;* consequently, for all intents and purposes of ornamental heraldry, the left. This confusion seems to lie behind such allusions as "Reeve Gootch was right and Reeve Drughad was sinistrous!" (*FW* 197.1), and Tristan's "sinister dexterity, light and rufthandling, vicemversem. . ." (384.26–27). See also *FW* 99.30.

difference. Modifications made to an heraldic field to distinguish it from a similar one; usually distinguished from **cadency,** which is the system of symbols used to differentiate the arms of blood relatives. Arms have been "differenced" by the addition of bendlets, fur spots, cantons, changes of tincture, and so forth.

dimidiation. One of two ways of combining two coats of arms on one shield. A "dimidiated" shield has halves of two shields; an example is the coat of arms of Connacht. In this arrangement, the charges are cut in half, so the arms of Connacht have half of an eagle displayed in the dexter (Illus. 5-A). In "impalement," on the other hand, the charges of two shields are shown side by side on a single shield, as in dimidiation, but the charges are whole.

displayed. Of an eagle, literally "spread eagle." The eagle in the Joyce arms is displayed, but Joyce (or Simon, or Stephen) keeps the word "displayed" in the blazon of the Dedalus arms, even though it is redundant (in fact, contradictory) given that the eagle is **volant** (See 15.3948–49 {572.16–17}) (Illus. 3-C, 3-D, 3-E).

Doubling all the time. According to McHugh, motto of Dublin, Georgia (seat of Laurens County); used in *FW* 3.8–9, when "topsawyers rocks" are said to have gone "doublin their mumper all the time." However, the Office of the City Manager of Dublin, Georgia, has no record of this motto ever having been used (letter to the author, 25 July 1984).

dragon. Canting emblem attributed to King Arthur in literature (as son of Pendragon); emblem of Wales. *FW* 24.5.

Dublin. The arms and motto of Dublin underlie one of *FW*'s most pervasive motifs. The charges on the arms are "three castles argent, flammant proper"; the arms are supported:

> On either side [by] a female figure proper, vested gules, lined or, that on the dexter side holding in her exterior hand a sword erect proper, pommel and hilt or, and that on the sinister a pair of scales, and each holding in her interior hand a branch of laurel. (Fox-Davies, *Public Arms* [1915] 246)

The motto is "Obedientia civium urbus felicitas." See Illus. 5-I, 6-A. The two female supporters in the achievement, and the three castles on the arms are clues in the first riddle in I.6: the subject of the riddle shows "two remarkable piscines and three wellworthseeing ambries" (127.35–36); he is also said to have "shot two queans and shook three caskles" (128.17). Similarly, the arms are the subject of the third riddle (139.29–140.7), the answer to which is one of the many variations on the motto in the *Wake:* "Thine obesity, O civilian, hits the felicitude of our orb!" Other allusions to the three castles: *FW* 22.34, 101.23, 420.31, 546.15–17, and 551.31. Hart (*Structure and Motif* 236) catalogues twelve variations on the Dublin motto. The supporters of the arms (the two women flanking the shield, who seem to be lifting their skirts) figure prominently in the *Wake:* they are in the Festy King's trial, when the litigants are "egged on by their supporters in the shape of betterwomen with bowstrung hair of Carrothagenuine ruddiness, waving crimson petties. . ." (87.27–29). Bernard Benstock ("Every Telling . . ." 5) connects one of the titles for the mamafesta (I.5) with the supporters: "*a Pair of Sloppy Sluts plainly Showing all the Unmentionability falsely Accusing about the Raincoats*" (107.6–7). In *Ulysses,* these well-known figures are evoked when Mulligan recalls:

> O, the night in the Camden hall when the daughters of Erin had to lift their skirts to step over you [Stephen] as you lay in your mulberrycoloured, multicoloured, multitudinous vomit! (*U* 9.1192–94 {217.17–19})

Dublin Herald. One of two heralds in the old Irish Office of Arms. See **herald.**

Ducal coronet. The wolf in the Joyce crest is "ducally gorged," meaning its throat is circled with the coronet of a duke (Illus. 3-D). Such a coronet is ornamented with "strawberry leaves" (as are the coronets of a marquis or an earl, but only a duke's coronet is exclusively ornamented with strawberry leaves: the other crowns alternate the leaves with balls). Shaun advises his sister "Look on a boa in his beauty and you'll never more wear your strawberry leaves" (*FW* 435.20–21).

eagle. The charge on the Joyce arms is an eagle displayed; the Joyce arms are remarkably similar to those of John Milton. The king of birds is probably the most frequently used heraldic beast. It was a preeminent symbol of empire: eagles were used as emblems in imperial Rome, and the two-headed eagle was the symbol of the Holy Roman Empire, the Russian Czars (the House of Romanov), Napoleon, and so forth. In *U*, Bloom's coronation procession in "Circe" is preceded by beaters bearing "*imperial eagles hoisted*" (*U* 15.1409 {480.7}). In *FW* I.1, Finnegan has a "bloodeagle waistcoat" (24.29; cf. the Napoleonic "elbaroom surtout" [52.25]). The eagle is a canting charge for Earwicker, by a circuitous route: McHugh points out uses of the Pan-Slavonic "orel" (eagle), which suggests "Perce Orielle" or "Persse O'Reilly"—HCE's aliases (See the entry in the catalogue of titles for ALP's mamafesta: "*Prszss Orel*" [105.10–11]). At 310.26–27, where HCE is "host of a bottlefilled" (the Tavern), he has "hunter's pink of face, an orel orioled." Shem (as Glugg) envisions himself "eagelly plumed" (231.13), and as Dolph, he is equated with the eagle emblem when he is called "the divver's own smart gossoon, aequal to yoursell and wanigel to anglyother" (300.4–5).

Earl Marshal. The hereditary head of the College of Arms (the post is held by the Duke of Norfolk). *U* 15.1438 {480.39}). See **herald.**

Earwicker of Sidlesham. I find no arms recorded for the actual Earwickers (to whom, we are assured, HCE is not related anyway: *FW* 30.7–8). But Roland McHugh notes an Earwicker rebus on the tomb of one of the real Earwickers of Sidlesham: ears of wheat (*Sigla* 15). Among the epithets directed at HCE from outside the gate is "*Wheatears*" (71.11); cf. ref. in HCE's speech at the end of "Yawn" (III.3) to "wheatears" (550.26), and "Good wheat!" (616.10).

earwig. Holme's *Academy of Armory* (2: 471) records an earwig as **canting** charges for "Earwigg"; see **canting arms.**

écu. French word for armorial escutcheon; *FW* 538.16.

Edward, the Black Prince. Son of Edward III and father of Richard II, Edward, the Black Prince predeceased his father and therefore never reigned; he was a Prince of Wales, however, and his "Shield for Peace," with its three ostrich feathers (*Sable, three ostrich feathers, their quills passing through escrolls argent bearing the words Ich Dien* [*Boutell* 77]) is the source of the badge of subsequent Princes of Wales (see **Wales, Prince of**). HCE is associated with the Black Prince ("the black prints, now extincts . . ." [*FW* 387.20]). This provides a link between HCE and his sons, who bear the three-feathered emblem.

Elephant, Order of the. The Order of the Elephant is a Danish chivalric order, the emblem of which depends from the royal armorial achievement. Edward VII appears in "Circe" wearing, amidst other regalia, "Elephant of Denmark" (15.4451–52 {590.18}). I do not know for certain that Edward belonged to the order, but his father-in-law did happen to be the King of Denmark.

embowed. Arched, as is the crown of rue on the arms of Saxony. The term is also used to refer to the arched posture of snakes, and this is likely the sense in which it occurs in *FW* 270.16.

ermine. One of the heraldic furs: a white field with black marks (as distinct from "ermines," which is black with white marks), for the ermine's tail. Ermine is the fur that lines royal mantling, both in heraldic achievements and, I suppose, in fact. See Bloom's "Circe" coronation regalia, including "a crimson velvet mantle trimmed with ermine" (*U* 15.1442–43 {481.2–3}). See also *FW* 339.29. See Illus. 1-C.

escutcheon. Heraldic shield.

Esquire. The honorific applied to members of the upper echelon of the gentry. Bloom styles himself a gentleman in his fantasies (see also Ithaca), giving his name as "Henry Flower Esq" (*U* 5.62 {72.31}); the "E" in HCE is often used for this title, as in "Humme the Cheapner, Esc" (29.18–19); see also *FW* 102.16, 205.22, 254.20, 557.1.

F.E.R.T. One of the heraldic mottoes most frequently used in *FW*, in various forms, of which Hart (*Structure and Motif* 224) has catalogued ten, including "In all fortitudinous ajaxious rowdinoisy tenaucity" (53.16–17), "Fulgitudo ejus Rhedonum teneat!" (610.6), and so forth. One of the clues of the first riddle of I.6 is that the subject "wrote F.E.R.T. on his buckler" (127.9–10). Atherton glosses the mysterious motto as that of the House of Savoy, saying that it "is interpreted in two ways, *Fortitudo eius Rodum tenuit*, and *Foemina erit ruina tua* (33). According to Brewer's (26th ed.), it is the motto of Sardinia; the current edition of Brewer's (1981) elaborates, giving the Savoy motto as "Fert" ("He bears"), and giving the initials F.E.R.T. as the motto of the sixteenth-century Italian Order of the Annunciation.

Falkiner. The arms of Frederick Falkiner, recorder of Dublin, are referred to in "Cyclops" (12.1873–74 {344.21–22}), but not described (see **crest**). They happen to be not only canting arms, but canting arms that refer to falconry. The blazon in Burke's *General Armory* for Richard Henry Fitz-Richard Falkiner is "Or, three falcons close ppr. in the center chief point a mullet gu. *Crest*—A falcon's lure ppr. charged with a mullet gu. between two wings az. *Motto—Fortunâ favente*." The tantalizing possibilities of this singular yoking of "the subtle and curious jargons of heraldry and falconry" (*P* 180) are heightened by references in the Buffalo notebooks to the recorder as "Frederick the Falconer" (Buffalo Notebook V. A. 8., 24r; Herring, *Joyce's Notes . . .* 174).

false heraldry. Blazon which places a color on another color, or one of the metals on the other. Heraldic practice is to alternate colors and metals for the purpose of effective contrast.

fess. One of the heraldic **ordinaries;** a horizontal band at the center of the field, occupying approximately one-third of the shield's height. It is a common ordinary in *FW:* see 5.8, 85.30, 546.7. Illus. 1-E.

field. The surface of the heraldic shield. *U* 3.336 {46.12}; 3.415 {48.25}; 3.418 {48.28}; 15.3949 {572.17}; *FW* 85.31, 99.29 ("fidd of Verdor"), 205.9, 546.8.

Finnegan. Dominic Manganiello has pointed out the occurrence of Finnegan crests in *FW* (30–31). "A hand from the cloud emerges, holding a chart expanded" (593.19) alludes to a Finnegan crest: "Out of a cloud a hand erect holding a book expanded proper." Also, on 604.3–5, Manganiello finds another Finnegan crest (listed under "Finncane" in *Fairbairn's Crests*): "The vinebranch of Heremonheber on Bregia's plane where Teffia lies is leaved invert and fructed proper . . ." The blazon for the crest of "FINNCANE" is "A vine-branch, leaved, vert, fructed, proper" (*Fairbairn's* 1: 181b). See also **O'Molloy.**

flanche. Also "flaunche," and called a "flasque" by Ruskin (Illus. 1-E); other writers consider a "flasque" a diminutive of the flanche. A division of a field by a curved line extending from the chief to the base.

flowers, language of. Bloom's emblematic code: *U* 5.261–66 {78.14–22}, 11.296–98 {263.32–36}; cf. "Mineninecyhandsy, in the languo of flows" (*FW* 621.21–22).

fret. An interlaced figure consisting of a **mascle,** a bendlet, and a bendlet sinister (Illus. 1-G).

fructed. Of a tree or a vine, used to distinguish the color of the fruit from that of the plant: Gogarty's olive branch is "fructed proper," meaning the olives are of natural color. Similarly, the vinebranch of *FW* 604.3–5 is "leaved invert and fructed proper". See **Finnegan.**

Fruiterers, Company of. See **Gough;** Illus. 5-B.

fumant. The term for smoking in an heraldic description; Gough (1894, 277) says that it is used in regard to a brick kiln. In *FW*, it occurs in the phrase "in tabinet fumant" (43.4).

fur. One of the stylized shadings and patterns that represent fur; examples are **vair** (Illus. 1-D), and **ermine** (1-C).

fusil. a **lozenge-**shaped charge.

Garter, Order of. A chivalric order founded by Edward III. Brewer (26th ed., 331b) says:

> The popular legend is that Joan, countess of Salisbury, accidentally dropped her Garter at a court ball. It was picked up by her royal partner, Edward III., who gallantly diverted the attention of the guests from the lady by binding the blue band round his own knee, saying as he did so, 'Honi soit qui mal y pense.'

This motto appears on the Garter worn by members of the Order (below the knee by the knights; by the Queen of England on her arm), and also appears in several forms in *FW*, such as "Honey swarms where mellisponds" (238.33–34) and "O'Neill saw Queen Molly's pants" (495.27–28; see Hart, *Structure and Motif* 227, for a list of allusions to this motif).

Heraldically, the Garter appears prominently in armorial achievements, including those of the English monarch and the Prince of Wales; in an heraldic achievement, the Garter encircles the escutcheon. In *U*, in his appearance in "Circe," Edward VII wears "the insignia of Garter" (15.4451 {590.17}). The Garter also appeared around the escutcheon of the Duke of Wellington (see Willingdone's "magnate's garters" [*FW* 8.19]); in other words, several of the aliases of HCE, Shem and Shaun are Knights of the Garter. The hen's gift of "a starr and girton for Draper and Deane" (211.1–2) includes two insignia of the Order. The "Star and Garter" was also a Dublin hotel; see *U* 7.535 {132.25}. The reference "so buckely hosiered from the Royal Leg" (*FW* 536.15) seems to be a Garter reference.

golpe. See **roundel.**

Gough. Author of the 1847 *A Glossary of Terms Used in British Heraldry*, revised in 1894 and published as *A Glossary of the Terms Used in Heraldry* by Henry Gough and James Parker. The reference to Gough at *FW* 271.29 would seem to be the heraldic Gough, not the Gough of a statue in Dublin (see Glasheen 108; McHugh, *Annotations* 271), since "This is the glider that gladdened the girl that list to the wind that lifted the leaves that folded the fruit that hung on the tree that grew in the garden Gough gave" seems to refer to two coats of arms in Gough and Parker under "Paradise": the arms of Macklean of Scotland, and of the Company of Fruiterers, London (Gough 442; Illus. 5-B), both have coats of arms depicting the serpent tempting Eve ("the glider that gladdened the girl") in the garden of Eden. Issy's note (271.F5) confirms the connection of this reference to her family arms, those of the O'Reilly's (see **O'Reilly;** Illus. 5-D): "Tho' I have one just like that to home, . . . a nice shiny sleekysilk out of that slippering snake charmeuse."

Greece. The heraldic colors of Greece—azure and argent—are represented in the cover of the first edition of *Ulysses:* white letters on a blue field. See *Letters* 3: 46, 72. These are also the colors of Zurich. See Illus. 4-A, 4-B.

gules. The heraldic color, red. The color of the charge in the Joyce/Dedalus arms, and the color of the royal livery. *GJ* 16; *U* 15.3949 {572.16♧, 15.4638 {597.14}.

gunstone. See **roundel.**

harp. See **Leinster.**

hatched. In heraldry, drawn with lines and dots to indicate tinctures. Many of the illustrations in this study are hatched: horizontal lines indicate azure; vertical lines, gules; dots, or; and so forth. See *U* 3.417–18 {48.27–28}: "coloured emblems hatched on its field."

hatchment. A representation of an armorial achievement on a lozenge-shaped frame, for funerary display. *FW* 139.30.

hauberk. A piece of armor to protect the neck. *U* 15.1915 {0}; 15.4507 {592.19}.

helm. The helmet of a suit of armour; usually found over the escutcheon in an armorial achievement. See *U* 15.1915 {0}; 15.4507 {592.19}: "Don Emile Patrizio Franz Rupert Pope Hennessy" appears "*In medieval hauberk, two wild geese volant on his helm. . . .*"

herald. Heralds are officers in the College of Arms and members of the Royal household; historically, they found their origins in officials who recorded and identified arms used in tournaments, and served certain diplomatic services. They do not now, nor have they ever, been called upon to blow fanfares on trumpets. Since 1943, the Republic of Ireland has had its own herald, known as the Chief Herald of Ireland. Prior to the establishment of this office, there existed the Irish Office of Arms (located in Dublin Castle, like its successor, the present Genealogical Office). According to Barron's *Encyclopaedia Brittanica* article, written while the old Office of Arms existed (as, for that matter, were all of Joyce's works), the chief heraldic officer, the Ulster King of Arms, held "office by patent, during pleasure [of the Sovereign]" (Barron 329a). Under the Ulster King two heralds, the Cork Herald and the Dublin Herald, served. The junior officer of the Irish Office of Arms was the Athlone Pursuivant; the Lynch-Robinsons also mention there having been a "St. Patrick Pursuivant" (117). In *Portrait,* Stephen defends his lineage by appeal to the authority of heralds: "Come with me now to the office of arms and I will show you the tree of my family" (*P* 202). In *U,* Mr. Best is described as "douce herald" (*U* 9.1059 {213.34}). One herald and one pursuivant are present at Bloom's coronation in "Circe": "the Athlone poursuivant and Ulster King at Arms" (*U* 15.1413 {480.12}).

The other Kings of Arms (except for Scotland's Lyon King, who enjoys the same type of autonomy as Ulster King had) serve under the authority of the Duke of Norfolk, who as Earl Marshal is hereditary head of the College of Arms. At Bloom's coronation, the procession of guilds and tradesmen (including "heraldic seal engravers" [15.1433 {480.34}]) is followed by "gentlemen of the bedchamber, Black Rod, Deputy Garter, Gold Stick, the master of horse, the lord great chamberlain, the earl marshal, the high constable carrying the sword of state, saint Stephen's iron crown, the chalice and bible" (15.1436–40 {480.37–41}). Officers of arms at the *Wake* are noted in the "Yawn" chapter: "Ulster Kong and Munster's Herald with Athclee Ensigning and Athlone Poursuivant and his Imperial Catchering" (*FW* 498.11–13).

The four annalists seem to function as heralds in their various genealogical inquiries; Markey Lyons shares a title with the chief heraldic officer of Scotland, the Lyon King of Arms. Also, the four are associated, like the officers of the Irish Office of Arms, with the four provinces: Ulster King, Cork [Munster] Herald, Dublin [Leinster] Herald, Athlone [Connacht] Pursuivant. The heraldic insignia of the provinces are prominent in III.3, when Yawn remarks "the three crowns round your draphole (isn't it dram disgusting?)" (521.7–8; three crowns of Munster), and Matt Tarpey is addressed "Gently, gently Northern Ire! Love that red hand!" (522.4; Ulster). See also 482.14–15: "Number four, fix up your spreadeagle and pull your weight." This seems to refer to the dimidiated (composed of the halves of two escutcheons) shield of Connacht, which bears half of a spread eagle, and a human arm.

Outside of the Irish Office, the title of the oldest King of Arms, the Norroy King of Arms, seems to occur in the reference to HCE as "Norreys" (*FW* 311.35), and to the four as "them four hoarsemen on their apolkaloops, Norreys, Soothbys, Yates and Welks . . ." (557.1–2). According to Anthony Wagner (*Heralds of England* 20–21), the earliest records (1338) of the Norroy King of Arms give his name as "Andrew Norreys or Norrois, King of Heralds. . . ."

heraldry. Once referring to all the functions of a herald, "heraldry" is now understood to encompass the field once known as "armoury": The art and science of devising, rendering, and identifying coats of arms and related emblematic devices.

> . . . it wounded [Stephen] to think that he would never be but a shy guest at the feast of the world's culture and that the monkish learning, in terms of which he was striving to forge out an esthetic philosophy, was held no higher by the age he lived in than the subtle and curious jargons of heraldry and falconry. (*P* 180)

See also "his crest of huroldry" (*FW* 5.6).

Honi soit qui mal y pense. See **Garter, Order of.**

Horse of Hanover. An emblem incorporated into the Royal Arms under the House of Hanover. " 'Gules, a horse argent,' really the arms of Westphalia, is popularly known in [England] as the coat of Hanover . . ." (*CG* 201). See "a kingbilly whitehorsed" (*FW* 75.15–16); cf. 347.1: "a white horsday where the midril met the bulg"; and 388.16–17, with "Lapoleon, the equestrian, on his whuite hourse of Hunover." This motif connects Willingdone's "white harse" (8.17, etc.) with the monarch. See Illus. 5–H.

Ich dien. See Wales, Prince of.

inescutcheon. A single small escutcheon used as a charge on an heraldic shield.

Ireland. National symbols of Ireland are popular as wearing apparel in *FW*. The republican tricolor (green, white, and gold), which dates from the mid-nineteenth century, is worn by the Shaun-like witness at the Festy King trial (sans the Orange): "upon letting down his rice and peacegreen coverdisk" (86.35–36), by Chuff in the "Mime" chapter: "Of all the green heroes everwore coton breiches, the whitemost, the goldenest!" (234.8–10), and again by Shaun in III.1: "a starspangled zephyr with a decidedly surpliced crinklydoodle front with his motto through dear life embrothred over it in peas, rice, and yeggyyolk, Or for royal, Am for Mail, R.M.D." (404.27–30). See also Butt's change at 344.11–12: "*his face glows green, his hair greys white, his bleyes become broon to suite his cultic twalette*"; "the gren, woid and glue" (596.21), and "greenmould upon mildew over jaundice" (582.10–12).

The traditional crest of Ireland was "On a wreath or and azure, a tower triple-towered of the first [or], from the portal a hart springing argent, attired and hoofed gold" (Illus. 4–C); this emblem figures in the hunt motifs of *U* and *FW*. See **buck.**

Joyce. Joyce of Galway bears "Argent an eagle with two heads displayed gules, over all a fess ermine" (MacLysaght, Plate XVII; see Illus. 3–E). The heraldic rendering owned by Joyce, however, features a deviation from this blazon, which comes from Burke's *General Armory:* "Ar[gent] an eagle disp[layed] gu[les] charged on the breast with a bar gemel erm[ine]" (Burke 550b; see Illus. 3–C, 3–D). The Joyce arms are the basis for the Dedalus arms as described in "Circe" (*U* 15.3948–49 {572.16–17}). The red eagle on the coat of arms used by Joyce is called a "phoenix" by Glasheen (233), and the phoenix motif in *FW* is probably related to the many eagles, red and otherwise, at the *Wake.* Cf. Finnegan's "bloodeagle waistcoat" (24.29), with "bester of redpublicans, at Eagle Cock Hostel" (53.28); and HCE's appearance as "host of a bottlefilled" where he has "hunter's pink of face, an orel orieled" (310.26–27); "orel" = Pan-Slavonic for eagle, according to McHugh. See also references to Shem as "eagelly plumed" (231.13), and as an eagle at 300.4–5.

lambrequin. See **mantling.**

Lancaster. The badge of Lancaster was a "red rose en soleil." In *P* (12) Stephen's class is divided into two sections, York and Lancaster, and they wear the two badges of those historical factions: "The little silk badge with the white rose on it. . . . —Right. Bravo Lancaster! The red rose wins. Come on now, York! Forge ahead!" See *FW* 94.35–36, where HCE is "behind the war of the two roses." See also **York.**

lapwing. See **Tweedy.**

leek. A Welsh national emblem, see discussion in Scott-Giles (118–19). Its most famous use in literature is by Shakespeare, who had *Henry V* promise Fluellen to wear the leek on St. David's day. Thus the "garlic leek" (462.29–30) whose smell enables Shaun to recognize Shem is a Celtic symbol: a "Gaelic leek," also "Gaelic League." The Welsh connotation of the symbol connects Shem's identity with the Prince of

Wales (see *FW* 463.3–4, where Shem has the "three white feathers"). See also **Wales, Prince of.**

Leinster. "Vert, a harp or, stringed argent" are the arms of the Province of Leinster, and the harp is a traditional symbol of Ireland. It is still found on an azure field as the Presidential flag of the Republic of Ireland; the harp on azure is also still quartered in the Royal Arms. The Citizen objects to what he calls "Henry Tudor's harps" (*U* 12.1308 {328.9–10}), and favors the arms of **Munster** as representative of Ireland.

letters patent. Letters Patent are, among other things, the instrument whereby grants of arms are made by the College of Arms. This is the significance of the frequent references to letters patent by HCE and Shaun, both of whom claim to be legitimate armigers. When Shaun carries "The Letter," it is described as "letter patent," and thus is the instrument of his noble pedigree and status as an armiger. Asked if he is able to read "those shemletters patent," Shaun replies "I'm as afterdusk nobly Roman as pope and water could christen me. . . . I am, thing Sing Larynx, letter potent to play the same backwards" (419.20–23). He asserts his noble and papal status, thus certifying himself as HCE's heir apparent; and the letters patent themselves would also do this. Cf. HCE's letters patent: 492.35 ALP testifies that HCE is "liable to succumb when served with letters potent"; and the motto of HCE's armorial achievement, which is in "letters portent" (546.10).

lion. The insignia of the English monarchy are lions passant guardant. Cf. "lions couchant" (*U* 2.429 {35.42}). The lion rampant is an heraldic charge in the arms of **O'Reilly** and **O'Molloy.** See *FW* 99.29–30, 223.19–20, 599.6–7. If, as Beryl Schlossman suggests, the lion is "an avatar of Shaun" (Schlossman 130), then he could be the heraldic counterpart to Shem as unicorn (see **unicorn**), which would make the brothers the two supporters of the Royal Arms.

livery. Attire in the heraldic colors of an armiger, worn by his servants and retainers. *U* 15.409 {443.17}; 15.1049 {466.24}.

lozenge. The diamond-shaped heraldic field employed by an heiress in her own right, or by a widow. The rhombus in the geometric problem on *FW* 293 is seen by Shaun as a lozenge: "it will be a lozenge to me all my lauffe" *FW* (299.27–29).

Lux upon lux. Bogus motto attributed to Leo XIII by Martin Cunningham in "Grace" (*D* 167); used by HCE in "Yawn" (III.3): "loomends day lumineused luxories on looks" (*FW* 548.27–28). The motto is from a prophetic motto ascribed to the 102nd pope (O'Kearney 106).

Lyon King of arms. The chief heraldic official in Scotland. Perhaps connected with one of the four annalists, Markey Lyons. See **herald.**

Macklean. See **Gough.**

manche. A stylized sleeve, used as an heraldic charge.

Man, Isle of. "Gules, three legs armed proper conjoined in the fess point at the upper part of the thighs, flexed in a triangle, garnished and spurred or." See "*Three legs of man*" (*U* 15.2179 {507.14}). In *FW*, references include two in II.3 (Tavern): HCE is described as "this ale of man, for him, our hubuljoynted" (310.31) (double-jointed conjoined legs); "The threelegged man" on 331.8; Butt's line regarding "the calves of Man!" on 339.27.

mantling. Stylized cascades of fabric that surround an heraldic achievement; also called the **lambrequin.**

metal. In heraldry, the two tinctures "or" (gold) and "argent" (silver) are metals, as distinct from colors.

morganatic marriage. Like Leopold Bloom in "Circe" (*U* 15.1508 {483.13}), HCE's elevation to royal status sometimes seems to exclude his wife: Bloom's marriage to Molly is deemed "morganatic" after his coronation (*U* 15.1508 {483.13}), and HCE, defending himself, alludes to "morgenattics litt" (*FW* 545.27 [morganatic bed]). A morganatic marriage is one in which the status of the male does not appertain to his wife or their issue; English law does not recognize this arrangement, the lack of which alternative was one of several factors that led to the abdication of Edward VIII (later the Duke of Windsor).

Mors aut honorabilis vita. The motto on Joyce's armorial engraving. I must confess surprise at not finding it in any of the works; he does quote it in a letter, however (*SL* 377).

Munster. "Azure, three antique crowns, or." In "Cyclops," the Citizen alludes to the arms of Munster as "the oldest flag afloat, the flag of the province of Desmond and Thomond, three crowns on a blue field, the three sons of Milesius" (*U* 12.1308–10 {328.10–12}). Hayes-McCoy traces the three crown device to the fourteenth century; it was borne by Robert de Vere circa 1386 when he was Lord of Ireland, and the three crowns "were borne as the arms of Ireland, in the funeral procession of Henry V in 1413" (Hayes-McCoy 20). The arms appear in *FW* in III.3, "the three crowns round your draphole (isn't it dram disgusting?)" (*FW* 521.7–8). See Illus. 4-E.

Napoleon. Napoleon bore an eagle as his heraldic emblem; nearly every eagle in the history of heraldry has its head turned to the dexter (excepting, of course, two-headed eagles such as those in the arms of the Holy Roman Empire, John Milton, and Joyce of Galway). Napoleon's eagle, however, faces sinister. In "Circe," Bloom appears "*with folded arms and Napoleonic forelock . . . with piercing eagle glance* (*U* 15.2721–22 {526.9–11}). See **eagle** for Napoleonic allusions in *FW*. Napoleon's famed three-cornered hat is also connected with heraldic emblems in *FW*, principally the Irish trefoil ("threefoiled hat" 10.8), and the three-feathered badge of the English heir apparent ("With its tricuspidal hauberkhelm coverchaf emblem on" [273.28–274.1]).

Newcastle. Like the arms of Dublin, Newcastle features three castles. See *FW* 18.6, 555.13.

Newman. See **Cor ad cor loquitur.**

Norfolk, Duke of. See **Earl Marshal, herald.**

Norroy King of Arms. As "Norreys," *FW* 311.35, 557.2. See **herald.**

Obedientia civium urbis felicitas. See **Dublin.**

ogress. See **roundel.**

O'Kirwan. The arms of the O'Kirwan sept (one of Galway's twelve tribes, like Joyce) are "Argent, a chevron sable between three Cornish choughs proper" (MacLysaght, Plate XVIII). Cf. reference at *FW* 352.33–34, to "the frustate fourstar Russkakruscam, Dom Allaf O'Khorwan, connundurumchuff." Taking the conundrum-chuff to be a reference to the chough, the "connundurumchuff" becomes a member of the "O'Kirwan" sept. A likely candidate would be Owen Kirwan, executed in 1803 with Robert Emmet (MacLysaght 203–4). See Illus. 5-F.

O'Molloy. The arms of the O'Molloy sept are featured in *Finnegans Wake*, but Dominic Manganiello's identification of a misleading article in the *Weekly Irish Times* as one of Joyce's sources suggests that the Molloy arms are being used as the arms of Finnegan. The Molloy arms are "Argent a lion rampant sable between three trefoils slipt gules" (MacLysaght, Plate XXI). Through creative genealogy, the *Weekly Irish Times* of 18 July 1936 (of which Joyce requested a back copy: *Letters* 3: 403) silently "granted" these arms to persons named Finnegan. Manganiello finds the arms at 599.6–7: "the liofant, when even thurst was athar vetals, mid trefoils slipped the sable rampant. . . ." I think there are hints of these arms on 223.19–22, where the "evangelion, sabre accusant" seems both the emblem of St. Matthew and a sable, heraldic lion, that, like the Finnegan lion, "would proffer to his delected one the his trifle [trefoil] from the grass." See Illus. 5-E.

O'Neill. The Citizen is connected with the O'Neill sept when he drinks and quotes "tribal slogan of *Lamh Dearg Abu*" (*U* 12.1211–12 {325.24})—"Up the red hand." See **red hand.**

or. The heraldic metal, gold. See **tinctures.**

ordinary. One of the geometric shapes conventionally used in the heraldic field, such as the **cross, saltire, fess, bend, pale, chief,** and so forth.

O'Reilly. HCE, a.k.a. Persse O'Reilly, bears numerous charges related to the O'Reilly sept. Dominic Manganiello (30–31) points out that HCE's murder by "the MacMahon chaps" is described in terms that link him with the O'Reilly sept: "On the fidd of Verdor the rampart combatants had left him lion with his dexter handcoup wresterected in a pureede paumee bloody proper" (99.29–31). Cf. blazon of O'Reilly sept arms: in Burke's (761) "Vert two lions ramp[ant] combatant or, supporting a dexter hand couped at the wrist erect and apaumée bloody proper"; see Illus. 5-C. The hand is cut off at the wrist, is standing palm outward (apaumée), is flesh-colored (proper), with drops of blood emanating from the wrist (indeed, as one might expect). Also, cf. "aslike as asnake comes sliduant down that oaktree onto the duke of beavers" (100.11–12) and the second and third quarters of the arms of O'Reilly of East Brefny: "Argent, on a mount an oak with a snake descending on the trunk proper" (Fox-Davies, *Armorial Families* 2: 1471; see Illus. 5-D). See also **Gough,** for further allusions to this latter charge in connection with the arms of London's Company of Fruiterers.

orle. One of the heraldic **ordinaries;** a hollowed escutcheon shape within the field (an escutcheon "voided"). Illus. 1-E.

pale. One of the heraldic **ordinaries;** a vertical band occupying the center one-third of the field. Illus. 1-E.

Papal arms. Harry Levin (65) pointed out that there is a hint of the arms of the papacy in the "Keyes" emblem that Bloom seeks to use in an ad for Alexander Keyes (*U* 7.141–58 {120}). See Helm: "The arms of the *Papacy* and *Vatican City* show the papal insignia [triple tiara and crossed keys] on a shield gules" (136). In "Circe," after having been crowned, Bloom receives "The keys of Dublin, crossed on a crimson cushion" (*U* 15.1520 {483.25–26}). The crimson matches the gules field of the papal arms. Bloom is also heralded by the "papal standard" (15.1410 {480.8}). A possible allusion is at *FW* 205.7–9: "Ellis on quay in scarlet thread linked for the world on a flush-caloured field" (the papal keys, on a red field, are linked by a cord). See also **Crivelli.**

party. Term to designate that a field is divided: a field "party per fess" is divided in halves by a horizontal line; "party per pale" is divided in halves vertically, and so forth. See *FW* 546.7: "partifesswise" is "party per fess."

peer. There are five ranks of peers in English aristocracy (making some peers more equal than others): listed in descending order, they are, Duke, Marquis, Earl (the equivalent of a continental count; his wife is a "Countess"), Viscount, and Baron. HCE is described as a peer by numerous clues; he is probably a "pee-er," from his Park activities. In the "Mime" of II.1, as HUMP, HCE has armorial bearings of a peer, complete with supporters: "cap-a-pipe with watch and topper, coat, crest and supporters" (220.26–27). Later, HCE proclaims his rank in the tavern: "confessedly in my baron gentilhomme to the manhor bourne" (365.4–5), a claim which is verified by his receiving a grant of supporters by the patrons leaving the pub: "whereas bigrented him a piers half subporters for his arms" (372.8–9). Clues in the first riddle (I.6) include that "hold as an earl, he counts" (128.5–6); Shaun is "dressed like an earl in just the correct wear" (404.16–17). Both are likely earls in right of Albert Edward, who, as Prince of Wales, was also Earl of Dublin. See **Burke.**

pelican. In heraldry, often represented as feeding its offspring on its own blood: the pelican is rendered either "in her piety" or "vulning herself." *U* 14.921 {409.24}. See Thornton 240.

pellet. See **roundel.**

pennon. Bloom's coronation procession is preceded by "pennons of the civic flag" (*U* 15.1411 {480.7–9}).

Per vias rectas. Deasy recalls that his ancestor, Sir John Blackwood, used the motto *Per vias rectas* (*U* 2.282 {31.32}). Thornton notes that this was the actual motto of Sir John Blackwood, Bt. (Thornton 36).

plate. See **roundel.**

pomme. See **roundel.**

Power. The label of Power's Irish Whiskey features "Gules, three swallows volant or." See *FW* 319.11. *Power's Irish: Blended Irish Whiskey.* Dublin: John Power & Son, n.d. (in the collection of the author).

proper. In the color of nature. The "Cornish chough proper" in the O'Kirwan arms is black with a red beak and feet; Adam and Eve in the arms of the Company of Fruiterers (London) are "proper" (flesh-colored), but not decent. The O'Reilly hand "bloody proper" in *FW* 99.31 is flesh-colored with red drops of blood, and so forth. See *U* 3.337 {46.13}; *FW* 99.31, 269.14, 270.17, 546.8, 604.5.

Prussia. A peculiar Prussian flag is on *FW* 8.11–12: "This is the flag of the Prooshious, the Cap and Soracer." The best I can do with this is the crown (cap?) and scepter (soracer?) borne by the two-headed eagle on the Prussian flag and arms. Prussian blue occurs at *FW* 305.14–15: "you were republicly royally toobally prussic blue in the shirt after." Garvin (137) connects this with the "Blue Shirts" headed by ex-Police Commissioner Eoin O'Duffy in 1933, and with the Nazi Blue Shirts; I don't know what type of crayons Joyce used in his MSS, but Prussian Blue was a color of a Crayola crayon for the first half of this century. Perhaps more relevant to *FW* is the rôle of the Prussian blue uniforms at Waterloo, where Napoleon miscalculated after mistaking the Prussian blue for that of his own men.

Pursuivant. See **Athlone, Bluemantle, herald.**

Rampant. The attitude of a lion (for instance) rearing on its hind legs, found in the second quarter of the royal arms (the Scottish lion), in the arms of the **O'Reilly** sept, and of **O'Molloy**). See *FW* 99.29, 599.7.

raven. McHugh notes that Danish pirates flew a flag with a raven as charge. According to G. A. Hayes-McCoy, the use of raven standards in Ireland dates from Norman invasions of Ireland, and circa 1913 a flag bearing "a black raven on a white field" was used by the Dublin County unit of the Irish volunteers. He adds that the arms of County Dublin now feature the raven on white. In *FW*, the subject of riddle No. 1 (I.6) "bears a raaven geulant on a fjeld duiv" (136.12–13); also see 480.1, "Her raven flag was out, the slaver."

rebus. A type of visual puzzle where an image stands for a word or name by homonymy (i.e., a picture of an eye to stand for the pronoun "I," and so forth), Perhaps the term derives from "*non verbis sed rebus*," as Brewer (26th ed., 740a) states, but the *OED* (2: 2435) questions this derivation. A verbalized rebus can be inferred from Athy's riddle to Stephen in *P*: "Why is the county Kildare like the leg of a fellow's breeches? . . . Because there is a thigh [Athy] in it" (*P* 25; this is a conundrum, as Patrick McCarthy points out [18]); a picture of a human thigh would be a rebus for "Athy." A famous rebus is that of Abbot Islip, in stained glass at Westminster Abbey: it pictures a man in a tree, holding a small branch (called a "slip"), and a human eye: eye-slip (*Boutell* 102). Heraldry is full of rebuses, in **canting arms.** For specific use of the term, see *U* 16.1234 {647.11}; and *FW* 523.20: the annalists demand of Yawn, "Perhaps you can explain, sagobean? The Mod needs a rebus." Yawn's lengthy piscatorial speech (523.21–525.5) is in reply to the query: Indeed, HCE's fish crest is a rebus of sorts for his salmon identity, and is an elaborate rebus/acronym for his divine identity ("Ichthus," Greek for "fish," but also an early Christian symbol for Christ, with the letters of the Greek word standing for "*I*esous *CH*ristos, *Th*eou *U*ios, *S*oter": Jesus Christ, God's Son, Savior)—certainly one of HCE's more ambitious identities.

Red hand. The cognizance of the O'Neill sept, and of the province of Ulster. The Citizen invokes the red hand as he drinks (see **O'Neill**), and, Robert M. Adams pointed out in this context, the red hand also graces the label of Allsop's ale (Adams 143). Before the Festy King trial, HCE appears on the Butt Bridge, "his alpenstuck in his redhand" (85.11–12); this is in token not only of his guilt (as in "caught redhanded"), but of Ulster and O'Neill. Cf. reference in the "*Book of Kells*" part of I.5: "wrasted redhandedly from our hallowed rubric prayer. . . ." (122.7–8).

regardant. The attitude of a lion whose head is turned back over its shoulder. *U* 3.503 {51.4}: "He turned his face over a shoulder, rere regardant."

Richard II. One of Richard II's badges seems to appear at *FW* 500.12–13: "The cry of the roedeer it is! The white hind! Their slots, linklink, the hound hunthorning! Send us and peace! Title! Title!" "The white hind" suggests the badge of Richard II, the king from whom the House of Lancaster seized power: "a white hart lodged, ducally gorged and chained or" (*Boutell* 210). Richard was the son of **Edward, the Black Prince.**

Robinson. The passage "The cubs are after me, it zeebs, the whole totem pack, vuk vuk and vuk vuk to them, for Robinson's shield" (*FW* 480.30–32), would seem to refer to a coat of arms. Of the fifty or so arms recorded in *Burke's* for families named Robinson, all feature stags trippant but one: the arms for Robinson, Provost of Banff, 1785, feature "Gu[les] on a chev[ron] engr[ailed] betw[een] three wolves' heads erased ar[gent] a cinquefoil az[ure]" (863a). This is the only "Robinson's shield" I find pertaining to the wolf pack references surrounding this allusion.

roundel. Any one of several round charges, the precise name of which depends on the charge's tincture. Roundel or = bezant, roundel argent = plate, roundel gules = torteau, roundel azure = hurt, roundel vert = pomme, roundel purpur = golpe, roundel sable = pellet, ogress, or gunstone.

Royal arms. See **Garter, Order of; Wales, Prince of; Horse of Hanover.** Illus. 4-D, 5-H.

S.P.Q.R. Featured on the arms of the City of Rome, these letters stand for "*S*enatus *P*opules*q*ue *R*omanus": the Senate and People of Rome. After Stephen is pandied, one of his companions declares, "—The Senate and the Roman people declared that Dedalus had been wrongly punished"

(*P* 53). In *FW*, the initials appear in such references as "Go in for scribenery with the satiety of arthurs in S.P.Q.R.ish" (*FW* 229.07); see also 455.28 "to begin properly SPQueaRking"; 484.22–23: "The W.X.Y.Z. and P.Q.R.S. of legatine powers." Hart (*Structure and Motif* 242) also cites 454.35. Brewer's *Dictionary* (the 1981 edition, but not the 26th ed.) also notes the interpretation of the motto as "small profits and quick returns."

S.S. Collar. One of Henry IV's emblems was a collar bearing the letters "SS"; he modified a Lancastrian Collar consisting of a series of S's to the so-called "collar of SS" by alternating the SS with portcullises. According to *Boutell* (192) the collar serves "as insignia of the Heralds, the Lord Chief Justice, and the Lord Mayor of London." See allusion to "his loose Eating S.S. collar" *FW* 292.29.

sable. The heraldic tincture, black. See *GJ* 16; *U* 3.281 {44.28}; 12.215 {297.39}; 15.4636 {597.12}; *FW* 223.19 ("evangelion, sabre accusant"); 546.6 ("vested sable"); 599.7 ("the sable rampant").

Saint Andrew Cross. Azure, a saltire argent. Bloom appears dressed in "shepherd's plaid Saint Andrew's cross scarftie" (*U* 15.537 {448.14}). Illus. 4-F.

Saint George Cross. Argent, a cross gules. The emblem of Spenser's Redcrosse, of Malory's Galahad, and according to some medieval and Renaissance writers, of Jesus Christ. It is one of the component crosses of the **Union Jack.** See "knights of the red cross" (*U* 15.4681–82 {599.1}). Illus. 4-F.

Saint Patrick Cross. Argent, a saltire gules. A cross of obscure origin; it has been suggested (cynically, and probably correctly) that when a cross was needed to complement those of Sts. George and Andrew in the **Union Jack,** St. Patrick's Cross came into being on the spot. Hayes-McCoy gives this subject its most comprehensive treatment to date (36–41), and suggests that the device was simply appropriated from the arms of Fitzgerald, which are identical to the blazon above. Its dubious origins notwithstanding, the red saltire was used on the flag of the Irish Volunteers from Down in 1916 (Hayes-McCoy 200). In *FW*, one of the two combatants in the altercation in the Park (whether HCE, Shem or Shaun, Buckley or the Russian General) takes on the appearance of the St. Patrick Cross when, having given "the Paddybanners the military salute" (84.13–14), appears with "the white ground of his face all covered with diagonally redcrossed nonfatal mammalian blood" (84.19–20). See also 228.5: "Cross of a coppersmith bishop!"; and Shem's "coat macfarlane (the kerssest cut, you understand?)" (180.10–11;

the MacFarlane clan arms features a red saltire between four roses on a white field). Illus. 4-F.

saltire. One of the heraldic **ordinaries,** consisting of a diagonal cross (X). In *Ulysses,* the crossed keys in the Keyes layout are heraldically "in saltire" (*U* 7.146–58 {120}). The "terce of lanciers" in HCE's arms have "their arms crossed in saltire" (*FW* 546.8–10). See also 567.34: "those puny farting little solitires" (soldiers and saltires). See also **Saint Andrew Cross, Saint Patrick Cross.** Illus. 1-E.

Seal. Properly the study of "sigillography" rather than heraldry, seals do come into heraldic study because most seals feature heraldic emblems, and because of the significance of a seal as a sign of authority. In *U,* Stephen transforms the blot on Sargent's paper into a signet: "Cyril Sargent: his name and seal" (*U* 2.130 {27.23–24}). The inquiry into HCE's history and genealogy in I.2 avails itself of sigillographic information: "The great fact emerges that after that historic date all holographs so far exhumed initialled by Haromphrey bear the sigla H.C.E." (*FW* 32.12–14). "Sigillum" (root of "siglum") is Latin for seal. See also the seal as an instrument of truth and foreplay: "but for my sealring is none to hand I swear, she is highly catatheristic and there is another which I have fombly fongered freequuntly and, when my signet is on sign again I swear, she is deeply sangnificant" (357.12–15), and HCE's use of a royal seal: "Wherfor I will and firmly command . . . upon my royal word and cause the great seal now to be affixed. . . ." (545.14–16). Finally, Hart suggests, that "Lps." (628.15) is, among other things, "Lord Privy Seal" (*Structure and Motif,* 205).

Semper paratus. The motto Bloom envisions on his heraldic achievement in "Ithaca" (*U* 17.1611 {715.32}). The motto is not distinctive, and is attributed to eighteen families in Burke's: Armitage, Armytage, Clifford, Constable, Elphinstoned, Fuller, Johnstone, Knowles, Lecky, Macreadie, Mounsey, Phillpotts, Postlethwaite, Purchas, Royds, Stuart, Upton, Usticke.

sept. Septs are the family groups of Ireland, sometimes compared with Scottish clans. Edward MacLysaght, former Chief Herald of Ireland, states that the Irish family groups were never as highly developed as their Scottish counterparts; he says

> The term 'sept' has never, as far as I know, been given an authoritative technical definition. It can perhaps best be explained by saying that it is a collective term describing a group of persons who, or whose immediate and known ancestors, bore a common surname and inhabited the same locality. (10–11)

The ancient families of Ireland—Joyce, O'Neill, O'Regan, O'Molloy, and so forth—may be spoken of as septs. Shem is said to be "the first of his sept" (*FW* 173.24); Shaun makes a note of "URGES AND WIDERURGES IN A PRIMITIVE SEPT" (267.R1), and Archdruid "Balkelly" sports a "septicoloured" mantle (611.6): both a coat of seven colors, and of the colors of a sept.

Shakespeare. "Or, on a bend sable a spear of the first, steeled argent" (Illus. 3-A). Joyce alludes to Shakespeare's arms (obliquely) in *GJ* 16; explicitly in "Scylla and Charybdis" (*U* 9.925 {210.3}), and, according to Vincent John Cheng (196), in HCE's arms (*FW* 546.5–11).

shamrock. See trefoil.

sigillography. The study of seals. See **seal.**

sinister. The left of the shield *as borne;* hence the right side *as viewed.* See also **dexter** for Joyce's use of this confusion in *FW*. *FW* 197.1, 384.26, 546.8.

sinople. Archaic (a relative concept in heraldic blazon) term for the color green. *FW* 546.10.

slipped. Of an heraldic flower, "slipped" means there is a visible stem. "Trefoils" are almost invariably "slipped," and Fox-Davies (*CG* 267) states that even where "slipped" is not specified in the blazon, trefoils are nevertheless thus depicted. See *FW* 599.7: "mid trefoils slipped."

Solomon, Seal of. Two overlapping triangles forming a six-pointed star; also the Star of David. See *U* 10.845 {242.36}. In *FW*, Dolph sees it in the geometry problem: "And if you flung her headdress on her from under her highlows you'd wheeze whyse Salmonson set his seel on a hexengown" (*FW* 297.1–4).

supporters. Figures of persons or beasts on either side of an heraldic shield, in the posture of supporting it. Perhaps the most famous are England's **lion** and **unicorn.** Supporters are common in corporate arms (cities, counties, etc.), but in personal arms, hereditary supporters are not granted to armigers below the rank of peer. HCE has supporters in *FW* 220.27, and 372.8–9. See also **Dublin,** for discussion of Dublin supporters in *FW*.

surcoat. The "coat" part of a coat of arms. Fox-Davies explains that the surcoat was a loose-fitting coat worn over mail, which "afforded another opportunity of decoration, and it had been decorated with the same signs that the wearer had painted on his shield, hence the term 'coat of arms' "; (*CG* 18). See *FW* 24.29, 52.25, 343.13, 559.9. See also **tabard.**

tabard. Surcoat worn by the officers of arms. *U* 12.1598 {336.28}; 15.1413 {480.11}; *FW* 99.12.

tartans. Not strictly heraldic, but as hereditary colors emblematic of allegiance, tartans are of interest to this study. Glugg's tantrum (*FW* 227.29–228.2) seems not only to pit him against the seven sacraments, but also against Scottish clans identified by their Tartans: he begins by diving "his head into Wat Murrey, gave Stewart Ryall a puck on the plexus . . . tel a Tartaran tastarin toothsome tarrascone tourtoun. . . ." The Murray and Stewart tartans would seem to be an allusion by Joyce to his own wardrobe: see *Letters* 3: 204–6 (To Mrs. Herbert Gorman, 22 October 1930; To Herbert Gorman, 30 October 1930).

tenney, or **tenné.** One of the so-called heraldic stains, tenney is the heraldic equivalent of orange. Heraldic purists (of the Oswald Barron school) sometimes use "gules" to cover orange. According to Campbell and Evans (20), tenné is part of the Irish republican tricolor: "It is sometimes spoken of as 'green, white, and gold,' but the gold is *not* yellow: it is a warm orange-gold, described by the heralds as *tenné*." It occurs in *U* 3.337 {46.13}; see also Bloom's "tawny red brogues" 15.538 {448.15}. In *FW*, Joyce connects tenné with William's orange in *FW* 361.24: "A lurk of orangetawneymen!"

Thistle, Order of. Chivalric order, the insignia of which represents St. Andrew and the St. Andrew's Cross. Edward VII wears the insignia of the Order in "Circe" (*U* 15.4451 {590.17}).

tincture. The general term for colors, metals, and stains used in heraldry. The five colors (azure, vert, sable, gules, and purpur) are distinct from the two metals (or and argent) but both classes of hues may be called "tinctures," as can the stains (tenné, murrey, sanguine, etc.).

torse. A wreath of twisted silk by which the crest is connected to the helm in an heraldic achievement.

torteau. See **roundel.**

trefoil. A three-leaved plant, typically a shamrock or clover, in heraldic blazon. See *FW* 10.8, 599.7 and 467.10–11: "And, whoa! do you twig the schamlooking leaf greeping ghastly down his blousyfrock? Our national umbloom! Areesh!".

trippant. The term used to describe a walking deer or dog. *U* 3.337 {46.13}.

Tweedy. The maiden name of Molly Bloom. According to Fox-Davies (*Armorial Families* 2: 1976–77), the crest of various individuals surnamed "Tweedy" is the lapwing, called here a "peewit rising proper" (found as crest of Arthur Hearne Tweedy, George Alfred Tweedy, and

Hugh James Tweedy). In his *Complete Guide to Heraldry*, however, Fox-Davies remarks "*The Lapwing*, under its alternate names of *Peewhit*, *Plover*, and *Tyrwhitt*, will be found in the arms of Downes, Tyrwhitt, and Tweedy" (*CG* 249). The lapwing is one of the birds with which Stephen Dedalus associates himself in *U* 9.952–54 {210.35–38}.

Ulster. The arms of Ulster feature a red hand, couped at the wrist, appaumée. In III.3, Matt Tarpey is addressed "Gently, gently Northern Ire! Love that red hand!" (*FW* 522.4). See also **red hand.**

Ulster King of Arms. The chief heraldic officer of the old Irish Office of Arms. See **herald.** *U* 15.1413 {480.12}; 15.3949 {572.17}; *FW* 498.11.

unattired. See **attired.**

unguled. Used in heraldry to blazon the colors of an animal's hooves where they differ from the principal tincture of the beast; the most famous example of the above reference is the sinister supporter of the Royal Arms: "a unicorn argent, armed [horned], unguled [hooved] and crined [maned] or [gold]" (*Boutell* 214). The Mookse and Gripes hurl these heraldic epithets at one another:

> "—Unuchorn!
> —Ungulant!"
>
> (*FW* 157.3–4).

unicorn. Mythical beast, resembling a horse, with a lion's tail and a single horn. In royal heraldry, the unicorn is the sinister supporter of the royal arms. See blazon under **unguled.** See *U* 15.4481 {591.21}; *FW* 157.3; also, 462.20, where Shaun observes that Dave (Shem) "would be the unicorn of his kind." If the brothers were heraldic supporters, it would be consistent for Shem to be the sinister.

Union Jack. Flag of Great Britain, incorporating the crosses of **Saint George, Saint Andrew,** and **Saint Patrick.** Worn by Tennyson in "Circe" (*U* 15.4396 {588.12–13}). In *FW*, the Mookse says to the Gripes, "Unionjok and be joined to yok! Parysis, *tu sais*, crucycrooks, belongs to him who parises himself" (*FW* 155.16–17). "Crucycrooks," an echo of Martin Cunningham's dog-Latin rendering of a bogus motto attributed to Pius IX ("*Crux upon Crux*" ["Grace," *D* 167]), is an apt description of the superimposed crosses of the Union Jack. Illus. 4-F.

Urban III. See **Crivelli.**

vair. An heraldic fur. Illus. 1-D.

vert. The heraldic color, green. See also **sinople.** *FW* 5.6; 34.25; 99.29; 270.16; 604.5.

vested. The heraldic term used to indicate the tincture of a charge's clothing: e.g., "a woman, vested purpur." The "two young frish" in HCE's crest are "vested sable" (546.6); the supporters of the arms of Dublin are "vested gules" (Fox-Davies, *Public Arms* [1915] 246).

vexillology. The study of flags, from Latin: *vexillum* = flag.

volant. In the attitude of flight; of a bird, or in some rare cases (including *FW* 24.5), a dragon. See *U* 15.1915 {0}; 15.3949 {572.17}; 15.4507 {592.19–20}; *FW* 339.29.

Wales, Prince of. The Prince of Wales is an excellent candidate for the *Census;* Glasheen identifies several kings who, in the natural course of things, were Princes of Wales; and she also identifies the **Black Prince** (Glasheen 32), who held no higher rank. But the position of the Prince of Wales, somewhat independent of the individuals who historically have held it, is conspicuous in *FW.* Shem, Shaun, or both, seem to be the Prince, since they bear versions of his badge, called by some the "Prince of Wales' crest" or the "Prince of Wales' feathers." Strictly speaking, the three ostrich feathers enfiled by a coronet are not the crest of the Prince of Wales, but rather his badge of office; nor is the badge that of the office of Prince of Wales *per se,* but rather is the badge of office of the Heir Apparent—who is customarily created the Prince of Wales. For the emblem's origin, see **Edward, the Black Prince.** The badge (which, for Joyce's purposes, is a crest) appears to be Shem's emblem at various points: he sports "trinity plumes on the right handle side" (180.9–10); amidst the debris in Shem's house "O'Shame" are "borrowed plumes" (183.32); cf. "the heron's plumes sinistrant" (233.16). Later, he appears as Dave the Dancekerl "showing the three white feathers" (463.3–4); on the previous page he had borne another Welsh symbol, "the garlic leek" (462.29–30): see **leek.** Whichever of the two brothers responds through Yawn in the passage blazoning Yawn's arms claims the emblem: "my High tripenniferry cresta and caudal mottams: Itch dean" (485.2–3). The skeptical questioners hear the motto as a fish: "Ichthyan!" (485.10).

The motto of the Prince of Wales, "Ich dien," also appears in HCE's word, "selvischdischdienence" (*FW* 357.25). HCE connects himself with an Albert Edward (as Edward VII was known as Prince of Wales) motif begun in *Ulysses* ("peace, perfect peace": see Thornton 421; Roby 112–13), and at the same time with Christ: both Christ and the Prince of Wales are Princes of Peace, for the purposes of the speech in which HCE equates himself with both, via references to "the prince of peace"

(549.7) and "peace, perfect peace" (549.12). See also **Edward, the Black Prince.** Illus. 1-H; Illus. 5-G.

Wappen. The German word used for coats of arms. See *FW* 339.10: Butt's Crimean war allusions contain the phrase, "With his cannonball wappents." Later, HCE asserts his prerogative to raise the "imperial standard by weaponright" (*FW* 539.19–20; weaponright implies "Wappen right": the right to arms, in both senses). See also "wappon," 566.22.

wavy. A type of line of partition in heraldic fields. *FW* 475.25.

York. The badge of York (A white rose en soleil) occurs frequently in Joyce's work. See *P* 12; *U* 3.315 {45.27}. In *FW*, the rose is especially prominent in the recapitulation of HCE's case between pp. 94 and 96: at 94.35–36 he is "behind the war of the two roses," and page 96.1: "The rose is white in the darik!"

NOTES

Chapter One

1. It is a bit of a mystery precisely why Irish heraldic authority continued to derive from the British sovereign for 20 years after the establishment of the Free State. In *Heralds of England,* Sir Anthony Wagner writes:

> from 1922 till his death in 1940 the Irish Government permitted Sir Neville Wilkinson, as Ulster King of Arms, a servant of the British Crown, to continue, personally or by deputy, to discharge his office in Dublin, occupying quarters in Dublin Castle, for which the British Treasury paid rent to the Free State. . . . (551)

In a letter to me (1984), Mr. Eilís Ní Dhuibhne, Assistant Keeper, Dublin Castle, said "There is no available [written] source on the recent history of this office. Oral sources suggest that the cause of the continued link with the College of Arms until 1943 was, quite simply, apathy on both sides."

2. While several writers have noticed the heralds in the individual works, I haven't seen it remarked that they appear in all three major works. See Ellmann (*JJ* 11), who remarks on Ulster King in *P* and *U;* also, Shari and Bernard Benstock identify the Irish heraldic officers in *U* (Benstock, *Who's He* . . . 50, 61). Gifford and Seidman (387) gloss the *U* reference to Ulster King and the Pursuivant; Ulster King was not, however, as Gifford and Seidman say, an officer of the College of Arms: unlike the Kings of Arms in the College, whose authority is through the Earl Marshal, Ulster King's authority came directly of the Crown. Finally, Roland McHugh (*Sigla* 24; *Annotations* 498) identifies Irish heralds at the *Wake.*

3. A symbol which, in the final passage of *The Scarlet Letter,* is actually described in the language of heraldic blazon: "ON A FIELD, SABLE, THE LETTER A, GULES."

4. Mr. Thomas Woodcock, Somerset Herald (College of Arms) has kindly provided me the details on this change to the arms of the Prince of Wales (letter to the author, 21 January 1985), in which the arms of the Principality of Wales replaced the arms of "the August House of Saxony" (the latter are shown in Illus. 1-H). College of Arms MS I.76, pp. 97–8, records the order of George V to change the arms of the Prince of Wales in this fashion (4 March 1911).

5. Fox-Davies, however, makes an entertaining (if not altogether convincing) case for the existence of white as a separate heraldic tincture; see *CG* 70–71.

6. Unless one's imagination permits one to see the "saltire" on p. 308 of *Finnegans Wake,* or the lozenge in the geometry problem on p. 293. Certainly Kevin/Shaun's imagination is capable of the latter, since he proclaims "it will be a lozenge to me all my lauffe" (*FW* 299.28–29).

Chapter Two

1. Prose translation:

After studying their faces, [I realized that] I didn't know any of them, but I noticed that from the neck of each hung a pouch containing a particular sign and color. . . . On a yellow purse, I saw, in azure, the face and figure of a lion. Then, proceeding with my study, I saw another bag, blood red, displaying a goose, whiter than butter. One of the men, whose little white sack bore as a sign a big azure sow, said to me, "What are you doing in this pit?" (Translation by Catherine L. O'Shea)

2. Sir Richard Le Scrope and Sir Robert Grosvenor, both claimed the right to the same coat of arms (*Azure, a bend or [Boutell* 106]). The transcript of Chaucer's deposition (*Chaucer Life Records* 370–74) indicates that the poset testified that during his military service, he had been familiar with Le Scrope's armorial bearings.

3. Malory never describes Lancelot's arms, given in numerous medieval French sources as "argent, three bends gules." See Brault 47.

4. Brault points out the use of a similar device by Chrétien de Troyes in *Cliges*, in which the hero, "wishing to remain incognito at the Tournament of Osnefort (Oxford), enters the lists on three successive days bearing first plain black, then plain green, and finally plain red arms, defeating in turn Sagremor, Lancelot, and Perceval" (30).

5. "Who comes through Michan's land, bedight in sable armour? O'Bloom, the son of Rory: it is he" (*U* 12.215–16 {297.39–40}).

6. Brault (23) traces the Arthurian crest of a dragon (used both in Malory and Tennyson) to Geoffrey of Monmouth, and considers it a possible (but unlikely) "canting" device (an heraldic rebus punning on the bearer's name; a rarity in twelfth-century blazon) playing on Arthur's patronymic, "Pendragon"; but Brault further notes that the dragon was also the traditional symbol of the Saxons.

7. Milton's angels can boast armorial bearings: in Book I, there are "Cherub and seraph rolling in the flood/ With scattered arms and ensigns. . . ." (*Paradise Lost*, 1: 325); and later, Satan's minions bear "Th' imperial ensign. . . ./ With wind and golden luster rich emblazed, / Seraphic arms and trophies . . ." (536–39). Milton's own coat of arms is of (coincidental) interest to this study because of its resemblance to the arms of Joyce of County Galway (discussed in Chapter 3): "Ar[gent] an eagle dis[layed] with two heads gules beaked and legged sa[ble]" (Burke's 689). For a discussion of Tennyson's use of heraldry, see O'Shea, 1983.

8. Scott-Giles remarks that posterity is fortunate that Shakespeare's arms exemplify the elegant simplicity of an earlier age, since such restrained design had become a virtual anachronism by Elizabethan times (Scott-Giles 33).

9. Cited by Angus Wilson in *The World of Charles Dickens*, 290.

Chapter Three

1. Sonnet 135: "Whoever hath her wish, thou hast thy *Will*, / And *Will* to boot, and *Will* in overplus." Shakespeare's identity also intrudes upon Sonnet 136 ("If thy soul check thee that I come so near, / Swear to thy blind soul that I was thy *Will*") and Sonnet 143 ("So will I pray that thou mayst have thy *Will*"). Stephen is not the only poet in *Ulysses* to be interested in this type of literary device, as Leopold Bloom's acrostic poem demonstrates:

> ***P**oets oft have sung in rhyme*
> ***O**f music sweet their praise divine.*

Let them hymn it nine times nine.
Dearer far than song or wine,
You are mine. The world is mine.
(*U* 17.412–16 {678.21–25}

2. Other canting arms are those recorded for Oliver St. John Gogarty, of Buck Mulligan fame: the escutcheon features "an olive branch fructed proper [bearing leaves and fruit (olives) of natural color]" (Fox-Davies, *Armorial Families* 1: 773): the olive branch puns on Oliver, the armiger's first name.

3. Anthony Burgess makes the pun explicit in his pseudobiographical novel on Shakespeare, *Nothing Like the Sun*, where he has John Shakespeare describe the arms as "A falcon shaking a spear and a silver spear on what they call a bend" (174). I assume that mistaking the gold spear "steeled [tipped] argent" for "a silver spear" is the error of the fictionalized John Shakespeare, and not of the author of *Nothing Like the Sun*.

4. An earlier echo of John of Gaunt's nominal puns is found in "The Dead," where Mr. Browne remarks, "Well, I hope, Miss Morkan, . . . that I'm brown enough for you because, you know, I'm all brown" (*D* 200).

5. Contrary to Tristram's apparent assumption, a bend sinister is not invariably a sign of bastardy, so Tristram's heraldic squeamishness reveals a "popular" understanding of the heraldic ordinaries. Nevertheless, because the popular association of bends sinister had become so pervasive, the ordinary is seldom used, so Tristram's discomfiture would not be out of place in an heraldically literate observer—particularly since the charge was indeed supposed to be a bend dexter (conventionally called a "bend," since bends, bendlets, and partitions per bend are assumed to be dexter unless specifially blazoned otherwise).

6. Taking to heart Lodwick Hartley's warnings against fabricating instances of Sternean influence on Joyce (" 'Swiftly-Sterneward' . . ." 37–47, *passim*), I continue to resist pressing the point of "influence," even in light of the similarity of the personal heraldic gestures in *Sentimental Journey* and *Ulysses*. Even though the former novel is often cited as the occasion of some parody in the "Oxen" chapter, Hartley convincingly argues that "the performance is so insensitive and ineffective as to make one wonder whether a parody of Sterne is actually intended" (41). Yet the temptation to see the Dedalus appropriation of the Joyce arms as an echo of Yorick's use of those of Sterne is far from diminished by Hartley's observation in the same essay that:

> [Joyce's] spelling of Sterne's name as *Starn* on page 303 [*FW* 303.6] might suggest that Joyce was remembering the famous starling of *A Sentimental Journey*, together with the fact (as Sterne himself humorously points out) that a starling was mounted on the Sterne family crest. (43)

Tempting as this suggestion of influence may be, however, the safest course would seem to be to conclude inconclusively, with Hartley, "Is Joyce *necessarily* referring to the starling and thus making a specific allusion to *A Sentimental Journey?* Who can say?"

7. According to Scott-Giles, 27, the 1599 grant is a draft of an "assignment of arms for Arden [the maiden name of Shakespeare's mother], to be impaled with those of John Shakespeare and quartered by his descendants. . . ."; the Shakespeare arms themselves were actually granted in 1596, not 1599 as Joyce's note suggests. Although Scott-Giles suspects that William Shakespeare may well have been entitled to quarter the arms of Arden with those of Shakespeare, there is no evidence that he did so: his tomb bears the Shakespeare arms only. For another Joyce's perspective on John Shakespeare's arms, and his son's role in obtaining the grant, see Stanislaus Joyce, *MBK* 237.

8. In a letter to the author (May 1984) Eilís Ní Dhuibhne, Assistant Keeper, Dublin Castle, indicates that during Joyce's lifetime, the English disposition on the use of arms

would have governed the question of entitlement to display the arms of the Joyce sept. While the Irish Genealogical Office now holds that any member of a sept may *display* the arms of that sept (as distinct from personally "bearing" the arms, as on stationery, silver, or other such use; only the grantee and his descendants may "bear" the arms), this distinction was not recognized until the first Chief Herald, Edward MacLysaght, established it after 1943. Thus Mr. Dhuibhne writes

> . . . it is probably safe to assume that Joyce and his father conformed to a common Irish habit of displaying their sept arms. . . . If they were at all akin in outlook to present day Irishmen, the question of "authority to use a coat of arms," would simply never have occurred to them.

While Joyce apparently knew about the question of heraldic authority (as is clear from Stephen's discussion of Shakespeare's arms), I agree with the tendency of Mr. Dhuibhne's suggestion: would Joyce have cared about such authority? Probably not.

9. I am indebted to Mr. Patrick J. Smyth of Dublin for obtaining this information from the Irish Genealogical Office; and to Dr. Robert Bertholf, Curator of the Poetry/Rare Books Collection at SUNY-Buffalo, for providing me with the particulars and a facsimile of the armorial drawing that Joyce owned.

10. Burke's *Landed Gentry of Ireland* (1899) seems to give the double eagle (unless an eagle could have two necks without having two heads) for Joyce of Corgary and Mervue: "Arg., an eagle displayed with two necks, over all a fess erm." (226)

11. See also description from the La Hune catalogue (1949) in Slocum and Cahoon, 132–33.

12. As Nathan Halper pointed out, the hawk emblem derives not directly from the Dedalus myth, but from the transformation of Dedalion into a hawk in Book XI of Ovid's *Metamorphoses* (Halper, "Note on 'The Hawklike Man' " 312).

13. See Buffalo Notebook VIII.A.5, (Herring, *Joyce's Notes* 21): the note "Circe—the hawk" is followed by a chart of correspondences between Egyptian gods and birds. See also Herring, *U Notesheets* 303: the notes designated "Circe 7" contain the reference "Ra (Phra) sparrowhawk"; also "Circe 11" (Herring, 1972, 325) contains "Circe=hawk=fate."

14. Kenner describes this eagle plaque in a program written for National Public Radio, entitled "James Joyce: A Portrait in Sound" (Kenner, 1980).

15. Stephen's seeming conflation of eagles and falcons would seem warranted by their treatment in heraldry and iconography: heraldic eagles and hawks are far more difficult to distinguish than their natural counterparts: *Boutell's Heraldry* notes, "The *Falcon* and HAWK are in heraldry indistinguishable, and closely resemble the eagle. . . ." (77)

Chapter Four

1. I am indebted to Patrick A. McCarthy for his assistance with this discussion, and particularly for his allowing me to read the typescript of his essay, "*Ulysses* and the Printed Page."

2. However, among the Trieste books was Brunetto Latini's *Il libro delle bestie* (Ellmann, *Consciousness of J* 116); this bestiary gives the legends underlying such heraldic beasts as the phoenix, the basilisk, the cockatrice, the pelican, and so forth. Stephen acknowledges his source for his basilisk when he thinks, "Messer Brunetto, I thank thee for the word" (*U* 9.374–75 {194.22}). See Thornton 176.

3. The "Legs of Man" are the arms of Man, and vice versa. They are "Gules, three legs armed [meaning colored, as if things weren't confusing enough] proper conjoined at the fess point at the upper part of the thighs, flexed in a triangle, garnished and spurred

or" (*Boutell* 62). A. Walton Litz discusses this motif (26). Joyce's reference is found in the notes labelled by Herring "Circe 7" (Herring, *U Notesheets* 303). The arms of Gibraltar are the apparent reference of "arms . . . castle & key": these arms are "Gules, a triple-towered castle on a rock argent, the port opened, and pendent therefrom by a chain, a key with ward downwards or" (Rothery 107). Joyce's note appears on the "Penelope 6" Notesheet (Herring, *U Notesheets* 511).

4. The only term used in "Proteus" that gives me pause is "rere regardant," Stephen's attitude as he leaves the Strand. None of the English sources to which I have referred uses the expression "rere regardant" (they simply use "regardant" to describe the lion looking back over its shoulder) except Barron (325a). But Barron is citing old French usage; the term is certainly not original with him, since he cites it to deride its use.

5. This curious description of a pelican derives from the myth that the female pelican would wound herself with her own beak, feeding her young on her own blood. For this reason the pelican became a symbol of Christ in Christian iconography (see Ferguson 23). The phrase "pelican in her piety" is the conventional phrase used in blazon where the pelican is shown "vulning herself." See Brewer's *Dictionary*, 26th edition, p. 668. *Boutell* gives this description as well. Joyce also would have found the legend (but not the conventional heraldic phrase) in Latini's *Il Libro delle bestie*, which was in his Trieste library (Ellmann, *Consciousness of J* 116). There is also an allusion to the legend in *Hamlet:* Laertes says "To his good friends thus wide I'll ope my arms / And like the kind life-rend'ring pelican / Repast them with my blood" (4: 5, 145–47). To make the phrase apply to Bloom, Joyce changes the conventional gender of the pelican, but the usual form ("pelican in her piety") is found in the British Museum Notesheets, along with the conventional heraldic description of a male peacock: "peacock in his pride" (Herring, *U Notesheets* 179).

6. Mahaffey (416, n.18) compares this reference to Stephen's silent comment to himself in "Scylla and Charybdis": he looks at his hat and his ashplant, and thinks, "My casque and sword" (*U* 9.296 {192.16}).

7. For an explanation of the origin of the Greek colors, arms, and the Kings of Hellenes, see Maclagan and Louda, 281–85.

8. Herbert Gorman notes that Mrs. Conway, who lived with the Joyces, and became *Portrait's* Dante, and *Ulysses'* Mrs. Riordan, kept "her green and maroon brushes named for Charles Stewart Parnell and Michael Davitt . . ." (21).

9. An interesting element of the two opposing colors in Stephen's imagination is that, in addition to their historical connotations, red and green are "complementary opposites" in color theory. Basically this means that together, green and red light would produce a white light; it also means that each of the two colors appears at its brightest intensity against a background of the other. I am grateful to Dr. John S. Crawford for calling this aspect of the red-green opposition to my attention.

10. Ellmann notes:

> Once [Joyce] said to Daniel Hummel, another friend, "Human beings sometimes appear to me to take the shape of animals." [Hummel asked] . . . "And do you have an animal in mind for yourself?" "Yes," Joyce replied, "a deer." (*JJ* 328)

11. Thornton (59) connects Stephen's image as an allusion to the myth of Acteon, who was transformed into a deer by Diana and set upon by his own dogs.

12. This is the *crest* as distinct from the arms: Azure, a harp or, stringed argent. The crest would be featured on top of the arms. Brault notes an intriguing parallel to this device in Arthurian literature:

> While Ider's shield in Chrétien's *Charrete* would appear to be a reference, then, to the White Stag episode in the same author's *Erec*, the peculiar attitude of the stag issuing from a gate is strangely identical with the arms associated with Ireland since the end of the thirteenth century. (28)

13. Racing colors emerge again in connection with Deasy, who appears clad in the modern colors of the Republic of Ireland (if one takes honey to stand for the white) in "Circe": he appears riding a horse, wearing "honey cap, green jacket, orange sleeves" (15.3981 {573.19}). In Buffalo Notebook V.A.19, p. 31r (Herring, *Joyce's Notes . . .* 244), he had sported "king's colours," riding a horse "caparisoned with the Union Jack" and wears "honey cap, red jacket, orange sleeves."

14. This title is one of two (the other being Duke of Saxony) conspicuously absent from the modern litany of title appertaining to the Prince of Wales. Thornton (288) notes that the title originated with Albert Edward, who was made Earl of Dublin by Queen Victoria in 1849.

15. The harp continues to form part of the royal heraldic achievement, in which it constitutes the third quarter. Contrary to Gifford and Seidman's note (290), Henry VIII did not quarter the harp in the royal arms: this use of the harp dates from the accession of James I (see Hasler 11; *Boutell* 213; Gough and Parker 340). Nevertheless, the Citizen is quite correct in associating the harp with Henry VIII. C. A. Hayes-McCoy wrote, "The harp appears first as an Irish emblem prominently displayed in Henry VIII's time" (22). Hayes-McCoy goes on to say that Henry substituted the harp:

> for the three crowns. . . . A facile explanation . . . is that Henry feared, after he had begun his reformation of the church, that the three crowns might be mistaken for the papal tiara and so abandoned them.

16. Note that this flag is more elaborate than that in the intermediate draft in Buffalo Notebook V.A.6 (Herring, *Joyce's Notes . . .* 184). Here the Citizen looks forward to "the first Irish battleship . . . breasting the waves with the green flag at her helm." See also British Museum Notesheets (Herring, *U Notesheets* 97), "Cyclops 4": "Prophecy: when 1st Irish gunboat is seen breasting the waves with the green flag at her helm."

17. In an essay in *Smithsonian*, Michael Olmert explains the legendary origin of the mysterious red hand of the O'Neills:

> Once upon a time, a few Celtic warlords were roving over the wide Atlantic. . . . When they spied a green headland, it occurred to them to race for the beach—the first one to touch land, it was understood, would acquire the whole place for himself and his descendants. But as one slower boat slipped slightly but inexorably behind in the churning surf, the brave O'Neill decided on a rash act. Deliberately wielding his battleax, he chopped off his own left hand and hurled it ashore, thus claiming the territory forever. (86)

According to *Boutell* (248) and Lynch-Robinson (179–80), the red hand of Ulster and O'Neill is a *dexter* (right, since this is from the standpoint of the bearer/charge), not sinister. The red hand that is used to difference the arms of the Baronets of England and Ireland, however, is a sinister hand. See Brewer (26th ed.), 741.

18. Levin says, "[Bloom] hits upon Saint Peter's symbol, a pair of crossed keys, also the insignia of the Isle of Man, and thus—if we are willing to follow the implications of a second pun—twin emblems of human isolation" (Levin 65). As I have noted earlier, the arms of the Isle of Man are those featuring the three conjoined legs. The insignia to which Bloom alludes is that of the House of Keys.

19. See Heim 136 ff.

20. Margot Norris has noted the connection between Stephen's civil and spiritual targets of revolt, and the paternal target. She refers to the scene in *A Portrait,* when Stephen and his father travel to Cork and Simon Dedalus is faced with the idea of his son's rising to take his place (the mythic archetype of the son killing the father). Simon Dedalus, speaking with an old acquaintance, brags, "There's that son of mine not half my age and I'm a better man than he is any day of the week." The acquaintance cautions him:

> —Draw it mild now, Dedalus. I think it's time you take a back seat, said the gentleman who had spoken before.
>
> —No, by God! asserted Mr Dedalus. I'll sing a tenor song against him or I'll vault a fivebarred gate against him or I'll run with him after the hounds across the country as I did thirty years ago along with the Kerry Boy and the best man for it.
>
> —But he'll beat you here, said the little old man, tapping his forehead . . . (*P* 95).

Norris notes that "Stephen Dedalus in *Ulysses* redirects his struggle toward the symbolic father ("*[He taps his brow.]* But in here it is that I must kill the priest and the king" [*U* 589])" (Norris 43).

21. The origin of the cross of St. Patrick is a deep heraldic mystery, and it has often (and plausibly) been suggested that it came into being when needed to simplify the design of the Union Flag. A thorough discussion of this emblem is in Hayes-McCoy 36–42. Hayes-McCoy suggests a connection between this symbol and the arms of Fitzgerald, Earl of Kildare, which bore "Argent, a saltire gules."

22. This livery appears once in Bloom's imaginings in "Circe," when Bloom explains to Mrs Breen that Molly would want "Negro servants in livery if she had the money." This is followed by the appearance of "*Tom and Sam Bohee, coloured coons in white duck suits, scarlet socks, upstarched Sambo chokers and large scarlet asters in their buttonholes*" (15.1412–14 {443.17–23}).

23. See Gifford and Seidman, 431, and Schneider, 309.

24. Compare this with the more elaborate garb in the intermediate draft of Buffalo Notebook V.A.8 (Herring, *Joyce's Notes* . . . 160):

> There entered the noble John Wyse O'Nolan, resplendent in verdant and silver garb. ~~He were the~~ Grand High Chief Ranger, he, of the National Foresters of Ireland. He doffed his whiteplumed helm. . . .

25. Cf. description of Bloom leaving Kiernan's at the end of "Cyclops," Bloom himself is described as "late of Messrs Alexander Thom's, printers to His Majesty . . ." (12.1816-17 {342.40–41}).

26. I am unable to suggest a good reason for the adoption of this particular motto; I believe Thornton is correct when he says "*Semper paratus* ('Always ready') is a Latin proverbial phrase that is too common to specify a single source" (476). Of the family names said in Burke's *Armory* to use "Semper paratus" as a motto (see Appendix to this study, *s.v.* "Semper paratus"), only Clifford (Bloom's correspondent is Martha Clifford) rings a faint bell. Strictly speaking, mottoes are not part of an armorial grant, so documentary sources on family mottoes are even less reliable than those for coats of arms.

27. A. Walton Litz discusses Joyce's revisions to this and the related passages in "Lotus Eaters" to expand and emphasize the floral motif. See *Art of JJ,* 47–49.

28. Brewer's gives as an example, "Ophelia gives the queen a daisy to signify 'that her light and fickle love ought not to expect constancy in her husband" (Brewer, 26th ed., 209a).

29. Gorman (33) recounts Joyce's own days at Clongowes, and notes ". . . he played his part in the scholarly contests of the two teams into which his class of Elements was divided—one wearing the white rose of York for insignia and the other flaunting the red rose of Lancaster. . . ."

30. Cf. letter from Joyce to Valery Larbaud, 5 January 1922: "In a shop at the corner of rue Jacob, rue Furstenberg you will see a picture of Molly *avec le vieux lion*" (*Letters* 3: 56).

31. Both Gordon (7) and Schueler (92) note that the attitudes of the dog in the passage following the "buck" blazon are also heraldic in character. Schueler quotes from a passage which includes 3.343–45 {46.21–25}:

> The dog yelped running to them, reared up and pawed at them with mute bearish fawning. Unheeded he kept by them as they came towards the drier sand, a rag of wolf's tongue redpanting from his jaws.

Schueler observes that "Stephen's descriptions of the dog's actions are references also to the positions of an animal emblazoned as a principal charge on a shield: passant, salient, rampant, regardant, etc." (Schueler 92). Specifically, "passant" is a synonym for Stephen's term "trippant," and means walking. Running, the dog is "courant." "Reared up" with its hind-feet on the ground, the dog is "salient" (springing). Ordinarily, "rampant" is not used in connection with a dog, but the dog's attitude when "reared up" and pawing the cockle-pickers is identical to the lion's posture when rampant. See Fox-Davies 204; *Boutell* 72–73.

32. "Tenney" covers a range of heraldic tinctures, including brown, orange, and certain shades of yellow. It has particular significance for Ireland, for, as Campbell and Evans remark, the Irish tricolor "is something spoken of as 'green, white, and gold', but the gold is *not* yellow: it is a warm orange-gold, described by the heralds as *tenné*" (20).

33. Ellmann (*JJ* 34) notes that "At the beginning of 1892 [John Joyce] moved his family to 23 Carysfort Avenue, Blackrock, a house called 'Leoville' because of the stone lion in front of its door."

34. This is clear from the notes from the British Museum. The "Circe 5" notes contain detailed references to the language of parasols ("handle shoulder= indiff. / high=daring/ drop to right=lean on you . . ." [Herring, 1972, 295]); and playing cards; "Circe 8" purports to give details on the language of handkerchiefs ("handk,drop = ?friends / both twirl = indiff / over cheek=love . . ."), [p. 311] but, as Herring points out [312n], "a fan would seem to work better for some of the gestures." Bella Cohen's fan "speaks" to Bloom in "Circe" (*U* 15.2754–2803 {527.15–529.11}).

35. Cf. references in *Stephen Hero:*

> There should be an art of gesture, said Stephen one night to Cranly. . . . Of course I don't mean art of gesture in the sense that the elocution professor understands the word. . . . I mean a rhythm. You know the song 'Come unto these yellow sands?'. . . . This is it, said the youth making a graceful anapestic gesture with each arm. (184)

Stephen's reference to "the elocution professor" suggests a source for aspects of Joyce's emblematic imagination, in his Jesuit education at Clongowes and Belvedere. In a study of the literary and emblematic work of a seventeenth-century Jesuit, Herman Hugo, S.J., Mark Carter Leach discusses the development of a highly sophisticated art of gesticulation, as a component of the study of rhetoric. He cites such works as the *Vacationes Autumnales, sive De Perfecta Orationis Actione et Pronunciatione* (ca. 1620) of Louis de Cressolles S.J., a "massive, . . . folio volume [which] treats the action of the orator, from the arching of the eyebrow to the overall pose of his figure" (Leach 29). In his discussion of Hugo's contribution to emblematic literature, he makes clear that the Jesuit order was the focal point of attempts to refine "visual rhetoric," through promulgation of "gesticulative language" (305). This possible background for Stephen Dedalus's "language of gesture" deserves serious study.

Chapter Five

1. Ian Fleming, *On Her Majesty's Secret Service* (New York: Signet, 1963). There is no Sable Basilisk (although there is a Rouge Dragon) in the College of Arms, but, except for his deliberate deviation from the titles of the College's officers (he also fabricates a "Griffin Or"), Fleming's characterization of the resources and methods of the College of Arms is amazingly accurate.

2. *Intelligible Heraldry* mentions there having also been a "St. Patrick" pursuivant in the Irish Office as well as Athlone (Lynch-Robinson 117); Ulster King was king of arms to the Order of St. Patrick, as Garter Principal King of Arms is king of arms to the Order of the Garter, and Lord Lyon king to the Order of the Thistle. Barron mentions only the Athlone Pursuivant (329a). I find no reference to St. Patrick Pursuivant in Joyce's writings.

3. See Northrop Frye, *Anatomy of Criticism*, 200: "[Eden's] heraldic colors are green and gold, traditionally the colors of vanishing youth. . . ."

4. Atherton gives as a likely source for Joyce's information on the Dublin arms A. C. Fox-Davies's *Book of Public Arms* (Edinburgh, 1894; new ed., 1915). Fox-Davies, who is at his worst (i.e., prejudiced, condescending, and inaccurate) in discussing Irish and American heraldry, gives two very different discussions of the Dublin arms in his 1894 and 1915 editions of *Public Arms*. The 1894 edition describes the arms ("AZURE, THREE CASTLES ARGENT, FLAMMANT PROPER. *MOTTO*, OBEDIENTIA CIVIUM URBIS FELICITAS"), and appends the following paragraph:

> The Town-Clerk [of Dublin] forwards a drawing of the Arms supported by a female figure vested, each holding in their interior hands a branch of olives, that on the dexter side representing "Law," and holding in her dexter hand a sword erect; that on the sinister side representing "Justice," and holding in her sinister hand a pair of scales. The Editor believes that no very extensive use is made of the Supporters, which, so far as he can ascertain, are of no authority. (26)

Fox-Davies was in error, and apparently merely assumed that the supporters were not authorized. He silently corrects his error in the 1915 edition, simply by giving the arms and supporters as used (245–46). Perhaps Atherton refers to the later edition as Joyce's source, but surely Joyce would have known the arms from long familiarity. We know he had a wood carving of the Dublin arms, a gift from Constantine Curran (Curran 99–100).

5. See Nathan Halper, "Of The Stuttering Hand," 7–8, for the connection between this reference and the Red Hand of Ulster.

6. I am grateful to Professor Bonnie Kime Scott for calling to my attention that Virginia Woolf had referred to Joyce as a "he-goat" in a conversation with T. S. Eliot (Woolf, *Writer's Diary* 173).

7. See the line "Bulloc sterteth, bucke verteth" from the medieval lyric "Sumer is ycomen in . . ."; this line—perhaps an antecedent for "in vert or venison" [34.25]—depends on the pronunciation mentioned above.

8. My thoughts on the possible connection between Joyce's "gentility" and the Festy King's "fesses" were prompted by a paper given by Susan Swartzlander at the 1985

Philadelphia James Joyce Conference ("Multiple Meaning and Misunderstanding: The Mis-Trial of Festy King").

9. See *The Index Manuscript*, Danis Rose, ed.: "O'Reilly / apaumee, bloody proper, / vert, 2 lions rampant / combatant, or, a dexter / hand couped at wrist, erect / oaktree, snake descending / proper, fortutidine et pudentia [sic] . . ." etc. (263)

10. For evidence of the Joyce family's acute consciousness of its descent from the twelve tribes, see Stanislaus Joyce, *Dublin Diary*, entry for 26 Sept. 1903:

> The twelve tribes of Galway are:
>
> Athy, Blake, Bodkin
> Deane, D'Arcy, Lynch
> Joyce, Kirwin, Martin
> Morris, Skerret, French
>
> Pappie is the only child of an only child . . . He takes pride in a family of some refinement, education and some little distinction on one side, and of some wealth on the other. (5)

11. Fox-Davies discusses the matter of such use of supporters:

> Whilst the official laws in Ireland are, and have apparently always been, the same as in England, there is no doubt that the heads of the different septs assert a claim to the right to use supporters. On this point Sir Bernard Burke, Ulster King of Arms, wrote: "No registry of supporters to an Irish chieftain appears in Ulster's Office, in right of his chieftaincy only, and without the honour of peerage, nor does any authority to bear them exist." But nevertheless "The O'Donovan" uses dexter, a lion guardant, and sinister, a griffin; "The O'Gorman" uses, dexter, a lion, and sinister, a horse; "The O'Reilly" uses two lions or. "The O'Connor Don," however, is in the unique position of bearing supporters by unquestionable right, inasmuch as the late Queen Victoria, on the occasion of her last visit to Dublin, issued her Royal Warrant conferring the right upon him. (*CG* 421)

12. See note in *The Index Manuscript*, Danis Rose, ed.: "coat, crest and supporters / Ulster (K of Arms)" (358).

13. *U* 15.4459 {590.26}. See Thornton 421, and Kinley Roby, "King Edward in Nighttown," for detailed discussion of this motif.

14. Brewer's *Dictionary* (26th ed.) traces the motto's origin not to its German meaning, but to a Welsh expression of similar sounds:

> According to a Welsh tradition, Edward I promised to provide Wales with a prince "who could speak no word of English," and when his son Edward of Carnarvon was born he presented him to the assembly, saying in Welsh, *Eich dyn* (behold the man). (432)

15. The badge of the Prince of Wales was apparently noted, but not used, by Joyce while he was writing *Ulysses*. One of the Buffalo notesheets for "Penelope" (Page 6) contains the note "God bless the prince of Wales 3 feathers" (Herring, *Joyce's Notes . . .* 71).

16. I base this observation upon renderings of the respective arms of the heirs apparent at the turn of the century (see Illus. 1–H, above; Rothery 273), and those in contemporary sources ranging from *Boutell's Heraldry* (Plate XV) to an official "Royal Marriage Souvenir" tea cup (England: Wood & Sons, 29 July 1981; in the possession of the author) featuring the arms of Prince Charles. The change in placement of the badge is not a matter of

policy: in a letter to me (2 July 1984) Sir Colin Cole, Garter Principal King of Arms, states:

> A badge can exist by itself, or it can be displayed in relation to the owner's Armorial Bearings, there being no position in particular which is laid down when this is done. In these circumstances it is possible that in the past in a number of achievements the Heir Apparent's Badge might have been placed above his Shield, and so given the appearance of being a Crest.

I am grateful to Mr. Thomas Woodcock, Somerset Herald, for searching the records of the College of Arms for practice as to placement of the badge of the Prince of Wales. In a letter to me (January 1985), he has confirmed that, while renderings in 1842 (College of Arms MS I.54, pp. 40–42), 1901 (MS I.73, pp. 189–90), and 1911 (MS I.76, pp. 97–8) show the badge above the armorial achievement, opposite the crest, in more recent renderings (e.g., in College MS I.82, p. 197 [1960]) the badge is at the bottom of the armorial achievement, in the "compartment."

17. The *OED* (1: 313–14) states that "cad" is "an abbreviation of CADEE, CADDIE, CADET," deriving from the sense of "cadet" as a younger son: literally,

> A gentleman who entered the army without a commission, to learn the military profession and find a career for himself (as was regularly done by the younger sons of the French nobility before the revolution).

Padraic Colum recalls Joyce's recounting his father's story of the "cad on a bicycle" who had asked him the time (the progenitor of the HCE/cad episode throughout *FW*), and wonders:

> But what did "cad" mean? A cadet, a younger son. And why should "younger son" amount to a term of abuse? "A cad on a bicycle"—Joyce was in a convulsion of laughter as he repeated it. Was the comedy in the fact that his father should be enraged because a young man on a bicycle addressed him? Or was it that dark expanse of garden, a man asking for a light, the ferocious reaction on the one accosted, suggested the comic side of a myth? Or was it the passage of "cadet" into "cad" that was comic? (159–60)

In *Ulysses*, Simon Dedalus invokes John Joyce's favored epithet in regard to Mulligan (*U* 6.49 {88.15}). Finally, an entry from Stanislaus Joyce's *Dublin Diary* (29 January 1904) illustrates the literal sense in which the Joyce household employed the root word for "cad": describing his deceased brother George, the young Stanislaus wrote: "He was the youngest—the cadet" (17).

18. Joyce was given an heraldic rendering of the "Breast Plate," which is actually a prayer: Mrs. Charles Joyce gave him "a pocket breast-plate in the new Irish colours [the Republican tricolor] with part of [St. Patrick's] famous prayer on it cut in the form of a shield" (*Letters* 3: 108). Ellmann's footnote relates this with Yawn's "patrician" coat of arms. For other "Roman Catholic arms," see John Garvin, *James Joyce's Disunited Kingdom*, 172–74; specifically, he finds the canting arms of Urban III (whose family name, Crivelli [seive], is alluded to by the seive in the arms; the arms had sows for supporters) in the Mookse and the Gripes episode: "Poor little sowseived subsquashed Gripes!" (*FW* 155.12–13; Garvin, 173).

19. I am resisting the temptation to draw conclusions from the occurrence of two *Wake leitmotivs*, "Ich Dien" and "Ichthus," on page *432* (the number being the date of Patrick's

coming to Ireland, and a numerical constant of *FW*) of Brewer's 26th edition. I cannot resist calling attention to my resistance, however.

20. Cautious medievalists insist on distinguishing between "sealing" and "signing"; one can always cause a scholar trained in sigillography to cringe simply by referring to John's "signing" the Magna Carta. King John did not *sign;* he affixed his seal, which carried far more clout than a mere signature. Indeed, we do not know with certainty that writing was among John's skills. In this spirit, a close reading of HCE's testimony in 545.14–23 will reveal that he causes "the great seal now to be affixed"; there is no explicit indication that he signs as well.

21. See Tindall 48, 53; Benstock, "Every Telling . . ." 5; Burgess 142; Norris 106; McCarthy, "Structures and Meanings . . ." 573.

22. *Letters* 1: 285: Letter to Constantine P. Curran, 22 September 1929: According to Gilbert's note, Joyce thanked Curran for his gift of "an eighteenth-century painted woodcarving of the Arms of the City of Dublin" (see Curran 99–100) and Joyce remarks "perhaps I may have it reproduced on the cover of the third of three or four fragments from *W in P* which I propose to issue at intervals."

23. The arms of Oldcastle (Kent) bear a single triple-towered castle.

24. This allusion seems also to place Shem's conflict in Joyce's wardrobe. In a letter to Mrs. Herbert Gorman (22 Oct 1930), Joyce asks her to buy him a plaid tie, and says "The plaid I prefer (I think it is the Murray) has a lot of red in it as a ground and of course blue and white and yellow all over it" (*Letters* 3: 204–5). The Gormans sent two ties, and Joyce acknowledged in a letter to Herbert Gorman on 30 Oct 1930 that "A.J. [Augustine John] started my portrait a few days ago with that highly treasonable Stuart royal tie" (*Letters* 3: 206).

Chapter Six

1. *See OED* 1: 228. The first meaning of "Blazon" is "To describe in proper heraldic language"; the second meaning given is "To depict or paint (armorial bearings) according to the rules of heraldry."

2. Cited by Hart, *Structure and Motif* 13.

INDEX